THE NEW MEDIUM OF PRINT

PRINTING INDUSTRY CENTER SERIES

THE NEW MEDIUM OF PRINT

MATERIAL COMMUNICATION IN THE INTERNET AGE

FRANK COST

RIT CARY GRAPHIC ARTS PRESS
ROCHESTER, NY

The New Medium of Print: Material Communication in the Internet Age
Frank Cost
Printing Industry Center Series: 1

Published and distributed by
RIT Cary Graphic Arts Press
90 Lomb Memorial Drive
Rochester, New York 14623-5604
http://wally.rit.edu/cary/carypress.html

Printed in the United States by RR Donnelley
ISBN 1-933360-03-8

Designed by Marnie Soom / RIT Cary Graphic Arts Press
Typeface: Whitney by Tobias Frere-Jones / Hoefler & Frere-Jones
Photographs by Frank Cost unless otherwise noted

Library of Congress Cataloging-in-Publication Data

Cost, Frank.
    The new medium of print : material communication in the Internet age /
Frank Cost.
        p. cm. — (Printing industry center series ; 1)
    Includes bibliographical references and index.
    ISBN 1-933360-03-8
    1. Printing—Technological innovations. 2. Printing—Social aspects.
    3. Digital printing. 4. Electronic publishing. 5. Commercial art. 6. Visual
    communication.   I. Title. II. Series.
    Z249.3.C67 2005
    686.2—dc22

                                                                2005014293

To my father, Emil, who taught me that presentation is the key to communication, and my mother, Elaine, who, as editor of our local weekly newspaper, gave me my first regular access to a printing press when I was nineteen.

CONTENTS

FOREWORD

Pʀɪɴᴛ ɪs ᴏᴜʀ ᴏʟᴅᴇsᴛ ꜰᴏʀᴍ ᴏꜰ technology-mediated communication. As printed communications have evolved over time, the
aura of that history is still tied to the printed word or image. The
word *imprimatur* is used to define a mark of approval or distinction.
It is derived from the Latin word that described the time when, in order to print and distribute ideas, publishers needed the permission
of the state. While this was a form of censorship in the 17th century,
today, if an idea or an image appears in printed form, it carries this
implication that it was important enough to be worth the time and
energy to produce and distribute it in this form.

The more recent forms of electronic communication and
satellite distribution allow for the uncensored and unedited distribution of ideas. Though this speeds the distribution of the ideas, the
disadvantage is that content distributed by these media are viewed
with skepticism by many. With the Internet allowing anyone to be a
publisher, the material communication provided by print still implies
that these ideas are worthy of our time. If we make it tangible and
enduring, it is viewed as important.

Material communication also matters in the everyday world.
This is nicely captured by a greeting card company slogan—when
you want to show how much you care, you send a card through the
postal mail rather than an e-card through the Internet. The tangible,
material communication adds something intangible. The means of
the communication enhances the meaning of the message. If it is
tangible, it conveys quality, caring, and effort. Because it took effort,
planning and forethought, it is valued.

This is why *The New Medium of Print* is an important book for people interested in understanding communication in this century. Frank Cost has a unique perspective on the industry that has evolved from his own intellectual and experiential roots in photography, journalism, history, computing, and printing technology. His writing reflects his passion for his subject mixed with a dose of irony. Audiences will find this book a pleasure to read as he presents his analysis with humor and accessible language.

I have enjoyed working with Frank at RIT over the past five years. He is a great colleague, a sought-after mentor to our students, and a frequent invited lecturer to the printing and publishing industries. The reader of this book will experience what it is like to take a class from him without the concern of taking any tests, or sit in his invited lectures without having to eat the rubber chicken. Enjoy!!

Patricia Sorce
Administrative Chair
School of Print Media, RIT
Co-Director
Printing Industry Center at RIT

PREFACE

B EFORE PEOPLE USED MEDIA OF ANY KIND THERE WERE ONLY WORDS, spoken with inflection, emotion, expression; sometimes sung; sometimes accompanied by instrumental music and perhaps even dance; sometimes shouted at a distance. But beyond the limits of shouting, a messenger was needed to traverse the distance, carrying words in memory and repeating them upon arrival at an intended destination, and making contact with an intended audience.

Thousands of generations later humans finally learned how to speak across continents and oceans and across the whole world. The telephone, radio, and television made it possible for people to finally do what they had always wanted to do. But these powers were not gifts from the gods. They were inventions of science. And science would never have been possible had people not invented ways to encode language in physical and portable form.

If the telephone, radio, and television had been embedded in the aboriginal landscape, like stones or trees, there never would have been the need for written language. This undoubtedly would have led to other historical consequences. The sitcom, for example, would surely have run its course thousands of years ago. Today, we inhabit a world saturated with electronic communication channels of all kinds. Yet the oldest form of mediated communication, fixing words and pictures to physical objects and then transporting them to locations in space and time where they can be viewed directly, still plays a vital role. Print is everywhere around us, and yet so familiar that it remains nearly invisible.

During the past quarter century of teaching I have often

wished for a small, fun-to-read book to give to people who were thinking about the world of print for the first time. Most of the available introductory books concentrate heavily on the technology, but say little about how people actually use print, let alone why. Until very recently it has been easy to overlook these questions. Asking why people printed was like asking why they farmed, or why they drank water. What alternatives existed?

Today we are living in the second decade of the Internet era. The impact of the Internet on printing promises to be as profound as the discovery of an electronic alternative to food would be on farming—for the first time in our long history on planet Earth we would be forced to ask fundamental questions about the enduring value of physical nourishment. Where will electronic substitution be most pervasive? Under what circumstances does the physical form work better than the electronic alternative? Where might the value of physical forms actually increase in the context of widespread adoption of electronic forms? How might the infrastructure that enables electronic solutions be used to revolutionize the way physical solutions are created and delivered?

If you are encountering print as a subject of conscious study for the first time, this book provides an introduction to the underlying systems for the creation and distribution of print in Part One, and an exploration of the many and varied contemporary uses of print in Part Two. If you are already familiar with the technologies of print, you may want to skip Part One and begin your reading with Part Two. However you use this book, my hope is that you will come away from it with a better understanding of how Internet-enabled print media serve a great variety of present-day needs, and deeper insight into how they will be likely be used in the future.

Frank Cost
Rochester, New York
April 2005

ACKNOWLEDGEMENTS

F OR THE PAST TWENTY-FOUR YEARS I have had the privilege of serving as a member of the faculty of Rochester Institute of Technology. During that time not a day has passed that I did not learn something new about the graphic communications industry from a colleague, a student, or a visitor. RIT has been a crossroads for the printing industry since 1937 when the Department of Printing and Publishing began offering diplomas at the Institute. My first acknowledgement, therefore, is of RIT itself. There is no better place to be, if your goal is to learn as much as you possibly can about this business.

During my time at RIT, I have worked with many generous people who have shared their knowledge freely. For twelve years, I had the wonderful experience of having Frank Romano just fifty feet down the hallway from my office. If I figure that on any given day I might have posed a minimum of two questions about the industry to Frank, and then do some multiplication, I probably asked and received answers to almost 4,000 questions over the years. And the good news is that even though Frank officially retired last year, he still answers my email questions in a matter of minutes on average, no matter where in the world he may be at the time. So Frank's contributions to this book and to my continued education were and are profound.

Many of the ideas in this book were formed in the daily dialog I have had over the past several years with Pat Sorce, co-director of the RIT Printing Industry Center and chair of the School of Print Media. As a professor of marketing with more than two decades of teaching at the MBA level in the RIT College of Business prior to the establishment of the Printing Industry Center, Pat brought the all-important question, "Why do we print?" to the forefront of my thinking.

Other RIT colleagues contributed significantly to the contents of this book. Professor David Pankow is the curator of the Melbert B. Cary, Jr. Graphic Arts Collection at RIT and a scholar of the history of print media. Most of the historical references in this book have their origins somewhere in the hundreds of conversations I have had with David over the years.

I have also enjoyed a fifteen-year-long running conversation about the enduring value of the book as a medium of human expression with Professor Owen Butler of the RIT School of Photographic Arts and Sciences. Owen's ideas and sensibilities are reflected at many points in this book.

Much credit is due many of the great proponents of the science of printing that I have had the honor of working with at RIT over the years, such as Roy Berns, Robert Chung, Ed Granger, Milton Pearson, Franz Sigg, Julius Silver, and Miles Southworth. Other members of the RIT faculty whose ideas are reflected within these pages are Barbara Birkett, William Birkett, Twyla Cummings, Mary Anne Evans, Franziska Frey, Michael Kleper, C.R. Myers, Fernando Naveda, Michael Peres, Douglas Ford Rea, Michael Riordan, Sandra Rothenberg, Patricia Russotti, Nitin Sampat, and Scott Williams. Thanks also to Greg Barnett, Chris Chapman, Hal Gaffin, William Garno, and William Pope for their contributions.

This book also reflects ideas expressed to me by academic leaders from some of the leading universities that offer programs in graphic communications related fields. Among these are: Harvey Levenson, director of the Graphic Communications program, California Polytechnic Institute; Alexander Tsyganenko, rector, Moscow State University of Printing Arts; Kong Lin Jung, professor, Shanghai Printing and Publishing College of Shanghai University; Ulf Lindqvist, research professor, Technical Research Center of Finland; and Douglas Holleley, professor, Visual Studies Workshop.

Many people from the industry have been generous with their time to offer perspectives and answer questions during the course of research for this book. These include the owners and chief executive officers of several companies: Bruce James, Public Printer of the United States; Regis Delmontagne, president of the Association of Suppliers of Printing, Publishing and Converting Technologies (NPES); Doug Smith, CEO of Merlin International; James Hammer, CEO of Hammer Lithographic Corporation; Ken McCurdy, CEO of Lazer Incorporated; Donald Samuels, CEO of Pictorial Offset Corporation; Chris Pape, CEO of Monroe Litho Inc.; Jon Buddington, CEO of Global Printing Inc.; Gerald Nathe, CEO of Baldwin Technology Company Inc.; James Kosowski, CEO of Rapid Impressions Inc.; Donald Roland, CEO of Vertis Corporation; K. Bradley Paxton, CEO of ADI LLC; Venkat Purushotham, president of NexPress, Inc.; John Lacagnina, president and CEO of ColorCentric Corporation; Robert Young, CEO of Lulu Inc.; and Mary Lee Schneider, president of RR Donnelley Pre-Media.

Thanks also to the following people who gave me significant amounts of time while I was working on this book: Heather Banis, Heidelberg; Chris Bondy, NexPress, Inc.; Frank Costello, RR Donnelley; Gart Davis, Lulu Inc.; Robert Eller, ExxonMobil; Howie Fenton, GATF; Dennis Floss, Gannett; Eddy Hagen, VIGC; James Hamilton, InfoTrends/CAP Ventures; Robert Hanlon, Rohm and Haas; Michael Hurley, NPES; Dov Isaacs, Adobe; Captain Douglas Jordan, U.S. Army Special Forces; Marty Kennedy, Thomson Legal and Regulatory; Helmut Kipphan, Heidelberg; Jim Kohler, International Paper; Larry Kroll, Heidelberg; Bill Lamparter, Printcom; Janice Mayo, Vertis; John McCracken, Konica Minolta; John Meyer, HP; Barbara Pellow, Eastman Kodak; Wolfgang Pfizenmaier, Heidelberg; Ray Prince, GATF; Rob Rolleston, Xerox; Richard Rosenberger, Sweetheart Cup Company; Bhima Sastri, MeadWestvaco; Leonid Shakhmundes, Cambridge Prepress; Kip Smythe, NPES; Alan Winslow, Weyerhauser; Mark Witkowski, Sheridan Group; and Trish Witkowski, Expert Finishing Group.

Several people read the entire manuscript and provided valuable suggestions for improvement. These include Owen Butler, Elaine Cost, Patricia Cost, Mary Anne Evans, Eddy Hagen, James Hamilton, Amelia Hugill-Fontanel, David Pankow, Pat Sorce, and Marnie Soom.

I would like to express my most heartfelt thanks to Joan Stone, dean of the RIT College of Imaging Arts and Sciences, who unburdened me of many of my regular administrative responsibilities during the research and writing of this book. I owe Joan at least two years worth of award dinners and committee meetings as her representative in the future.

My final and greatest thanks must go to Patricia Cost, who edited this text and read through it more times than any human being should have to read anything. Thanks also to Patty for the countless hours she has spent discussing and refining many of the ideas expressed within these pages.

INTRODUCTION

IN 1998 I WAS INVITED TO MAKE A PRESENTATION on the future of print at a symposium in Barcelona celebrating the 500th anniversary of the founding of the printers' guild in that Mediterranean city. My presentation focused on the promise of the new generation of digital production color printing devices to enable new markets for custom-printed products that were not governed by the traditional economics of mass production. In 1998, the Internet had only been open for commercial activity for a few short years, few people were connected to it, broadband was something only large organizations could afford, and computers were still far too slow to process graphic information efficiently enough to make effective use of digital printing. But all of the ingredients necessary for a revolution in print communications were in place. All we had to do was to wait a few years for the computing power and network infrastructure to catch up with the promise.

In 1498, the year the Barcelona printing guild was founded, the Portuguese explorer Vasco da Gama sailed around the horn of Africa to open the first maritime trade route to India. Christopher Columbus had visited the new world for the first time only six years before. The new mechanical technology of printing was spreading throughout Europe, and was enabling a revolution in communications that empowered the written word and the people who commanded it.

The invention of printing opened a channel of communication between individuals and audiences that provided a mechanism for accelerating the evolution of mass culture. During the next half-millennium, the print medium served as a foundation for the construction of a global order that mirrored the architecture of the medium itself. Print provided one-way, one-to-many communication. This enabled a small number of people to broadcast messages to large populations. The first generation of print publishers used the technology exclusively to broadcast tried and tested biblical messages. By the end of the 15th century, publishers began to realize that the greater power of the medium lay in its ability to transmit new messages to large audiences.

The first new messages transmitted by print were political or social commentary, often disguised as allegorical literature to evade the censorship that was claimed as a divine right by the ruling classes. With the gradual assertion of the idea of natural rights that began in the early 18th century, print was used increasingly as a medium for direct political expression. The purpose of the expression was to influence the political behaviors of large groups of people.

It didn't take long for people to realize that if political behavior could be influenced by printed messages, why not commercial behavior as well? Thus was born print advertising. The first advertising piggybacked on existing print channels. These were established and cultivated by editorial content. They were then exploited by advertising. For the past two centuries the print medium has grown to comprise tens of thousands of publications targeting distinct audiences defined by common interests and values.

In the 20th century, print advertising was joined by radio and then by television. For a few decades from the 1930s through the 1960s, print, radio, and television were able to assemble huge national mass audiences for advertisers. A common picture of the typical American home of the mid 1950s contains the following required details: the television sat in the corner of the room tuned to one of the two networks; *Life* magazine sat on the coffee table; consumers sat on the couch believing that there were substantive differences between Oldsmobile and Ford, or Crest and Colgate. National advertisers used print, radio, and television channels to reach large mass audiences of undifferentiated consumers to exert influence over their commercial behavior.

Print had one clear advantage over television at the time. In addition to the mass consumer audience, print was able to target a growing number of smaller special-interest markets. Television was not able to begin along this path until the cable revolution in the 1970s. By then, print had already defined hundreds of smaller audiences that advertisers could reach with more focused marketing messages.

Since 1970, the mass audience that was once such a rich target for mass advertising has become increasingly fragmented and diverse. Print has followed this trend by proliferating new titles that more effectively target emerging special interests. But there is trouble brewing across the whole spectrum of traditional print media. Circulations for all of the major consumer magazines have been falling for more than a decade. Daily metropolitan newspaper circulations have also been falling. More than 60 percent of the magazines offered for sale on newsstands are never sold.[1] The vast majority of printed catalogs and direct mail pieces end up in landfills without ever being read. If the Sierra Club and Greenpeace didn't rely almost exclusively on direct mail for their own fundraising efforts, the printing industry might find itself at the top of their lists of "corporate evil-doers."

The essential problem with the traditional print medium is that it supports only one-way communication. Because print first defined the audiences that became the markets for the products of industry, and because it continues to participate in the industrial economy as a mass-produced commodity, it is both parent and child of the Industrial Age. As such it shares all of the strengths and weaknesses of the industrial model.

Traditional manufacturing and distribution systems attempt to predict the size of future markets for products, and then produce and *push* the product into the marketplace. Automobiles, television sets, potato chips, and most printed products are mass-produced and distributed before they are offered for sale. If the manufacturers correctly predict the volume of sales and keep the distribution channel full enough to meet the demand, they will maximize the number of units sold. But there is always the risk of overproducing and pouring excessive amounts of money into inventory that sits in warehouses or on store shelves and might never be sold. The automobile industry pushes tens of millions of cars into the market every year, and tens of billions of dollars worth of unsold vehicles sit aging on car lots throughout the world at any given point in time.[2]

Print production services were first offered commercially to outside clients early in the 16th century. This began a trend toward commercialization and fragmentation of print communication services that continued through the next five centuries. This trend reached its peak in the first few decades after the Second World War. To effectively use the print medium, one had to coordinate the work of many separate businesses that provided component goods or services. To publish a book in 1975 required the publisher to interface directly with copy editors, indexers, illustrators, book designers, typesetters, color separators, printers, bookbinders, distributors, and retailers. The process was linear, laborious, and lengthy. Today, as we will learn, it is possible for a publisher to achieve the same results by interacting with a single website.

In some markets, there is simply no alternative to the mass manufacturing push model. This is because the decision to buy the product is made only after the product is in the consumer's hand. The product has to be on the shelf before someone decides to buy it. Supply precedes demand. Most food products and many manufactured goods can only be sold this way.

Other products and services lend themselves more naturally to a *pull* production and distribution model. Build-to-order production systems have existed for centuries. Before the era of mass manufacturing, this was more the rule than the exception. However, it is only relatively recently that build-to-order has been implemented in manufacturing. Perhaps the best known example is the system that Dell uses to custom-manufacture computers. When you order a computer from Dell, the assembled computer system does not yet exist. Your order sets in motion a custom assembly and distribution process. Dell does not have to tie up capital maintaining inventories of completed systems in anticipation of future demand. This gives Dell a key advantage over competitors that rely on traditional mass production and distribution channels.

Digital technology has the power to reverse the trend that began with the Industrial Revolution to disintegrate the processes by which wealth is created into myriad sub-processes that required ever-increasing amounts of mediation by an ever-expanding army of mediators. In a disintegrated world, mediated experience became the norm, because no single person had a view of the whole of anything. The re-integration of processes enabled by digital technology eliminates the need for mediation. Digital technology replaces mediated communication with direct communication, and mediated experience with direct experience. It diminishes the need for production-oriented work and opens the future to new creative vistas. It rescues us from the unpleasant disintegrated world of the Industrial Age and returns us to the hearth.

The place of print in this emerging world will change. Until recently print has been under the exclusive control of the mediators. Digital technology is transferring control of the medium into the hands of its users. What the users of communication channels want more than anything else is to engage in a two-way dialog with their customers and constituencies. The traditional print medium does not support this desire.

I am confronting this very reality as I sit here writing this book. You, the reader, remain invisible and silent to me throughout the long and laborious process of writing. I must rely upon a storehouse of knowledge that I have accumulated over many years about how people respond to ideas expressed in written form, and about the needs and wants of the audience I envision for this book. I use this knowledge to guide the writing process. When I have finished writing, I must then place my trust in the hands of other people who will design and market the product. By the time this book reaches you, your response to anything that I write will have no influence over the content. You may be compelled to send me an email responding to the book. (You can reach me at *cost@mail.rit.edu*.) But, in the traditional publishing model, your response can't influence the content until the publisher decides to do the next edition.

The one-way nature of traditional print communications leads to a lot of wasted effort and overproduction. The publisher of this book is reasonably sure that you exist, and that there are enough other people out there like you who will purchase the book and justify all of the effort and expense of writing, designing, manufacturing, and distributing it. But what if the publisher is wrong? What if you don't exist? What if there is no audience for this book? All of our effort will have gone to waste. The copies of the book that we print and cannot sell will make a slow, painful journey from warehouse to recycling plant or landfill where billions of unsold books and other printed products have gone before.

Although recycling reduces the volume of paper that ends up going directly into landfills, the energy required to collect and convert waste paper into recycled paper products is considerable. Printed paper once discarded therefore places a burden on the environment whether it ends up in a landfill or in a recycling plant. If the messages carried on the paper are never seen before the paper is discarded, the burden on the environment associated with its manufacture and disposal can easily be seen as being completely without redeeming benefits.

There has simply got to be a better way! And there is. We are witnessing the emergence of a new medium of print made possible by digital printing, the Internet, and the global infrastructure that supports high-speed digital communications among a rapidly growing percentage of the world population. Without the Internet, print must be pushed out into the world based on a prediction of its ultimate impact. Publishing this book without the help of the Internet is like making a break shot in a game of billiards. Once we hit the cue ball, we have no choice but to stand back and trust in the laws of physics. (This may not stop us from occasionally yelling at the breaking balls in a vain attempt to influence their behavior.) To extend this metaphor, the Internet makes it conceivable to engage each ball on the table in a separate dialog that will influence its path. If we figure out how to harness the interactive power of the Internet, we might live to see the day when we can convince every ball on the table to find a pocket.

The traditional medium of print uses the power of mass production and distribution to achieve economies of scale that counteract the huge material waste that results from a one-way push approach to mass print communication. The new medium of print uses the interactive platform of the Internet to harness the power of custom production and targeted distribution to make print a far more efficient vehicle for delivering value that is actively desired or demanded by the consumer.

To demonstrate our confidence in the long-term potential of the new medium of print, we will transform this very book from a traditional print media product to an exemplar of the new medium of print during the course of publishing it. The book will itself serve as a bridge from old to new. As a result, you and I, reader and author, will see our relationship transformed. This book will start its life as a traditional print product, but soon after its initial publication, it will begin a process of evolution that will be shaped by the interactions that happen among a community of people interested in pursuing the ideas first crudely articulated in these pages. This transformation will be explained and initiated in the last chapter of the book.

This book has two purposes. The first is to survey the various capabilities and uses of print media in the world today, paying special attention to the forces at play in each domain of application. The second is to construct a new model for understanding the role of print in the emerging networked digital world. The book draws a picture of the current state of print communications, including discussions of the critical technology demands and trends in each market segment. The book has two parts. Part One describes common means of print production and distribution in current use. Part Two describes how print is used by organizations and individuals today, and illustrates the role of print as a component in new media solutions that serve emerging communication needs and wants.

The evolution of the print medium as a service to human communications from the middle of the 15th century to the present is a story of the gradual disintegration of the production process into narrowly focused crafts that each took a share of the value of the final product. We are at the beginning of a radical redistribution of power enabled by digital technology and the Internet that sets the stage for the emergence of an entirely new industry. This new industry seeks to reintegrate the production and distribution of print with the businesses that are served by it. The industry will be dominated by companies that provide the technologies that will enable this to happen.

In nearly every current application domain for print media there are powerful forces for change. Interpreted through the filter of old models, the collected forces resemble barbarian hordes descending upon the printing industry from all sides. For many in the industry, the natural impulse is to take a defensive stand and look for solace in the many proud centuries of history where print stood unchallenged as the sole medium of mass communication. From this standpoint, print looks like the proverbial glass half-empty (and leaking). However, the opportunities for print enabled by digital technology appear to be an entirely new, potentially much larger glass that we are just beginning to fill.

PART ONE:
THE CREATION, PRODUCTION, AND DISTRIBUTION OF PRINT

I N THIS FIRST PART OF THE BOOK we will follow the path of graphic expression from point of origin to point of consumption. Everything that you see in print has made a journey that originates in the mind and is transformed from idea to physical reality with the use of technology. As you read this sentence, you are encountering a message that has passed through four distinct phases of life before reaching you. All printed media must pass through these four phases before they can fulfill their function. The four phases are:

1. **Mental phase.** All printed messages originate as impressions, expressions, or the consequences of human thought. As hard as I try to think of an exception to this rule, I cannot.

2. **Digital phase.** Although some expressions of human thought will first take an analog form such as pencil on paper, paint on canvas, or film in camera, most of what gets printed today goes directly from mental to digital through the exercise of computer keyboards, voice recognition software, digital cameras, or graphic design software. Analog expressions such as drawings, paintings, and conventional photographic images are converted to digital by scanning.

3. **Material phase.** Digital information must be rendered in physical form before it can be seen. There are only two ways to do this. One is to use electrons to illuminate materials such as phosphors or light-emitting diodes. The other is to distribute light-absorbing materials on surfaces. Computer monitors do the former and printing does the latter.

4. **Dissemination phase.** Once printed, a message must travel to a physical location where it is within viewing distance of the intended consumer. A million books stacked in a dark warehouse do not communicate anything to anybody.

The most exciting points in the transformation of information through these four phases are at the phase changes. The phase change from mental to digital is where all of the creative work is done. Companies like Adobe and Kodak constantly strive to increase the intelligence of the tools that creative people use to transform their ideas and impressions into data. The intelligence built into the current generation of Kodak digital cameras incorporates almost everything that the company has learned about photographic imaging over more than a century. Likewise, Adobe creative software applications such as Photoshop, Illustrator, InDesign, and Acrobat preserve the complete legacy of technical knowledge accumulated by the printing industry since the time of Gutenberg.

The changes from the digital to the material and the material to the dissemination phases are increasingly dominated by technology that is automated and hidden from view. The goal of each successive generation of technology is to eliminate craft, and improve the performance and ease of use of print as a medium of communication.

Within each phase from the digital phase to the dissemination phase there are a number of transformations that occur that move the information closer to the exact geometry and location of its final appearance in print. In the following chapters we will start with content creation and proceed through each subsequent transformation as we follow the content on its journey from point of creation to point of consumption. On the way we'll learn about the most common technologies for creating, editing, assembling, formatting, printing, finishing, and disseminating printed information.

CHAPTER ONE

CONTENT

C ONTENT IS THE FOUNDATION OF THE VALUE CHAIN. Without it, all
subsequent discussion in this book would be pointless. Most
content is created by people. However, some content is generated by machines. Not robots wielding feather pens, but computer
programs cranking out the results of computations: tables of stock
quotations, for example.

TEXT

My first real job in publishing was working for our weekly hometown
newspaper as a writer and photographer. I used an IBM Selectric
typewriter to write stories or to retype stories that were submitted by other writers in various paper formats. (The oddest format
was the weekly "police blotter" that was submitted on Tuesday
afternoons in the form of blotchy typewritten text on sheets of pink
construction paper.) I used a special font ball on the typewriter to
type onto ruled sheets of paper that could be scanned by an optical
character recognition (OCR) system that would produce a digital
file. This file was then used to set the type for the newspaper. I never
saw the computers that were used to convert the typewritten text
into digital files. They were hidden in the bowels of a production
facility that was strictly off limits to technologically-challenged editorial workers like me.

Today, thirty years later, I sit with my laptop computer and a
cup of coffee performing what would have been sheer magic back
then. As I press the keys, letters appear on a perfect facsimile of a
page displayed on the screen. In less than a minute I can publish this

IBM Selectric type ball.

text to a web server where people anywhere in the world can have access to it immediately—if only they have some way of knowing that it is there.

METHODS OF TEXT INPUT

Although most text input today is performed by humans using keyboards, there are alternative methods. For example, I am inputting this particular sentence to the computer using a microphone and speech recognition software. I am speaking slowly and clearly in a quiet room using software that I trained to recognize my voice. Get off that! (Sorry, the cat just jumped up on the piano.) Speech recognition is constantly being improved, but it requires a quiet, isolated environment and a different kind of mental discipline than the keyboard.

Writing is one of the most challenging things that people do. The conversion of thought into external text happens at an interface where the writer uses an instrument of some kind. Physical command of the instrument is critical to the process. I have one colleague, a prolific writer, who can only write with sharp number-two pencils on yellow legal pads. Another colleague has written dozens of books dictating into a tape recorder. I am dependent upon the keyboard at this point in my life. I've tried dictation, but my brain freezes up when I try to talk into a microphone, especially if there is anyone else in the same building at the time. And since I am the only person who can read my handwriting, there is no alternative to the keyboard.

The most challenging and desirable form of text input involves anonymous speech recognition or handwriting. Much of the original research for this book was in the form of interviews with experts and industry leaders. I recorded these interviews with a digital recorder that can be connected directly to the computer. To transcribe these interviews, I had no choice but to listen to the recordings and key the text into the computer. My dream would be to have a software utility that could read the sound file and convert it to text. But this is likely to remain impossible for the foreseeable future. Voice recognition software relies on a dictionary of sound patterns that are created from the actual voice patterns of an individual speaker. Even with extensive training, voice recognition is never 100-percent accurate. The accuracy of the best voice recognition software with a new voice for which it has not been trained is very low. Add background noise and the tendency for people to mutter and the task becomes impossible.

Handwriting recognition is similar to voice recognition in degree of difficulty. The most accurate systems are those that can be trained to recognize the handwriting of a specific person. These systems are employed extensively in hand-held devices such as personal digital assistants (PDAs) and pocket computers. Where handwriting recognition is most difficult and potentially most valuable is in the processing of hand-written paper forms such as census and tax forms. In the 2000 United States Census, a system that involved optical scanning and automated handwriting recognition was employed for the first time.[3] The design of the system took the better part of the decade of the 1990s. It involved the creation of specialized scanning technologies, forms design, and sophisticated software algorithms for recognizing handwriting, whether written by an accountant in perfect block lettering with a sharp black pen, or by a shaky senior who scrawls barely legible letters in red ink and draws smiley faces over all the lower case i's. Try writing a computer program to handle that range of diversity!

Textual content can come into existence without being explicitly created by a human being. Content of this kind relies on systems that collect, organize, and analyze data, and then produce output that can in some cases be published directly. A typical monthly mobile phone bill is a good example. The bill contains a printed record of every call made or received that month, with the call destination number, elapsed time, airtime charges and any additional charges. The content is generated without any human contribution. The system that assembles and formats the content was designed by humans. But the content itself was created by a machine.

The digital encoding of text is easy to understand. If you count all of the characters on your keyboard, including the space bar and all of the punctuation marks and special symbols, you will come up with less than a hundred characters. If each of these characters is given a unique number, each character can be represented by a single byte. The entire text of this book has less than half a million characters, so it can be represented by a file about a half a megabyte in size. To put this into some perspective, one uncompressed photograph from a typical two-megapixel digital camera represents more than ten times the amount of data (six megabytes) as this book's entire text. In other words, one picture is worth a lot more than a thousand words. It's worth closer to a million words.

IMAGES

Long before humans were putting their thoughts down in the form of written words, they were drawing pictures. Pictures are the earliest form of human graphic expression. The letters of the alphabet are themselves abstractions of pictures.[4]

The more primitive origin of pictures is sometimes cited in arguments about the regressive nature of modern culture with its obsession with image. I will leave these arguments for other writers to ponder. Suffice it to say that we can more easily envision a late Pleistocene-era cave dweller painting a picture than writing a poem. This is not to suggest that poetry cannot be produced by Neanderthals. Much has been over the years. And it should also be noted that painters and photographers are often some of the most refined and literate people in the present world, even though they continue to practice the earliest form of graphic communication.

Let's begin this discussion by recreating our own first experiences making images. Before you read further, put this book down and take a short trip to your nearest supermarket or drugstore and buy yourself a box of crayons. For the purposes of this assignment, you can get away with a small box of 8 or 16 crayons, but if you really want to indulge your inner child, buy yourself a big box of 64 Crayola Crayons, the kind that have the crayon sharpener built into the back of the box. I'll wait...

Now open the box and take out one of the crayons. Pick your favorite color, or pick my favorite: bittersweet. The crayon is made out of a mixture of wax and a finely ground material called a *pigment*. The pigment composition is different in each of the crayons in your box. People have been grinding up materials to make pigments for many thousands of years. To make the resulting powders adhere to surfaces, the pigments are mixed with sticky materials called *vehicles* or *binders*. Cavemen did it. Raphael and Van Gogh did it. We do it today and it is a good bet that people will still be doing it thousands of years from now.

Now take your crayon and use it to color in the box. If you were to use an electron microscope to inspect the layer of waxy coloring that you have applied to this page, you would find that the pigment particles resemble colored boulders suspended in a transparent support. In the crayon, the pigment boulders are opaque, so light only reflects from the surface and does not penetrate. All pigments are not opaque. Some pigments are transparent. Light passes through them and is filtered. A red transparent pigment allows the red light to pass through and absorbs the other colors of the rainbow.

Another kind of colored material that can be used in place of a pigment is called a dye. Rather than having to grind up dyes into powder, dyes dissolve in liquids such as water or alcohol. The inks in fountain pens and most desktop inkjet printers use dyes as the colored materials. Dyes must be suspended in vehicles that bind them permanently to surfaces.

All of the printing machines in the world today do essentially the same thing you did when you used your crayon to color the box. They apply thin layers of colored materials to surfaces to selectively alter the way the surfaces absorb and transmit light, thus creating visible images.

REPRODUCTION OF IMAGES

We are reasonably sure that people have been making images since Paleolithic times. We do not, however, know when the first system for making multiple copies of the same image was invented. There is archeological evidence of printing from carved blocks or through stencils that can be traced back a few thousand years at most. The idea might have occurred to any observant person walking with wet feet across a dry surface, leaving a trail of footprints.

I am reminded of a bit of personal history. When I was a child, my father decided to paint our basement floor, and then decorate it in a way that would distinguish our family from all of the others in our neighborhood. After painting the floor dark gray and letting it dry, he directed my two brothers and me to step into three different colored puddles of paint and then walk on the cold concrete floor. We covered the gray floor with colorful footprints. Mine were yellow. In my reconstructed narrative of personal mythology thus began my lifelong passion for print.

IMAGE CONTENT FOR PRINT TODAY

There are essentially three kinds of original image content that find their way into print: content that is captured through some kind of photographic process, content that is synthesized by human beings, and content that is generated by computer programs. There are many ways that these different types of image content can be combined. For example, a film camera can be used to capture an image from the natural world, the image can be scanned and manipulated on a computer, and then the image can be automatically processed by a computer program to produce a replicated pattern that will be used in a decorative application. Most images that appear in print today result from a complex image creation path such as this.

Photographic image capture was once the exclusive domain of film. Photographic images were captured on film from the natural world, in the studio, or on a copy board. Most natural world and studio photography today is performed with digital cameras. Film still dominates certain niche markets, but will soon disappear from commercial use altogether. For images to be usable in print publishing applications they must first be in digital form. Images captured with digital cameras are born this way. Film images have to be converted through a process of scanning.

Scanning technology has improved dramatically in terms of price and performance in the past few decades. The first digital scanners were massive, expensive, slow, and extremely difficult to operate by current standards. Today it is possible to purchase for a few hundred dollars the same functionality that in the mid-1980s would have cost a few hundred thousand dollars. Scanners, being computer-based devices, have followed the same price/performance trends as all other such devices. I purchased a scanner recently that ended up costing me, with discounts and rebates, a grand total of $49.

However inexpensive the hardware may be, scanning remains a labor-intensive activity. This is because each original piece of film must be individually handled, and digital images produced by the scanner always require some additional work such as the manual removal of digitized dust particles and scratches. As the cost of digital camera technology rapidly approaches that of film camera technology, the advantages of digital photography are quickly consigning film to the dustbin of graphic arts history. As with all discarded graphic reproduction technologies, film will most likely enjoy a long retirement from commercial work as a fine art medium. The darkroom will evolve into a sacred space where ancient rituals of alchemy and conjuring are performed by a chemical-saturated priesthood. I have recently considered re-establishing my basement darkroom as a hiding place from the harsh realities of everyday digital life. We'll see.

The digital imaging revolution is enabling the emergence of new industries that take advantage of the portability and reusability of digital assets. The rapid proliferation of digital images, accessible online and available for use by anyone willing to pay the license fee, makes their use an increasingly attractive option for publishers seeking imagery. Why hire a photographer to produce original images, if stock images exist that will fulfill the same need? The stock images can be procured in a matter of minutes versus the weeks that it would take to procure originals. Easy electronic access to mil-

Corbis maintains one of the largest collections of image resources in digital form. Corbis images can be found and licensed at www.corbis.com. Corbis also offers extensive client advisory services including subject matter and conceptual research, rights management and clearances, and production expertise.

lions of existing images has changed the behavior patterns of people seeking photographic imagery. Many photographers see the stock industry as a threat. Others see it as an opportunity.

The use of stock photography does not stop at the borders of the rectangular packages that define all photographic images. Designers increasingly view images as repositories of image data that can be mined with creative tools such as Adobe Photoshop. Most traditional photographers would prefer to think of their images as sacrosanct rectangles of creative property that should not be compromised. Simple cropping is bad enough. Imagine then the horror of seeing a designer ransack an image for content that is needed, leaving the plundered remains to rot away in digital oblivion.

However, designers increasingly do view images in this way. They simply have no decent respect for the sensibilities of photographers who labor hard to produce great rectangles full of great content. Progressive commercial photographers embrace the notion that the value they create is in the form of boxes of content that can be used in any way their clients wish. They do not wince when they see pieces of their work scattered across the landscape like the body parts of a gazelle in the aftermath of a hyena dinner party. They simply collect their fees and move on to the next assignment.

Most digital image content is encoded in the form of large arrays of numbers that represent the color and tonal value of the image point by point. I have a digital camera, for example, that captures a rectangular array of numbers exactly 2,560 wide by 1,920 high. The total number of points in the array is 2,560, multiplied by 1,920 = 4,915,200, or close to five million. Each point is a *pixel* (a contraction of the words picture + element). Each pixel contains a color represented by three separate values: red, green, and blue. A camera that is able to capture five million pixels in a single frame is said to have a resolution of five *megapixels*. Digital photographs are always represented in this form, sometimes called a *raster image*. Raster images are produced by digital cameras and scanners or with software such as Adobe Photoshop.

Photoshop runs on both Apple Macintosh and Microsoft Windows computer platforms and includes tools that enable the creation of anything imaginable in the two-dimensional world of pixels. In some cases, Photoshop is the only software application required to design a printed product. Posters, for example, often lend themselves to the Photoshop-only approach. If it all fits on a single page or panel, Photoshop will do the job. Photoshop includes tools for drawing, painting, typesetting, compositing, and automating the production of images for print and electronic presentation. There is likely no room in your house, nor in your place of work, nor in any retail establishment, where images made with Photoshop are not present.

THE AUTHENTICITY OF IMAGE CONTENT

Our ability to assemble and edit images today is only restricted by our imagination and skill with the digital tools available. With the proper editing, even bad originals can be made to look much better. This capability is a godsend to imaging professionals and to people like Cher and Madonna.

The ease with which images can be digitally altered raises several issues. There is an ongoing debate about the truthfulness of photographs and what kinds of alterations are ethical if the photograph is supposed to convey something that actually happened. Photojournalists are particularly concerned about these matters. Most news organizations have strict codes that forbid alteration of the content of photographs. Picture editors have gotten into deep trouble for the subtlest violation of these rules: for example, removing an empty soda can from a desk or moving an element in the photograph slightly to improve the composition. Most of these incidents result from an innocent effort to improve the graphic appearance of a photograph and not a sinister attempt to manipulate audience perceptions or interpretations. If audience manipulation is the goal, that can be accomplished far more effectively by simply choosing a different frame.

In advertising, none of these restrictions apply. You will almost never see a straight reproduction of an original photograph in advertising. Often, a single image is constructed out of numerous pieces of other images. Managing these editorial processes and keeping track of all of the intermediate edited versions of a final image can be daunting. Managing the intellectual property rights of original image creators when pieces of their images end up in composites requires sophisticated approaches to *rights management* that ensure that individual contributors are appropriately compensated for their work. Specialized *digital asset management* software makes it easier to manage large repositories of image content as it is developed and distributed. We will look at this in more detail in the next chapter.

HYBRID IMAGE CONTENT

Some digital images that find their way into print are represented as collections of mathematically described outlines filled with solid color values. An image of this type, sometimes called a *vector image*, resembles a paint-by-number painting. Vector images are created with drawing software such as Adobe Illustrator. Many of the images you see in print and displayed on computer monitors are originally described in this way. The image masters of the characters you are reading at this moment, for example, are each described as outlines filled with solid black. Vector-based outlines can also be stacked together to form complex images.

Creative artists using sophisticated tools such as Adobe Illustrator and Adobe Photoshop can produce hybrid digital images that combine both raster and vector elements. Hybrid images may also contain text elements. The illustration on page 194 is a printed rendering of a hybrid image created in Adobe Illustrator. Hybrid images can only be viewed and manipulated within their native applications and must normally be converted to simpler formats before they can be distributed and used broadly.

DIGITAL CONTENT INDIRECTLY CONNECTED TO PRINT

Many print media products today are integrated with digital media that feature other forms of content. In some cases the content is on a physical disk format such as CD-ROM or DVD-ROM. In other cases the content can be accessed on the Internet. Thus print can be packaged with, or reference, a variety of other forms of digital media. Textbook publishers will often include digital media products such as software programs, databases, videos, and games with their basic print media products. In many cases these bundled digital media products cannot be sold separately because there is no stand-alone market demand for them. However, they can be used to justify higher prices for the print products.

Print can also point to content on the web. Nearly all printed advertisements do this. There have even been attempts to make it possible to scan a printed 2D bar code with a specially-designed wand that automatically inputs a web address to a web browser such as Internet Explorer, thus saving the reader the need to retype the address. But after an initial period of experimentation with such technologically clever approaches to connecting print to web, people seem to have settled on manual input as the preferred method. Marketing experts assume that if people are not motivated enough to retype a simple web address into their browser, they probably aren't going to be very desirable customers.

When print is bundled with digital media or points to it on the web, it breaks out of its traditional boundaries. Print can't sing a song, show a video clip, or play a game. But it is often the only practical way to invite people to experience these things on the web.

Relationships that begin on the web can be strengthened and expanded through subsequent print communications. Print sometimes initiates a relationship that flowers on the web and then is consummated back in print. How these scenarios all play out in reality will depend upon what the users of media are trying to accomplish. But one thing is for certain: there will be few occasions where print will stand apart from the web in the future.

CONTENT MANAGEMENT

Digital technology accelerates the proliferation and aggregation of content. Digital photography, for example, removes the consumable costs from the process of capturing an image. With film-based photography, the high cost of consumables imposed a discipline on the photographic process that limited the rate of image content production. Photographers exercised judgment when shooting with film to optimize the cost/benefit ratio. This need for critical judgment about when and when not to release the shutter was a constant source of anxiety. Digital cameras eliminate the incremental costs associated with film and remove the anxiety. The mantra of the digital photographer is "shoot first and ask questions later."

Given the tendency that I described earlier of designers to view digital images as repositories of raw data that can be mined creatively for content, the potential value of any given image is no longer as easy to determine at first glance. A horribly-composed image that would never find its way into print in its pristine rectangular state might very well contain elements of value to a creative designer searching for parts. The digital photographer charged with the task of supplying usable image content will be increasingly motivated to preserve images that have the slightest potential for future application.

Thus digital photography encourages the proliferation of image content and shifts the burden of judgment about what is worthy of being preserved downstream in the process. The growing practice of image data-mining among designers encourages the preservation of raw image data. The challenge becomes how to manage the content in a way that will allow easy access to appropriate content for maximum value creation in the future.

Content management is something that begins the moment

we are confronted with more than one piece of information that we need to preserve for future reference. Today, for example, exactly eight pieces of mail were delivered by the U.S. Postal Service to my mailbox. There were two bills, one reminder from the dentist that I have an appointment next Tuesday, one monthly statement from an investment fund, and four pieces of direct mail. I temporarily placed the two bills into a folder that I keep for unpaid monthly bills. I tacked the dental appointment reminder to the bulletin board near the telephone in the kitchen. I filed the statement from the investment fund in a folder that I keep for statements for that particular fund. I opened one of the direct mail pieces because it looked like a check from the federal government on the outside. When I discovered that it was really a promotional piece trying to sell me a limited edition collectible plate with a portrait of Elvis painted on it, I threw it and the other three unopened pieces of junk mail into the trash.

The system that I have for keeping track of my incoming mail has both good points and bad points. My file of unpaid bills, for example, makes it easy to know what my current accounts-payable situation is at a moment's glance. But since the bills are all due on different days of the month, I have to continually paw through the entire file to make sure that I am keeping up to date with my bill paying. It would be better if the bills were somehow organized according to when they are payable. I could devise a system that would do this, but at this point I am not willing to spend the time. Besides, there would inevitably be tradeoffs.

How we ultimately organize our stuff is for most people and organizations an ongoing struggle that never ends. (This task often falls to the next generation once we have permanently departed their company.) We are constantly striving for better organizing schemes, and we realize that there is no one perfect scheme. That is why it is so useful to have the ability to change the organizing rules on the fly. I do this all the time with my various email collections. Sometimes I need to search by date, sometimes by subject, sometimes by sender, and sometimes by size. The organization of data into multiple-field records that can be sorted on any field is one of the greatest inventions of all time.

However, this organizing principle is more difficult to implement when data are not contained within the neat structure of a relational database consisting of tables of uniformly structured records. Much of the content that ends up in print is in the form of text files and image files that are not explicitly related to one another. We must impose relationships by how we organize them. This is where we enter the labyrinth of the computer file system that originated with Unix back in the 1960s, and which still reigns on every computer that exists today from the tiniest pocket PC to the largest and most powerful server.

This system associates files by co-locating them in directories organized in a hierarchical fashion. The organizational structure is entirely arbitrary, even though operating systems such as Microsoft Windows attempt to suggest some organizing ideas such as, "Put all of your pictures in the directory named *My Pictures* and all of your documents in the directory named *My Documents*." Thanks for your help, Microsoft. But I have thousands of documents and tens of thousands of pictures. If I dump them all into those directories, I will never be able to find them again. So immediately I am forced to start to organize my directories into sub-directories and sub-sub-directories, and on and on in a recursive spiral that leads to oblivion. No matter how smart I try to be in organizing my files, I know that I'm still going to have trouble locating content when I need it.

To deal with this problem *digital asset management* (DAM) systems take various approaches to indexing and organizing digital content so that people can work with it more easily. DAM is sometimes called *media asset management*. This yields a more feminine-sounding acronym that has not yet made it into the common lexicon. The range of DAM solutions is very broad, from software that runs on a single desktop and serves the needs of a single user, to enterprise-wide software that serves large organizations or even networks of organizations.

The simplest systems provide a way of indexing digital content so that it can be searched for and retrieved using simple methods. These systems transcend the physical directory structure by creating a virtual indexing system on top of it. This liberates the user from having to worry about where files are actually located in the file system. Textual descriptions and thumbnail images of individual pieces of content are stored in a structured database with pointers to the actual files. The files can reside anywhere on a hard drive, local network, or on the Internet.

Digital asset management becomes more complex as the variety of uses of content and the number of parties supplying and accessing the content increases. The most sophisticated DAM systems store the assets themselves inside a database that is capable of providing data security, ensuring data integrity, and enforcing rules about how the assets are used. These systems serve publishers and advertisers who need to have repositories of digital assets simultaneously accessible in real time to large numbers of users. The architecture of high-end DAM systems must be customized to meet the requirements of specific organizations and workflows. A publisher of legal books and Internet products has quite different needs from the packaging design division in a consumer products company. A company that sells digital assets such as stock photography over the Internet needs a different kind of DAM system than a museum that maintains a repository of digital photographs for scholarly and research purposes.

Many publishers also make heavy use of open-source data obtainable from the Internet. This is where the search engine comes into play. With a search engine, it no longer matters where content is located, just as long as it is located somewhere and it stays put. The search engine periodically runs through the Internet, visiting each accessible site and creating a catalog based on the text content at each site. Search engines rely on the fact that the Internet uses a numerical system to identify computers connected around the world. Numerical addresses are mapped to names of sites by *domain name servers*. For example, the domain name *www.rit.edu* directs requests to computers with the Internet Protocol address *129.21.2.245*, which identifies the computer at RIT that hosts our website.

The search engine performs the job of a good reference librarian. You tell it what you want, and it tells you where to find it. This method of organizing content is what makes the web so useful. Every file on the web has a unique location indicated by an address called a URL or Uniform Resource Locator. If you know the address, you can go directly to any file on the web. Here's the address of a file that contains a picture of me:

http://www.rit.edu/~fjcppr/newmediumbook/frank.jpg

How would you ever find this file, if I hadn't given you the exact URL? There is only one way possible. If I wanted to enable you to find a picture of me on the web, here's what I would do. I would attach some text metadata to this file that would describe it as a "photograph of Professor Frank Cost of Rochester Institute of Technology, co-director of the Printing Industry Center at RIT and author of the book, *The New Medium of Print: Material Communication in the Internet Age*." Then I would wait for the search engines that catalog the Internet to find the file and index it based on the keywords in the text metadata part of the file. If I wanted to make sure that my file was indexed, I could also take proactive steps to getting the file catalogued. I could sumbit the URL to Google, for example. By relying on the power of the search engine to find and catalog things and by adding information to my file to make it easier to catalog once it is found, I can be reasonably sure that a person searching for my picture would be able to find it.

It would be even better if you could search for images of me using descriptive criteria such as "good-looking middle-aged guy," or "resembles George Harrison, except with Ringo Starr nose." Attempts have been made to create search engines that catalog generic image data based on an analysis of the actual content of the image. However, none of these has worked well enough to become commercially viable. It is relatively easy to detect image content characteristics such as "predominantly reddish in hue," or "contains many straight lines." It is much more difficult to distinguish pictures of Lhasa Apsos from pictures of Shih Tzus.

Image-based search engines are most useful in highly constrained applications. The best example that I can give you is the system that the FBI uses to search for fingerprint matches. All of the images in the database are fingerprints. The search criteria are also images of fingerprints. The search engine is specially designed to match fingerprint patterns. One can imagine constructing similar systems for identification of samples from constrained sets of objects such as butterflies, tree leaves, coins, stamps, etc. In each of these cases, the search criterion must be almost identical in appearance to a unique record in the database in order for the search to succeed.

CHAPTER TWO

FORMATTING

A S I WRITE THIS BOOK, I am not thinking very much about how it will appear in its final form. I am using a simple text editor to contain my words as they dribble painfully from my brain, through my fingers, and into the computer by way of the keyboard. (Sometimes, thankfully, the words flow a little easier. For example, this sentence seems to be coming out without much suffering on my part at all.)

Although my prime purpose at the moment is to produce text for this book, I am also aware that elements of my writing may also find their way into other presentation forms. At the moment, I am concentrating on producing raw content. Later, I will worry about marrying that content to specific formats. My first experiences as a writer were before the age of personal computing. Back then I had two choices about how to generate content. I could either write with a pen or pencil on paper, or try to channel my thoughts directly into a typewriter and onto a finished page. Because my approach to writing can be described as "one step forward and two steps back," the direct input to the typewriter method was always guaranteed to lead to an episode of violence.

When I wrote an article for publication in the mid-1970s I would struggle with pencil, paper, and eraser to get the words out initially. Then, I would create a typewritten manuscript from my handwritten scrawl. I would submit this typed manuscript for publication. Everything that happened after that point was a black box to me.

Within that box, here's a quick description of what happened. A specially trained person called a *typesetter* would read my typed

manuscript and re-key the text at a special keyboard that would punch holes into a long strip of paper tape. The punched holes represented coded characters and formatting commands specific to a particular typesetting system. The punched paper tape would be fed into a typesetting machine that would produce long strips of white photographic paper bearing the latent image of a column of type. These strips of photographic paper would be fed into a chemical processing system that would develop and fix the image. The dried photographic paper strips, called *galleys*, would be fed through a machine that would apply a thin layer of tacky wax to the back. The galleys would be cut apart and laid out on large ruled sheets of heavy paper called *mechanicals*. These were the masters from which the printing plates were made through a complex photographic process that I will not discuss for fear of losing your attention.

Sometimes I would have the opportunity to proofread the mechanicals and make corrections. The cost of making a change at this point was very high, so I would normally only check for corrections of errors that were made by the typesetter misreading my manuscript, because I would not be charged for them. I would often be tempted to change a word or rewrite a sentence after first seeing my words in printed form. Words look different when formally dressed than they do when they first get out of bed in the morning.

Now fast-forward to the present. I am watching these words appear magically on my computer screen all dressed up in typeset form. I can read what I have written instantaneously and make changes to my heart's content. There is simply no excuse for me to subject you to a poor choice of word or an awkwardly written sentence. However, since I do not yet know what the final presentation format of this book will be, I cannot give a complete guarantee that everything will be perfect. For example, the book designer may choose a terrible typeface that is difficult to read, or design a page format that makes the lines of type so long that you have a difficult time reading from the end of one line to the beginning of the next. In either of those cases we will both have the designer to blame for your unhappiness.

The formatting of image content for presentation presents another whole set of issues. In the days of film photography, the original image content was in the form of a photographic print or transparency. This original defined the expectation for all subsequent presentation formats. There was a fundamental problem with this expectation, however. It was never possible to match the appearance of an original photograph when reproduced in print. In the age of digital photography, original images are first seen displayed on computer screens. Although print is capable of resolving more fine detail than a typical computer screen, it still can't reproduce the same range of available tones or colors.

Thus, when we prepare images for display in print we are set up for disappointment from the start. No matter how hard we try, we will not succeed at making printed images look the same as photographic or computer-displayed originals. We either need to lower our expectations of what is possible, or find ways to compensate for the inherent shortcomings of the print reproduction process. Fortunately there are many ways to improve the appearance of printed images by adjusting tonal contrast, edge sharpness, and color rendering. These adjustments can be built into image-processing software and applied automatically to optimize images for specific print reproduction conditions.

BINDING CONTENT TO PRESENTATION FORMATS

At some point between this moment when I am creating content by pressing the keys on my computer keyboard and the moment when you consume the content I have produced, the content must be formatted for presentation. This binding of content to presentation format can happen instantaneously as I press the keys, or later on. In my current mode of operation, I am temporarily binding this content to a default document format in Microsoft Word. I can see the results instantaneously on the screen. I am relying on the word processor to render my raw text using a specific typeface and typographic settings. If I press the print key, the word processor communicates with the print driver to produce a printed document that appears almost identical to what I see on the screen.

However, this format is only serving my temporary needs for feedback so that I can easily review what I have written. I mostly rely on the screen for this first level of review. There is nothing preventing me from accepting this format as the final appearance of the document. If this were a technical report or a business document, it might be appropriate to stop here. However, I am creating this content primarily for publication in book form and will need a more sophisticated formatting capability for that purpose. The book you hold in your hands was formatted with Adobe InDesign. Although it is possible to input keystrokes directly into InDesign, I prefer to keep the content separate from the final design while I am struggling to create it. I don't need the added distraction of trying to make pretty pages this early in the process. Most authors prefer to work in this manner.

There are three other reasons why I prefer to create my text content in Microsoft Word. First, Word provides tools such as spell checker, thesaurus, and grammar checker that I have come to rely on heavily. I can't think of the last time I used a printed dictionary or thesaurus. I am also not embarrassed to admit that I have a rather nasty habit of using the passive voice when I should be using the active voice, and the grammar checker in Word alerts me to this.

The second reason for using Word is to add structure to a document, making it easier to work with the content later on. Titles and paragraphs can be tagged with headings to indicate their respective levels in the hierarchy of the document. These headings can then be used to automatically generate outlines and a table of contents. Words and phrases in a text can be marked for automatic generation of indexes. Footnotes and endnotes can be inserted and maintained easily. Hyperlinks to other locations in the same document, or other documents, can also be included in the text.

The third reason I prefer to use Word for writing is that everyone in the world with whom I need to share files also uses Microsoft Word. It's the de facto standard for word processing. So when I send this manuscript out for editing or review, I am sure that the person receiving it will be able to read it. At this point I can sense danger arising from certain quarters where what I have just said is fighting language. So before someone leaps out of the bushes and attacks me I will try to act preemptively and explain myself.

If I wished to ensure that anyone in the world with web access could read my files, I would choose a different format than Word. Word files can only be read with the Word application software. People who do not own Word software cannot read Word files. However, anyone can read a PDF (Adobe Portable Document Format) file because the software required is available free for any kind of computer. PDF files can be generated easily from all word processing or graphics applications, accurately conveying all of the subtle graphic detail in the original application files.[5] So PDF is the universal choice for widespread distribution of documents, regardless of the application software used to produce the originals.

The primary reason for distributing Word files for review is that they can be edited and sent back with changes. Much of my writing is done collaboratively with other people. We bounce documents back and forth until they are finished. Word makes this easy. Although PDF allows a reader to add commentary to files, it is not editable in the same way as Word. Thus PDF works best if the master document is built in one place and editorial changes are suggested by readers through commentary added to PDF documents and returned to the person responsible for building the master. The choice of Word or PDF as an interchange format during content creation therefore depends on the particular workflow. Multi-author workflows favor Word. Single author/single editor workflows also favor Word. Single author/multiple editor workflows favor PDF.

The simplest way to design the print formatted version of a book would be to do the whole thing in Microsoft Word. If this book contained only text, that is probably the choice we would have made. Word offers a rich array of functions that make it easy to organize and manipulate the content of a book. By using custom-designed templates, and tagging all of the content so that it can be automatically formatted, design adjustments can be applied to the entire book with a few mouse clicks. Word also makes it easy to create and manage footnotes, endnotes, indexes, and tables of contents.

With this book, the choice was made to do the final page layouts in Adobe InDesign. This program allows for finer control of typography and page design than does Word. A book designer using InDesign has more freedom to fine tune the spacing of letters and words, the flow of text around illustrations, and the precise alignment of graphic elements on the page than with Word.

The key to the efficient conversion of a Word document into an InDesign document is to structure the content in the Word file so that the structure can be preserved when the content is imported into InDesign. This is easily accomplished by creating a custom list of text styles in Word and tagging all of the text with an identified style. Each style is identified by a name. When the style is applied to a block of text, it has the effect of labeling or tagging the text. A matching list of text styles using the identical style names can then be created in InDesign. The tagged text from Word can then be imported into the InDesign document.

The book designer assigns specific typographic parameters to each text style when creating a design template for the book. These include typeface, size, letter and word spacing, line spacing, line length, indents, and the stylistic treatment of initial letters. Text pasted into these containers automatically assumes all of these predetermined attributes.

By tagging each block of text with the appropriate style in the Word document, and creating a corresponding style sheet in InDesign, the transfer of text content from Word to InDesign is relatively painless. However, this book required additional manual work to incorporate the illustrations and adjust the flow of text around them to optimize the legibility of each page. Because the final pagination can only be known after all of the illustrations are included, InDesign was used to automatically generate the table of contents and index after the layout was finished.

COMMON DOCUMENT TYPES

For some publications this labor-intensive workflow is not the best solution to the problem. If, instead of this one book, we were producing a multitude of publications that all shared the same basic structure, or a single publication that consisted of a multitude of similar parts, we would benefit from a more structured relationship between the authoring format and the publishing format. If, for example, this book were part of a large series of books that shared the same design look and feel, a different approach would be warranted. Fortunately there is an information structuring format that enables automated workflows of this type. This is called *XML*.

XML stands for Extensible Markup Language. It is the foundation for publishing systems that automate the flow of content from creation to final presentation, whether in print or on the web. XML provides a mechanism for tagging all of the separate pieces of content in a document so that they can be inserted automatically into a design template for the final publication. XML also captures the hierarchical structure of a document, so it knows exactly where every piece of content goes. In most applications XML is hidden from view. The user interface can be as simple and foolproof as filling out an electronic form or interacting with a web interface. XML holds promise for my dream of someday being able to write a book by playing a book-writing video game. My interactions with the game would generate content that would be packaged in a specially designed XML file. This content would then be processed automatically and formatted into a book. As fantastic as this may sound, the technology already exists to make this possible today.

FROM DESIGN TO META-DESIGN

Contemporary graphic designers use design tools such as the Adobe Creative Suite to convert content into formatted files for print production. The designer of this book, Marnie Soom, started the design process by developing a number of alternative page designs using different sets of typographic and geometric styles for each design. She then created some sample page spreads with text and graphic elements to simulate the appearance of the finished book. We evaluated the different ideas and picked one that we liked.

We placed some constraints on the design from the beginning. We decided that the book was going to measure approximately 6 by 9 inches, that it would be printed in black and white, and that it would be paper-bound. These decisions were informed by the concept and business plan for the book. When I completed this text, I transmitted the Word file to the designer and she imported it into Adobe InDesign. She then placed all of the illustrations into the document. When she completed the layout she used the automated features in InDesign to generate the table of contents and the index. When the design was complete, she exported Adobe PDF files directly from InDesign and transmitted them to the printer over the Internet.

Adobe InDesign represents a document as a set of pages containing boxes or frames that hold various graphic elements such as text, drawings, and images. Each page in a document can contain an arbitrary number of boxes. Text boxes on one page can be linked to boxes on other pages so that stories can flow from page to page throughout the document. The text on this page, for example, flows continuously from this text box to the text box on the next page. If I insert a sentence here, the text at the bottom of this page will move or re-flow to the top of the next page because the text boxes on this page and the next are linked. If all of the text boxes in a book are linked from page to page from beginning to end, an insertion at the beginning of the book will result in text re-flowing like dominoes from page to page all the way to the end of the book. Such power makes it difficult to stop inserting text—even when the text has no added value, like this sentence, for example.

In addition to text, boxes can also contain images and drawings that are created with other programs such as Photoshop or Illustrator. These images and drawings remain in files external to the document. The document file contains pointers to these external files and they must be included when the document is transported from place to place. For this reason, InDesign includes a simple way to collect all of the files associated with a particular document and put them into a common folder with all of the links intact. This folder can then be transported on disk or over a network.

Like the snake eating its tail, the illustration on the next page is a screen shot of the InDesign layout of pages 34 and 35. If you are disturbed by the self-referential circularity of this experience, just imagine how disturbing it was for the designer to design this part of the book! She couldn't produce the illustration until the chapter was complete, but the chapter wasn't complete until the illustration was

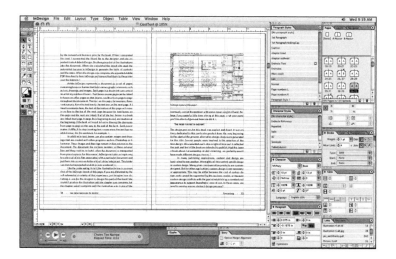

InDesign layout of pages 34 and 35.

in place! She eventually solved the problem with some clever sleight of hand. Perhaps if you spend a little time staring at this page, or at your navel, you'll be able to figure out how she did it.

THE NEED FOR META-DESIGN

The design process for this book was explicit and direct. It was entirely dedicated to this particular product from the very beginning. At the start of the process alternative design ideas were generated for this title. Several people were involved in the selection of the final design. We evaluated each idea in light of how well it reflected the look and feel of the book we intended to publish. Had this been a book about horsemanship or doll collecting, we probably would have made different design choices.

In many publishing applications, content and design are hard-wired to one another. We might call this *content-specific design* or *custom design*. Many print communication products are custom-designed. But for other applications custom design is not necessary or appropriate. This may be either because the cost of custom design work cannot be supported by the business model, or because custom design conflicts with the goal of establishing a standardized appearance to support branding or ease of use. In these cases, we need to employ a more abstract design process.

Meta-design is the process of creating designs that are content-independent. The most familiar example of meta-design is a Microsoft PowerPoint template. PowerPoint includes several dozen standard templates with names like clouds, ocean, competition, teamwork, and kimono. Each combines background graphics, typeface, layout, and type style choices. The names convey the general character of each design. Many of the designs address a rather narrow window of potential uses. Kimono, for example, may only be suitable for presentations about Japanese formal wear or flower decorating. Other designs have greater versatility.

Many PowerPoint users will create their own custom templates to achieve a corporate brand look. This takes advantage of the meta-design capabilities built into the program. This feature allows for relatively easy enforcement of design standards throughout an organization, while leaving individuals free to make their own documents using their own content.

Meta-designs in the form of templates also reinforce the concept that content can be completely separated from presentation format. The clean separation of content from presentation format is a fundamental building block of all emerging Internet-enabled print applications. Combined with the use of XML as a vehicle for structuring content, template-based meta-design eliminates the need to bind content exclusively to a specific presentation format. Thus content is maintained as structured data that can be viewed in a variety of ways. The choice of viewpoint results in the automated flow of selected content into a specific template. Both web and print presentation can draw from the same content database.

CHAPTER THREE

THE PRINT PRODUCTION INPUT SUPPLY CHAIN

W<small>E NOW TURN OUR ATTENTION TO</small> the manufacturing process itself. There are three distinct components to the input supply chain. These are:

1. Content
2. Information about what to do with the content
3. Raw materials

Most content is in digital form, packaged as a set of Adobe InDesign or PDF files, for example. However, there may also be discrete pieces of content that are still in their original "pre-digitized" form such as a photographic print, transparency, painting, or an object that needs to be photographed. Some catalog printers, for example, provide studio photography services for their clients. In such cases, it makes sense to consider physical product samples as part of the input supply chain.

Information about what to do with the content may take many different forms, from handwritten notes and order sheets prepared by a salesperson to digital files transmitted over the Internet. The Job Definition Format (JDF) was developed to provide a standardized digital container for all such information. The most simplified and elegant input data stream encompassing both content and information about what to do with the content that is currently available is a single PDF file for the content and a single JDF file that tells what to do with the content. Thus it is theoretically possible to contain all of the necessary digital information required to produce

any job in just two files. This book, for example, could be fully specified with the following two files:

1. New_medium_of_print.pdf
2. New_medium_of_print.jdf

(The contents of a book like this would more typically be contained
in multiple PDF files, with separate files for the cover art and the set
of inside pages. This is because the geometry of the cover includes
the front, spine, and back covers joined together in a single panel.)

A JDF file attached to a print job has the capacity to carry all
of the information about the job that may be needed at any point
during its planning, scheduling, production, and distribution. In other
words, it is an information container for job *meta-data*. A JDF file can
replace all other sources of information about a job necessary to its
successful completion.

Most current applications of JDF are intended to reduce setup
times on discrete pieces of manufacturing equipment by using the
information in the JDF file to perform machine setups automatically.
But the most significant promise of JDF is to provide a standardized
integrated communication channel between users and producers
of print communication products and services. This allows users
to specify such attributes as the exact form of the finished product,
product approval requirements, and production and distribution requirements. Without a standardized way to encode this information
in a digital file, it is impossible to contemplate a clean web interface
that allows users easy access to print communication services. The
minute you have to get on the phone and call someone, the efficien-
cies of the Internet are seriously compromised.

Because JDF is nothing more than a standardized information container for job meta-data, its role can easily be performed
by alternative proprietary methods of structuring the same type of
information. If you asked 1,000 computer scientists to each invent
a file format that would contain the same information as a JDF file
without showing them the architecture of JDF, you would end up
with 1,000 unique file formats and no standard. The real value of
JDF is that it standardizes the communication of job meta-data from
order entry through fulfillment. The standard promises to simplify

the construction of interfaces between Internet-based communication services companies and geographically distributed print production facilities. The organization responsible for creating the JDF
standard and promoting its adoption is called CIP4. You can learn
more than you thought you would ever want to know about JDF at
the following web site: *www.cip4.org*.

FILE TRANSMISSION

There are two ways to transmit files from one place (the designer's
desktop, for example) to another (the printer). Files can be shipped
physically on writable media such as CD or DVD, or over the Internet. Most commercial printing companies today have the ability to
receive files via Internet File Transfer Protocol (FTP). In some cases,
large file sets are transmitted physically on disk, and corrections or
changes are then transmitted via FTP.

There are a number of ways to provide security for files transmitted over the Internet. These are all based on a scrambling of the
file contents before they are transmitted and an unscrambling after
they are received. This takes place quietly behind the scenes. Current techniques for scrambling and unscrambling files are so secure
that there is effectively no possibility of failure.

The distinction between corrections and changes is important. A correction implies a fix, whereas a change is often the result
of a change of mind on the part of the print buyer. These changes of
mind can happen at any point in the print production process. The
later in the process this occurs, the more expensive the change.
The most expensive kind of change is one that is made after the
presses have started to run. The exclamation "stop the presses!"
has a dramatic ring for that very reason. Once those cylinders start
turning, this command has a similar effect to lighting a bonfire of
high-denomination banknotes. It's the very last thing some people
say before their print-buying careers come to an abrupt end.

One of the greatest promises of the emerging world of Internet-based print communication services is the elimination of
the liabilities associated with traditional print buying. The goal is to
provide simple foolproof interfaces between buyers and sellers of
print and eliminate the possibility that human error will undermine
the integrity of the final product. In this new world, file transmission

occurs automatically as a consequence of the transaction of business, and is not something to which anyone has to consciously attend.

FILE PREPARATION AND PREPRESS

So what happens to the file sets once they enter the print production process? We will now turn our attention to the complex set of digital operations performed on a set of files produced by a layout program such as Adobe InDesign. But first permit me a brief digression. Designers use a variety of tools to create documents that end up in print. Among these is the Microsoft Office suite of applications including Word, PowerPoint, Excel, etc. These office-type applications were not originally intended to drive high-volume commercial printing processes. However this has not prevented creative people from using them to do just that.

If you ask typical commercial printers what kinds of application files they will accept from their customers, the answer will almost always be, "Anything they send." If you want to create a book using Photoshop where each page is a separate Photoshop file, you can do that, and most commercial printers will be able to work with your files. They may also laugh at you behind your back for using such inappropriate tools for the job, and will most certainly charge you for the extra work required to prepare your files for print.

On the highest level, the *prepress* or print preparation process can be viewed as a black box that inputs application files from programs such as Adobe InDesign, Microsoft Word, or QuarkXPress at the front end, and outputs printing masters at the other. These masters may be physical plates that are mounted on mechanical printing presses, or digital masters that are used to drive digital printers. In either case, the masters must conform perfectly to the geometric requirements of a specific printing device and the dimensions of the material that can go through the device. The masters must also anticipate all of the nuances of the printing process with regard to the reproduction of graphics. One of the most critical nuances is the way a printing process reproduces color. Print buyers can be very difficult to please when it comes to color.

The transformation of application files into printing masters can therefore be very complex. The computing power required for this task is formidable. The file sizes associated with printing masters are enormous. Few computing applications require more raw power than the manipulation of the massive graphic files that are used in print production. Still, today's highest performance computer technology often leaves human operators waiting. The price/performance trends in computing will soon close this gap.

The conversion of application files into printing masters requires all of the following things to happen:

1. Color information in the file must be transformed into formats that work with the chosen printing process.

2. If the printing is to be performed on conventional printing equipment the dimensions of images must be minutely adjusted to compensate for the natural vibration and mechanical drift that occur when the press is running at high speed. This is called *trapping.*

3. Images must be arranged geometrically to take best advantage of the maximum sheet size that can be printed. When printing publications such as books, magazines, and catalogs, the individual pages must be positioned on the sheet in the correct orientation so that when the sheet is folded, the pages appear in the correct order. This is called *imposition.* Imposition gets complicated as the sheet size increases and the number of pages printed on a single sheet goes up. In packaging applications, one sheet usually contains many repeated pieces arranged to maximize the yield of individual pieces while still allowing them to be cut apart. The entire printed image is called a *form.*

4. Control devices for measurement and process control and guide marks for cutting and folding must be added to the form.

5. Printing plates must be made for conventional printing processes requiring a physical master. We will learn about specific plate-making processes for each of the printing processes described in the next section.

THE REPRODUCTION OF COLOR

When you look out into the world you see a great range of colors. The colors you see are the result of specific mixtures of light that

Press form for RIT student magazine.

emanate from each point in your field of vision. The most direct way to reproduce the colors you see in the natural world is to find materials in the world that have the exact colors you want, grind them up into powder, and then suspend the powder in a liquid base so that it can be applied to a surface. This is the principle behind the formulation of oil paints used by artists.

To reproduce a complex scene with many thousands of different colors in it, finding all of the right colored materials with which to formulate the paints would be an impossible task. Fortunately, a large number of colors can be formulated by starting with a relatively small number of base colors, and combining them in various proportions. You've probably experienced this when you buy paint for your house. You pick out a specific color from a large array of swatches. Your color is then formulated by the addition of precisely metered amounts of colored pigments to a white base. It is rare that more than two or three different pigments are needed to mix almost any color you might want.

Some printing inks are formulated the same way. The *Pantone* system provides a standardized color swatch book that is widely used in graphic communications. Designers specify colors by using Pantone numbers. Printers then use Pantone inks formulated to match the specified numbers on the press. There are more than a thousand colors in the standard Pantone set, so designers have a lot of options. However, each color is reproduced with a separate ink, so designers can't go wild with their color choices if they intend to have them reproduced in this way.

Fortunately there is another way to obtain a wide range of printed colors using only four process color primaries: cyan, magenta, yellow, and black. All color printing devices from the smallest desktop inkjet printers to the largest gravure presses use combinations of these four colors. This is the only practical way a printing process can be used to reproduce all of the different colors in a photograph.

The range of printable colors can be extended by adding a few more ink colors to the basic set of four. The Pantone Hexachrome system, for example, adds orange and green inks to create a six-color process that reproduces a larger range or *gamut* of colors. With six base colors, the Hexachrome system can be used to reproduce most of the colors in the Pantone set without the need to formulate and stock special inks.

Designers may also specify inks that are metallic or pearlescent. These must be specially formulated from materials that have the necessary properties to give the desired effect. Metallic inks, for example, are formulated with powdered aluminum or bronze. The most expensive printing jobs may combine process color inks with Pantone inks, metallic or pearlescent inks, and clear varnishes. Brochures for expensive cars often combine all of these to convey extreme elegance and quality. If you find yourself lusting after a Lexus, my recommendation is to first get a brochure from the Lexus dealer and see whether you can cure yourself by sleeping a few nights with it. The dealer's hope is that the brochure will amplify your desire and drive you back into his showroom. However, if you are able to live vicariously through the brochure, you can settle for a facsimile of the car and avoid the payment book.

Designers first visualize the colors they want by looking at a Pantone book or at the images they create on the computer screen. The printer has to formulate inks and calibrate the reproduction process to try to match the designer's intent. This is not always possible. The designer's computer monitor shows a much greater range of colors than the printer can reproduce with process color inks. The most brilliant colors on the designer's monitor cannot be reproduced by any printing process. This causes all kinds of problems. Experienced print designers understand the limitations of the printing process and design products that work within them.

The only effective way to bridge the gap between what the designer wants and what can be rendered in print is to use *color management* software to calibrate the designer's monitor and inkjet printer to provide an accurate preview of what will be printed. This software adjusts the colors produced by a computer monitor or digital printer to closely match the colors produced by a printing press when rendering the same graphics.

CONSUMABLES

An old cliché about print media is that it relies on a primitive process of "smearing dead dinosaurs on dead trees." The dead dinosaurs refer to the petroleum-based materials used in printing ink, and dead trees are the principal component of paper. I remember being amused the first time I heard this. But then I started to think more carefully about it. Printing does not always rely upon this simple relationship between dead dinosaurs and dead trees. In some cases we may find ourselves smearing dead trees on dead dinosaurs, or dead dinosaurs on other dead dinosaurs.

Like all things, the products manufactured by the printing industry are composed of materials that derive from two primary sources: agricultural products grown on the surface of the earth, and petroleum and minerals extracted from below the surface. Paper, for example, is primarily made of wood. But nearly all printing papers also contain minerals that impart desirable qualities such as surface smoothness, opacity, brightness, etc. Some specialty papers may also be coated with materials that are derived from petroleum.

The papermaking process employs the same fundamental mechanisms as it has for hundreds of years. However, continuous improvements have been made in the technology and the control of the variables of the process. Paper can be made out of almost any natural fiber. Cotton, linen, hay, and hemp fiber all work. Most papers used for printing are made from wood fibers. The papermaking process therefore starts in the forest. Paper companies such as

Weyerhaeuser and International Paper maintain vast tracts of forest that are managed to produce a steady flow of raw material on a perpetual basis. Mature trees are selectively harvested and new trees planted without cutting down or "clear cutting" the forest. Trees are bred, cultivated, and harvested for the express purpose of making paper.

The harvested trees are debarked, mulched, and then chemically and physically processed into pulp. Raw wood pulp looks like oatmeal. If you tried to make paper directly out of wood pulp without further refinement, it would be brown and somewhat lumpy. To make smooth white opaque paper, the pulp must be bleached and blended with mineral fillers. This pulp blend, consisting mostly of water, is then formed into paper in a continuous process in a paper-making machine. The machine automates a simple process that has been practiced for thousands of years.

You can easily make paper in your own kitchen. I must first, however, issue a warning: You may become addicted to hand papermaking once you have given it a try. If, a year from now, you find yourself obsessively searching the world for ever more exotic sources of fiber to make your next batch of hand-crafted paper, I am hereby absolved of any responsibility. Here's the simple recipe. You will need the following items:

- Ten sheets of white bond laser paper
- Large bowl
- Blender
- Square cake pan
- Small piece of window screen
- Bath towel

First, soak the ten sheets of white uncoated laser paper in a bowl of water for an hour. Next, pour the water and soaked paper into a blender and blend for a few minutes on medium. Now take the square cake pan and cut a rectangular piece of window screen small enough to fit into the pan and rest on the bottom. (You can create a deluxe model of this papermaking contraption by building a wooden frame for the screen. The deluxe model will yield a more uniform sheet of paper with well-formed edges.) Pour the slurry of re-pulped paper into the pan and gently lift the screen out of the pan through the slurry. The pulp will collect on the screen and you will be able to easily transfer it in a sheet to a towel that will act as a blotter. You can then let the paper dry on the towel.

Paper can be further processed after formation. It can be flattened between metal rollers and coated with various mineral-based materials to alter the surface characteristics. The slightest variations in the paper surface can have a profound impact on the print characteristics. Thus it is imperative that the papermaking process be rigorously controlled, from the breeding and growing of the trees, through the formation and finishing in the factory, to the storage and shipping to the final destination.

The ultimate goal of the paper industry is to produce consistent and uniform surfaces for printing. The predictability, consistency, and uniformity of the printing processes depend upon it. On top of this, the demand is for ever lighter, stronger, and more opaque grades of paper. Given the perpetually rising costs of transportation and mailing, this quest will likely never cease. The perfect piece of paper for many applications would be bright white, perfectly opaque, smooth as glass, strong as steel, and weigh nothing. Many magazine and catalog publishers would die for paper like this, as long as it didn't cost them more than what they are currently using.

The paper I have described in the previous paragraph is intended to be as invisible to the end user as possible. When you pick up a copy of *Time* magazine or the JCPenney catalog, you rarely give a thought to the paper. You are focused on the content, and the paper acts as a transparent carrier. The paper is the equivalent of a clear television signal or a high-fidelity sound system.

This is not always desirable. Sometimes we want the paper to be more visible or physically present. We want the consumer to notice the paper, and in doing so we hope that the paper will exert subtle influences that cannot be conveyed by the printed message alone. For example, a designer might use a thick textured paper to convey elegance, or a colored paper to convey permanence. The look and feel of the paper can sometimes be as important to the message as the print itself—sometimes even more so. (Think of a wedding invitation.)

The paper industry offers a vast assortment of specialty papers to meet these demands. In most cases, these papers are speci-fied exactly by the product designer. Working from a sample book provided by the paper manufacturer, the designer will choose the paper that best imparts the tactile and appearance qualities sought.

There are two ways that paper is procured for print produc-tion. The printer may purchase paper directly from a paper mer-chant and then use it to produce the product sold to the print buyer. Alternatively, especially in high-volume publishing applications, the print buyer may purchase the paper directly and supply it to the printer. With specialty print orders, the print buyer will normally specify the exact paper required. For standard papers such as white gloss-coated sheets, the printer may query multiple suppliers and buy based on price and availability.

Digital printing devices often require special papers that are designed to work exclusively with them. These papers have coatings or treatments that are applied to optimize print quality on a specific digital printing device. The potential markets for such papers are not often large enough to justify the development and manufactur-ing setup costs. Thus, digital printing devices that are capable of printing on a variety of standard papers have clear advantages over those that require proprietary papers. The general trend is toward digital printing machines that "know" more and more about how to adjust themselves to generic papers, and papers that are therefore required to know less and less about the machines that will be used to print on them.

PLASTIC SUBSTRATES

In some product segments, paper substrates are increasingly giving way to plastics. This has little to do with graphics. The wood fibers in paper act like little sponges, and can absorb large volumes of water quickly. In their natural state this is their primary function. However, in most paper applications this becomes a liability. The exception, of course, is in functional products like tissues and paper towels.

Printed paper surfaces are often treated with coatings to pro-vide a moisture barrier. These can be waxes, varnishes, or plastics. Milk cartons are made of plastic (polyethylene) coated paperboard. The plastic coating provides an impervious barrier between the liq-uid contents and the wood fiber in the paper. The paper provides stiffness and strength at relatively low cost. Without the plastic coating a milk carton would quickly be reduced to a soggy pile of paper pulp surrounded by a puddle of milk.

In applications where we do not need the strength and stiffness of paper, but do need the moisture barrier properties of plastic, pure plastic substrates become attractive. Flexible packaging and outdoor advertising are two of the fastest growing markets for plastic substrates. Three of the most common plastics are vinyl, polyethylene, and polypropylene. These materials are all organic polymers derived primarily from petroleum.

INKS, TONERS AND COATINGS

One simple way of looking at the manufacturing side of the printing business is as a series of operations performed on blank rolls or sheets of substrate that progressively add value to the material. Chief among these operations is the application of inks and coatings to alter the way the substrates reflect or transmit light as well as their structural properties.

Depending on the process, inks may enter the plant in ready-to-use or concentrated form. The control of ink formulation is a key variable in the printing process. The slightest variation in the concentration or composition of pigments in inks can cause unacceptable variations in the color attributes of the printed graphics. Tolerances for variability of this kind have become so small that out-of-tolerance variability can often barely be seen. Precise color measurement instruments called *spectrometers* (alternatively called *spectrophotometers* or *spectro-densitometers*) are used to quantify the color and density of a printed layer of ink. Often, especially in color-critical applications like packaging, the target numbers and tolerances are included as requirements in the contract.

Printing inks range in sophistication from relatively simple materials such as black newspaper ink that is little more than powdered carbon suspended in an oil base, to extraordinarily complex chemical formulations that are designed to work only in specific printing devices. Digital color printing devices commonly require proprietary liquid inks or powdered toners that are supplied by the manufacturer of the device and cannot be purchased as a commodity on the open market.

This brings us to an important distinction between companies that manufacture conventional printing presses such as those used to produce newspapers, magazines, catalogs, and packaging materials, and companies that manufacture digital printing devices. Because conventional printing processes are able to work with commodity substrates and inks, the manufacturers do not expect to make money selling proprietary consumables to their customers. Manufacturers of digital printing devices, on the other hand, expect that most of their profits will come not from the sale of the devices, but from the sale of high-tech proprietary consumables. (That explains why they can afford to sell you that super-sophisticated color inkjet printer for $79 after rebate.)

Many printed surfaces are subsequently overprinted by clear coatings, to protect the printed images on book and magazine covers, paper labels, packaging materials, and any other products that must stand up to rough handling and exposure to the elements. We will take a more detailed look at coatings in Chapter 5.

Printers typically work very closely with their suppliers of consumables, even when the consumables are commodities like papers, inks, and coatings. In many cases the consumables suppliers consign materials to the printer and manage inventories in the printing plant, transferring ownership of the materials to the printer only when they are used. The careful monitoring and control of the quality of all incoming materials is essential for any printing or package converting company that wishes to be competitive in the global marketplace.

CHAPTER FOUR

PRINTING PROCESSES

PRINTING DEVICES COME IN A VARIETY OF sizes and speeds to produce printed products in quantities ranging from a single copy
to millions of copies. In this chapter we'll focus first on mechanical devices used to produce the everyday products we'll be talking
about in Part Two of this book. Then we'll take a brief look at digital
printing devices that are used in commercial print production. We
won't spend any time looking at desktop and office printers because
these are familiar to everyone.

RELIEF PRINTING

The oldest and most familiar printing mechanism is *relief printing*,
or printing from a raised surface. The rubber stamp is the simplest
relief printing device. The ink transfer mechanism is simple. The
stamp is pressed into an inkpad and ink adheres to the relief surface
of the pad. This surface is then pressed against a piece of paper
with enough pressure to transfer a layer of ink from the stamp to
the paper. Just the right amount of pressure is needed. Too little
pressure and the ink will not transfer well. Too much pressure and
the ink will ooze out around the edges of the image elements, forming unsightly blobs. Uneven pressure and the resulting print will
not be uniform. It is interesting to note that all of these defects are
sometimes used as deliberate design elements. This trend peaked
in the late 1990s with the grunge movement, a particularly regrettable moment in human evolution.

Relief printing comes in two basic forms: *flexography* and *letterpress*. Flexography uses soft rubber-like printing plates and thin fluid

WACK SLACKS Lamestain
SWINGIN' ON THE FLIPPITY-FLOP
ROCK ON TOM-TOM CLUB

Grunge typography.

ink to print on continuous rolls of paper or plastic substrates. These rolls can be as narrow as a few inches or up to five or more feet wide. Flexography is particularly good at printing color graphics on smooth plastic surfaces. This makes it an ideal process for many packaging and label applications. Many of the flexible packaging materials you find in your local supermarket are printed by flexography.

Letterpress was at one time the core technology of the commercial printing industry. Up until the middle of the 20th century, letterpress was the dominant process used for the production of books, magazines, newspapers, and most other printed products. Before the Second World War, when people said "printing," they meant letterpress. Letterpress is the outgrowth of the original printing process developed by Gutenberg. Many newspapers throughout the world are still produced on old letterpress equipment that has one overwhelming advantage over newer offset presses—they are long paid for.

While largely supplanted today by other processes in publication printing, letterpress is still used in special niche applications, mostly in the packaging and label markets. For example, the hundreds of billions of aluminum soda pop cans consumed each year are printed in specialized high-speed letterpress machines called *decorators* that produce multicolor printed cans at speeds approaching 2,000 cans per minute.

GRAVURE

During the Renaissance, a method of printing called *copper engraving* was invented and perfected for making multiple reproductions of images. The engravings were made by artisans using sharpened steel tools to cut grooves into the surface of smooth polished copper plates. Five hundred years later, massive *gravure* printing presses

This eight-color Mark Andy flexographic press is used for conducting research and teaching at RIT. This type of press is used primarily to print high-quality labels for commercial products.

employ computer engraved copper-plated cylinders to print color magazines and catalogs at blinding speeds. These presses can print on rolls of paper up to three meters wide at speeds approaching one mile of paper every two minutes. Gravure presses are also used to apply rich color graphics to packaging materials, simulated wood grains, vinyl floor coverings, wallpaper, and other materials used in the manufacture of decorated surfaces.

Gravure cylinders are made of steel with a thin layer of copper electroplated on the surface. The cylinders are engraved on special computer-controlled engraving machines that cut millions of microscopic cells into the polished copper surface. These cells transfer the ink to the paper, plastic, or other substrate being printed. The printing process itself is about as simple as it could possibly be. The cylinder rotates in a pan filled with ink. A sharp steel blade scrapes off the excess ink. The ink remaining in the engraved cells transfers directly to the substrate under extreme pressure. The printed substrate then passes through a furnace to dry the ink. When printing the color pages of a magazine using four process colors on both sides of the paper substrate, this printing and drying sequence happens eight times in a matter of a couple of seconds as the paper travels through the press.

Gravure inks have a high percentage of solvent in them to make them flow easily. This is essential for proper transfer of the ink from the engraved cells on the cylinder to the printed substrate. Most gravure inks use petroleum-based solvents to suspend the pigments and resins. The ink is mostly solvent which must be removed from the printed substrate before it emerges from the press. This is accomplished by passing the substrate through a furnace to raise the temperature enough to vaporize the solvent. The vaporized solvent can then be either recycled or burned. If the solvent is burned, the energy produced can be recycled.

Some gravure inks used water as the primary solvent. These inks present special challenges. It takes a lot more energy to dry water-based inks. If the inks start to dry in the engraved cells, the dry ink will not re-dissolve when flooded with wet ink. This may inhibit the proper transfer of ink from the engraved cells to the substrate. If the ink in a single cell fails to transfer, it will show up as a tiny white void in the printed image. It is critical to control the flow properties of gravure inks to ensure the effective transfer from cylinder to substrate. Solvent-based inks are generally more forgiving and easier to work with than water-based inks. The downside of solvent-based inks is the solvent itself. It's expensive, toxic, and explosive. Water is cheap, nontoxic, and, with the possible exception of the Cuyahoga River in Cleveland, doesn't catch fire.

OFFSET LITHOGRAPHY

Lithography means literally "stone writing." This word was coined by an eccentric Bavarian inventor named Alois Senefelder more than 200 years ago. Senefelder had a burning desire to leave his mark on the world in the form of an invention that would become his eternal legacy. He documented this quest in a book entitled *The Invention of Lithography*.[6] I refer you to this book, which is still in print, because it is entertaining to read and will help to keep Mr. Senefelder's memory alive.

Senefelder came up with an idea to make a relief printing surface by etching a smooth slab of limestone with acid. By protecting the parts of the limestone surface that represented the image he wanted to print with a greasy acid resistant substance, he would be able to remove the surrounding stone through chemical means. The basic idea was to use acid to do the work of cutting away the non-printing areas of the master.

What Senefelder discovered accidentally along the way was that it was not necessary to physically remove the non-printing areas to prevent them from transferring ink. As long as he kept these areas wet, they would repel an oil-based ink that would only adhere to the protected image areas. This chance discovery of a new printing mechanism more than 200 years ago enabled a creative explosion in the graphic arts in the 19th century and a revolution in commercial printing in the 20th century.

Today lithographic printing is accomplished with machines that range from small single or two-color presses that print on cut sheets of paper in two-page formats, to massive machines that print on wide rolls of paper at speeds measured in thousands of feet per minute. All modern lithographic presses use flexible metal or plastic plates that are the descendents of Senefelder's stone. The plates can be made quickly and inexpensively in computer-to-plate (CTP) devices that use computer-controlled lasers to fix the image to the surface of the plate. The plate transfers ink from a set of rollers to a soft smooth rubberized cylinder called a blanket cylinder. The ink can then be transferred from the blanket to paper, plastic, or metal media. The "offsetting" of the ink from plate to blanket before being transferred to the printed medium is the reason why the process is often called *offset lithography* or, more commonly, simply *offset*.

Offset presses that print on sheets of paper, plastic, or metal are called *sheet-fed* presses. Presses that print on continuous rolls of material are called *web* presses. The fastest sheet-fed presses currently available produce approximately 15,000 single-sided sheets per hour. The fastest web presses produce nearly 70,000 double-sided sheets per hour. Web presses also fold the paper and cut it into sheets before delivery, ready to feed into a book binding machine. Sheet-fed presses are used to produce a great variety of printed products including books, magazines, folding cartons, labels, posters, and annual reports. Web presses have traditionally had

This six-unit, 57-inch-wide Goss Sunday 2000 Web Offset Press is located in the Printing Applications Laboratory at Rochester Institute of Technology. The press can produce 70,000 24-page folded magazine-sized signatures per hour in six colors. That makes it almost a thousand times faster than the fastest digital color printing presses. For high-volume applications requiring photographic image quality, like mass-circulation magazines and catalogs, this will be the preferred technology for many years to come.

a much narrower range of applications—basically magazines and catalogs, and anything else that looks like a magazine or catalog. However, in recent years the web offset process has been successfully adapted to print labels and packaging materials.

The best demonstration of the stunning graphic capabilities of sheet-fed offset printing that I can think of is a glossy brochure for an expensive automobile. The next time you have the opportunity to visit a car dealership, take a walk through the showroom and pick up some brochures for the priciest vehicles they sell. This will provide you a great example of the current state of the art in sheet-fed offset printing.

The easiest way to assess the current state of the art in web offset printing is to pick up a copy of *Time* or *People* magazines. The print quality may not be as stunning as the premium sheet-fed examples from the Lexus dealer, but in one respect web offset takes the prize over sheet-fed offset. Because web offset prints on a continuous roll, the paper can be extraordinarily thin. This is of great importance for printed products that are distributed through the mail. (Mailing costs are a function of weight, and postal rates continually defy the laws of gravity in that they always go up, and never come down.) It would be nearly impossible to feed a sheet of *Time* magazine paper though a sheet-fed press. Yet as thin as the paper is, it is also incredibly opaque. As you contemplate these words while inspecting the paper in your copy of *Time* magazine, imagine a 57-inch wide roll of that paper flying through a web offset press at 30 miles per hour being printed with four colors on both sides simultaneously. I see this happen with my own eyes every day in the web offset lab at RIT and I still don't believe that it's possible.

SCREEN PRINTING

With all of the previous printing processes I have described, ink is transferred from one surface to another. Ink is either transferred from the raised areas of a plate (letterpress and flexography), recessed areas of the plate (gravure), or from areas of a flat plate that are chemically prepared to attract the ink (lithography). There is one additional way to make multiple mechanical reproductions of an original image: Ink can be pushed through a stencil. It is likely that people have been using stencils for thousands of years.

Screen printing is a form of stencil printing where the stencil is supported by a fabric, plastic, or metal screen mesh through which the ink is pushed onto the print medium. The process was traditionally called "silk screen printing" because silk fabric was used as a support for the stencils. Modern industrial screen printing employs screens made of synthetic fabrics or metal. Depending on the press configuration, screens can be either flat or cylindrical. Cylindrical screens made of thin etched metal can be used to print on continuous rolls of material at high speed. Flat screens are used in a wide range of devices from simple manually-operated presses to high-speed automated multicolor printing presses.

You can make a primitive screen printing press by taking one of your window screens and using a brush to paint with thick, fast-drying glue onto the screen in the areas where you want to prevent ink from reaching the print substrate. Then you can lay this screen over a large piece of paper or fabric and use a squeegee to push some thick screen printing ink or paint through the screen onto the paper. You can make as many copies as you want this way. If you want to add a second color, just take down another screen and repeat the process. I have enough windows in my house to supply me with enough screens to make a 20-color screen print.

Screen printing today is used to apply graphics to a variety of products from textiles to signs to three-dimensional containers. One of the outstanding characteristics of screen printing is its ability to apply an extremely thick layer of material to a surface—hundreds of times thicker than other analog and digital processes are capable of applying. Screen printing units are sometimes integrated with other printing processes such as flexography or electrophotography. The screen units are used to apply thick layers of varnish or ink to meet special durability requirements or achieve special tactile effects. Screen units can also be used to selectively apply adhesives to surfaces.

Screen printing once dominated the market for large-format signs and posters. For some high-volume applications, the screen process is still viable. If the goal is to produce thousands of copies of a large sign, for example, screen printing may offer the best economy of scale. For shorter runs, wide-format inkjet devices now dominate the market. Digital printing eliminates the high setup costs of screen printing and allows for profitable production in small quantities, down to a quantity of one.

The most familiar and ubiquitous examples of screen-printed products in our daily lives are articles of clothing such as T-shirts and sportswear decorated with printed graphics. Digital alternatives to screen printing of apparel are used for short-run, on-demand production of standard or custom products. This allows retailers to maintain large digital inventories of graphics and modest physical inventories of unprinted garments to offer a broad selection of products without carrying the traditional inventory costs.

DIGITAL PRINTING PROCESSES

There are only two fundamental ways to form an image digitally.

One is to use a computer-controlled energy source such as light or electrical current to selectively alter the physical characteristics of a surface. The other is to use a computer-controlled device to selectively apply ink directly onto a surface. I distinguish between these two broad categories by calling the first *energy-writing processes* and the second *material-writing processes*.

ENERGY-WRITING DIGITAL PRINTING PROCESSES

Energy-writing processes use energy sources and matching materials that change when exposed to the energy source. This change is then exploited in some way to produce a visible image. Photography is the original energy-writing system. The word *photography* means writing with light. Before the electronic age this could only be accomplished by controlling the exposure of photographic materials to light using lenses and shutters. Today there are a multitude of digital devices that use computer-controlled lasers or *light emitting diodes* (LEDs) to form images on photographic materials. These devices enable the photofinishing industry to produce photographic prints directly from image files created with digital cameras.

The basic principles of photographic imaging are the same today as they were 150 years ago. Exposure to light causes the silver-based photographic material to undergo a subtle change that is invisible. This change is amplified by millions of times in a wet chemical development process. The developed image is then chemically fixed, and the fixed image is washed and dried. All of this happens rapidly in automated processing machines. The science and technology required to manufacture the photographic materials and design the required software and hardware systems is formidable, and there are only a handful of companies in the game. The three largest players are Kodak, Fujifilm, and Agfa.

Computer-controlled lasers or LEDs can also be used to expose other kinds of light-sensitive materials called *photoconductors*. These materials have interesting electrical properties. They can store a static charge and then surrender the charge when exposed to light. An invisible image (sometimes called a *latent image*) can be drawn onto a photoconductive surface by exposing it to a moving laser beam that can be switched on and off. This latent image can then be developed by flowing a statically charged ink or toner over the surface. The charged particles in the ink will be attracted to the image formed by the laser beam. This image can then be transferred to a piece of paper or plastic to produce a print. This digital printing process is called *electrophotography*, or sometimes *xerography*, a word coined by the inventors of the process from the Greek words for dry (*xero*) and writing.

Devices that employ electrophotography range from small single-color desktop laser printers to large commercial production printers capable of producing hundreds of pages per minute. The fastest machines print in black and white on continuous rolls of paper and can produce approximately 2,000 printed pages per minute. These are used to produce a variety of products from books to financial statements.

Energy forms other than light can also be used to write latent images onto surfaces. It is possible, for example, to apply a static charge directly to a surface made of a material called a *dielectric* that will hold the charge. The charged surface can then be used to form and transfer an image. This is similar to electrophotography minus the photo part and is called, appropriately, *electrography*. Electrography is suitable for large-format printing applications for the production of printed panels for outdoor display. It is also employed in high-speed, single-color devices for statement printing. The fundamental weakness of electrography is the lack of precision in the control of the imaging process. The result is similar to what you would produce if you used one of your crayons, instead of a fine pen, to write your signature. The only way to do this with some grace is to write really big. That's why electrography is most useful for making very large prints such as those used to decorate the sides of buses and trucks.

Direct *thermal printing* processes use computer-controlled arrays of heating elements to selectively apply heat to a surface to cause a chemical change that yields a visible image. Many fax machines use special paper that is coated with a material that darkens when exposed to heat. The fax machine prints an image by controlled application of heat to the fax paper. This simple single-color printing mechanism is employed in a large number of applications such as receipt and barcode printing in the supermarket.

Another form of energy writing is employed in devices that

are used to create printing plates for lithography, flexography, and gravure, and is called *laser ablation*. When lasers are used in photography and electrophotography, they only need to be powerful enough to form a latent image that must be further developed. Ablation employs much more powerful lasers to selectively burn or *ablate* material from a surface. This allows for the direct imaging of offset lithographic plates that do not require any further processing before they can be used. Ablation can also be used to write an image directly onto the surface of a photopolymer flexographic plate or a gravure cylinder. These images then act as stencils that control subsequent exposure to ultraviolet energy, or to the flow of an acid etching solution to form the printing surfaces.

MATERIAL-WRITING DIGITAL PRINTING PROCESSES

If the progenitor of all energy-writing processes is photography, material-writing processes all claim a common ancestry that goes back to Neolithic cave painting. Giotto, Rembrandt, and Picasso were all material writers. Material-writing processes use energy to physically transfer colorants to a surface. There are two broad categories of material-writing: *thermal transfer* and *inkjet*. The analog progenitor of all thermal transfer processes is the carbon paper that was once used to create multiple copies of handwritten or typewritten documents. The analog progenitor of all inkjet processes was born the day some long-forgotten avant-garde painter first got the idea to trade his paint brush for a squirt gun.

Thermal transfer processes use heat to transfer materials from one surface to another to form visible images. Thermal lasers can be used to transfer colored dyes or pigments from plastic ribbons directly to a surface that is specially designed to receive the transferred material. This is the underlying technology in the Kodak Approval color proofing system.

Thermal transfer printing processes use computer-controlled arrays of heating elements to selectively apply heat to a surface to physically transfer colored materials from a ribbon to a receiver. Dye sublimation photo printers are the most common example of thermal transfer printing. In these devices heat is used to transfer colored dyes from ribbons to specially coated sheets of paper or plastic to form photographic quality images.

If we took the painter's squirt gun away from him and gave it to a robot that we could control digitally, we would have an inkjet printer. An HP inkjet printer is nothing more than a refinement of this idea. Instead of only one nozzle, a typical desktop inkjet printer today has a print head with hundreds or thousands of microscopic nozzles that can all be controlled independently. The printer incorporates a mechanism for moving the array of nozzles back and forth while simultaneously transporting the print medium through the device. Each nozzle is supplied by a tiny ink chamber that can be made to eject the ink mechanically by a command from the computer. The printer creates a printed image by spraying millions of tiny droplets of ink onto the print medium. Because the computer can control precisely when each nozzle ejects a droplet, these types of printers are sometimes described as *drop-on-demand* printers.

Drop-on-demand inkjet processes are very precise and convenient to use for printing sporadically in low volumes. For continuous high-volume applications these will not do. We need to replace the squirt gun with a fire hose and then we need to figure out how to control it.

Eastman Kodak is the undisputed master of this domain of digital printing technology. Kodak manufactures high speed *continuous* inkjet printers under the trade name Versamark that can print in full color on continuous rolls of paper at speeds approaching 1,000 feet per minute. The print heads in these devices are as wide as a page (nine inches) and contain thousands of nozzles that each ejects a continuous stream of droplets at rates of 100,000 droplets per second or faster. To control the application of ink onto the paper to form images, the print heads employ an ingenious mechanism for removing unwanted droplets from the continuous stream before they have a chance to hit the paper.

Although these high-speed continuous inkjet printers are many hundreds of times faster than the desktop drop-on-demand inkjet printers, they are not capable of producing the same photographic-quality graphics. The print quality is more than adequate for statement and book printing applications where extremely low page cost and high throughput are the most important factors. The holy grail of printing technology might be an inkjet printer with the throughput and page cost of a Kodak Versamark machine with the image quality of an HP desktop photo printer and the wide format of an HP inkjet plotter. Whoever invents such a machine will very quickly become the king of the world.

CHAPTER FIVE

PRINT FINISHING

T HE PRINTING PROCESSES DESCRIBED IN CHAPTER 4 produce stacks or rolls of printed material that must be further processed. All of the production steps that happen after the product emerges from the printing press are described by the term *finishing*. Most printed products are useless before they are finished and small errors in the finishing stages of production can destroy all of the value that has been invested in the product up to that point. But creative finishing solutions also present an area of rich opportunity for adding value to print products.

In the packaging arena, the term *converting* is used to describe the finishing stages of production. The sheets or rolls of printed material are converted into products that are compatible with the packaging operations that usually take place in the customer's manufacturing facility. In packaging applications, the most exquisitely printed products are worthless if they are not properly converted so that they perform flawlessly on the packaging line. The slightest error in the positioning of a fold line or die-cut will sometimes result in a catastrophic failure at the point where the product is used in the manufacturing facility. It can therefore be argued that the finishing operations are far more critical than the printing operations in packaging applications.

COATINGS AND VARNISHES

Even though we have defined finishing as everything that happens to a product after it emerges from the printing press, I consider the application of coatings and varnishes as part of finishing, even though this normally happens in the press or inline with the printing operation. Coatings have two primary functions. One is to add durability to printed surfaces to make them less vulnerable to scuffing and abrasion or exposure to moisture and other solvents. The covers of paperback books, for example, are almost always protected by a thin coating of varnish for these reasons.

The other function of a coating is to alter the appearance of the surface to add visual appeal. A glossy coating of varnish applied to a printed image increases the contrast and strengthens the darker areas of the image. A glossy coating also gives the appearance of greater depth to a printed image, making it appear slightly three-dimensional.

Coatings can be applied to the entire surface of a printed sheet or selectively to specific areas. The selective application of a clear coating is called *spot varnishing*. While full-sheet clear coating is often intended to impart protective properties to a printed surface, spot varnishing is always intended as a design element to add visual effect. The best place to see spot varnishing is in the luxury automobile brochures that you collected earlier. The subtlest use of a spot varnish is when it is applied to unprinted paper to change the light-reflecting properties. Sometimes this can only be seen when the light hits the page at a certain angle. In the eternal quest for visual novelty, designers may even use clear varnish to reproduce type that conveys important messages. The elusiveness is part of the appeal. Struggling to read words rendered in clear on white may, in some cases, make the message stick better than if it were rendered in black on white.

Clear coatings are not always glossy. They are sometimes intentionally designed to dry with a matte surface. This imparts a certain look and feel to a surface that can be very attractive. A matte spot varnish can be used to differentiate selected areas of a glossy surface to draw the viewer's attention.

The most commonly-used clear coatings are cured instantaneously following application by exposure to powerful ultraviolet or electron beam energy sources. Beyond coatings, some printed surfaces are laminated with clear plastic layers that provide the ultimate in protection from the elements. Laminated paperback book covers are the most recognizable example.

In some applications, adhesives are an important input to the print production process. Nearly all packaging materials must be selectively coated with adhesives that enable the package to be partially assembled in the packaging printing (converting) plant and then sealed when it is filled with product on the manufacturing line. Adhesives are also used for bookbinding, and countless other applications where printed materials must be joined together to form the final product.

STAMPING

On your next trip to the supermarket take a stroll down the aisle with all of the hair coloring products. Until I did this myself, I hadn't realized that there were so many hundreds of different varieties of blond. All of the boxes are beautifully printed by sheet-fed offset lithography with glossy clear coatings. But many of the boxes also have shiny metallic accents incorporated into the design. These are the result of a finishing process called *foil stamping* or *hot stamping*.

Foil stamping is accomplished with a machine that uses a heated metal die that transfers a layer of metalized material from a plastic ribbon to the receiving surface. The temperature and amount of pressure are carefully controlled to achieve a complete and sharply-defined transfer. The judicious use of foil stamping can add immeasurably to the appearance of a package.

Foil stamping is also frequently employed as an anti-counterfeiting device. The covers of most passports have intricate hot-foil-stamped seals as the principal design element. You may think that counterfeiting is only a problem with currency and security documents, but it is a large and growing problem in packaging as well. In many parts of the world, especially where Western intellectual property laws are not rigorously enforced, counterfeit products in counterfeit packaging are very common.

Some rigid packaging materials are made by printing on paperboard that is laminated with a thin film of aluminum foil. By overprinting the metallic surface with transparent colored inks, a wide range of metallic colors are available. Gold, for example, is usually achieved by applying transparent yellow ink to an aluminum surface. It is also possible to use metallic inks. However, these are not capable of achieving the same mirror-like appearance of hot foil stamping or foil-laminated board.

There is one additional finishing feature that is related to this discussion of hot foil stamping. A growing number of packages and security documents incorporate holographic images in the design. These are made by mechanically pressing the holographic image, called a *hologram*, into a metalized plastic substrate with an etched metal roller. The process is similar to the mechanical process used to press commercial CDs and DVDs. The holograms are applied to finished products in machines designed especially for the purpose. Most holograms are intended to add anti-counterfeiting security features to products. However, holograms on cereal boxes are almost entirely designed to inspire young children to hound their poor parents to death in the supermarket aisle.

EMBOSSING

The April 5, 2004, issue of *Fortune* magazine contained an advertisement for a financial services company that consisted of two sheets of heavy white textured paper that were both completely blank. There was not a drop of printing ink or varnish to be found anywhere on these two sheets. Yet the advertising message was clearly legible and, to judge from the fact that I am telling you about it here, profoundly memorable. Now here's the riddle: How could a blank piece of paper deliver an advertising message so effectively?

The answer is that the paper was *embossed*. This is accomplished by passing the paper between a set of rollers that deform the surface of the paper to create a raised image. This particular example of embossing consisted of a small amount of text in a very classical-looking typeface. On the left-hand page were the words "Behind the Scenes. Above the Fray." On the right-hand page were the words "U.S. Trust. Quietly Building Wealth for Individuals and Families Since 1853." At the bottom of the page was a contact name and phone number. The choice of embossing as a way of communicating this particular message was a stroke of genius. Because of its sheer novelty, it would be simply impossible for a reader of that magazine to miss this advertisement. The extreme subtlety of the advertisement also fits perfectly with the message.

Embossing is used extensively in high-end folding carton packaging, and in the book publishing industry to add design appeal

Embossed ad from Fortune *magazine.*

to book covers. Embossing is also used on labels, very often in conjunction with hot foil stamping. Sometimes the only real difference between an embarrassingly cheap bottle of whisky and one that costs five times as much lies in the quality of the printing, embossing, and foil stamping on the label and box. The other difference is in the amount of money that the manufacturer spends on magazine and outdoor advertising. Let's face it. If your guests didn't know that you were serving them spirits that costs sixty dollars a bottle, would you really spend that kind of money?

Up to this point we have been discussing all of the various things that can be done to add value to a blank sheet or roll of paper or other material. This includes printing with process color inks, printing with special color inks, coating and spot varnishing, foil stamping, and embossing. Now we will turn to finishing processes that convert the printed materials into assembled products ready to ship.

CUTTING

Most printed products must be cut into smaller units that are compatible with downstream finishing processes. Some cutting functions happen before the product emerges from the press. Web offset presses, for example, cut and fold individual sheets from the web at the end of the press.

There are three basic types of cutting employed in the production of printed products: die-cutting, chop cutting, and guillotine cutting. *Die-cutting* employs a steel die that is either flat or cylindrical. The geometry of a die can be almost any shape, although given the laws of physics as they are, flat dies are limited as to how intricate they can be. Dies are designed on CAD systems and manufactured by specialty companies that serve large numbers of customers with similar needs. Any cut edge that is not straight is a die-cut. The little star stickers that your first grade teacher used to put on your homework papers were die-cut. Cylindrical die-cutting is accomplished by passing a roll of material between a cylindrical die-cutting roller and a pressure roller. Flat die-cutting can be configured to die-cut printed sheets. Depending on the total cutting area, flat die-cutting can cut multiple sheets simultaneously. The smaller and simpler the die-cut, the more sheets can be cut together. I have seen die-cutters cut stacks of thousands of small wine labels at a time.

Straight cuts are made with either *guillotine* cutters or *chop* cutters. A guillotine cutter is used to cut stacks of sheeted material such as paper or plastic. They come in a broad range of sizes. Seeing a guillotine cutter slice though a stack of 5,000 sheets of paper like a hot knife through butter is one of the more pleasurable experiences you can have in a printing plant. Guillotine cutters require a human operator. Chop cutters are more automated and are designed to make smaller cuts more rapidly. A special kind of chop cutter called a *three-knife cutter* is used to trim three edges of a book or magazine (top, right, and bottom) simultaneously. For paperback books and magazines, the chop cutter is the last step in manufacturing before final packaging for delivery.

FOLDING

How many different ways are there to fold a piece of paper? How many angels can dance on the head of a pin? There is no easy way to answer these questions. In *The Origami Handbook*, there are hundreds of different ways shown to fold pieces of paper into finished structures that are recognizable models of things.[7] Each of these structures can

New York City map book showing unique oblique fold.

be made by following a set of step-by-step instructions.

Most of the folding geometries used in print production are simpler than those described in the origami book. For the most part they do not include oblique folds. Folding in print production is a pretty rectangular undertaking. This is partly because it is far easier to automate rectangular folding geometries. A good mechanical engineer could probably design a machine that could automatically produce origami peacocks, but you would have to order a second dedicated machine if you wanted to switch to elephants. Complex oblique folding often serves to differentiate a product from competitors in the marketplace. Most products of this type today are produced in places where manual labor is inexpensive.

The *New York Insideout Guide* contains one of the most interesting complex folds of any book of its kind.[8] The book was manufactured in China, where the inexpensive manual labor required is available. Without the complex fold, it is doubtful that the book would compete very effectively in the marketplace.

Folding can be an intermediate step in a print production process, or it can be the last step. If folding is an intermediate step, it is normally only the concern of industrial engineers working in the printing plant. If it is the last step, the designer will be largely responsible for specifying how it must be done. Books and maga-

These folded signatures from the web offset press at RIT contain 24 pages. Signatures emerge from the press in this form at a rate of approximately 70,000 per hour.

zines, for example, are assembled from folded sheets of paper called *signatures*. The folding operation may be integrated with the printing operation or not. Brochures and newsletters are examples of products that are almost always folded at the end of the production process. The designer's choice of fold will determine how the folding operation must be realized in the plant.

Trish Witkowski, a graduate of the RIT School of Design with a graduate degree from the RIT School of Print Media, has created the first rational system for describing the range of folding options available to designers. In her 2002 book *Fold*, she describes hundreds of different folds that are used in publication design.[9] This book can be used in conjunction with a web-based service that enables designers to obtain templates for any of the fold geometries described in the book. The templates are automatically customized to the exact dimensions specified by the designer.

PRODUCT ASSEMBLY

Most publication products such as books, magazines, catalogs, and newspapers ship from the production facility in their final consumer-ready form. The binding and finishing operations may be performed in a separate facility from where the materials are printed, but once the product is shipped it is ready for use. Printed packaging materials, on the other hand, are shipped in an intermediate form that is compatible with the manufacturing processes where they will be employed. They are not finished goods.

I will describe the steps taken to deliver this book from the point where the paper emerges from the printing press to its current resting place in your hands. Two different printing processes were used to produce this book. Everything except for the cover was printed on a web offset press optimized for high-speed single-color book production. The cover was printed on a sheet-fed offset process in four colors plus a clear coating. The covers were delivered in flat sheets on pallets. The insides were delivered in folded signatures stacked on pallets. At the time I am writing this description of the production process, I can't be any more specific about the details of the print production. The specific machines that are employed for the production of this particular book will be designated very close to the time when production begins.

So let me make some assumptions that will help move this discussion forward. A common folded signature size for a book of this type is 32 pages. To produce a 32-page signature from a sheet of paper, the paper must be folded four times. (Remember that in web offset printing the signatures are folded inline.) If you count the total number of pages in this book, you will be able to easily calculate the number of 32-page signatures that were required to make this book by simply dividing by 32. Thus books produced on a 32-page signature web press can be produced in page-count increments of 32 (32, 64, 96, 128, etc.). If you wrote a book to be printed on this kind of press that was 129 pages in length, you would either be encouraged by a wise publisher to edit down to 128, or you would have to add 31 blank pages for "reader's notes" at the end of the book.

At the moment, my target page count for this book is 256 pages. This will require eight 32-page signatures. These will be stacked on separate pallets and delivered to the bindery along with the printed covers. The signatures must first be gathered into sets of eight. This is performed on a gathering machine that assembles signature sets that will then be loaded (automatically or by hand) into hoppers on a machine called a *perfect binder*. This machine clamps the eight signatures together, grinds off the back edge to form a rough gluing surface, and glues the covers to the book using a molten plastic adhesive called *hot melt* that solidifies when cooled. The bound books are trimmed on the three remaining edges. The finished *perfect bound* books are then packed for shipment. They may be shipped to the publisher, to a retail outlet, or directly to a consumer. I will further describe these different shipping options in the section on distribution below.

It is possible to produce a hard-cover or *case-bound* version of a book by taking the signatures through a different finishing operation. The cases are produced on specialized machinery that assembles heavy paperboard, decorative and structural paper, cloth, foil stamping, and other appropriate materials into cases that are then delivered in pallets to a case binding machine. The signatures are prepared separately for casing. They are gathered together, bound, and trimmed to final size before they are sent to the binding machine where they are joined with the finished cases.

There are many variations on these two basic themes in bookbinding. The methods described above all rely on adhesives that are modern inventions. Before the development of these strong synthetic polymers, books were bound with a combination of pastes made from grains such as wheat or rice, and animal glue (made from the gelatin derived from boiled animal parts). Because these adhesives were limited in strength, most book bindings were also sewn together with thread. Today, a sewn binding combined with modern adhesives produces a more flexible and permanent binding than simple glued bindings. Many contemporary case-bound "coffee table books" printed on glossy coated paper with full color on every page feature bindings with sewn signatures. Glossy coated paper covered with ink is notoriously difficult to hold together with adhesive alone.

An alternative to gathering and gluing signatures and cover together to form a perfect binding is called *saddle stitching*. Saddle stitching does not involve adhesives. Instead wire staples are used to attach the pages together. One or more signatures are positioned straddling an angled metal plate where they are stapled through the binding fold. With the lightest, thinnest grades of magazine paper available today, this binding method can be used to assemble books containing hundreds of pages. However, saddle stitching works best when the page count is below 200. Some magazines are bound with saddle stitching up to a certain page count and perfect bound beyond that. The number of advertising pages contained on a weekly basis in the *New Yorker* magazine, for example, determines what binding method will be used. The publisher would prefer to see the magazine perfect bound every week.

It is helpful to know as much about the specific steps that will be taken to create the finished product as possible when the product is being conceived and designed. The cost of alternative methods and materials will always influence decisions made early in the design process. Let me again use this book as an example.

When I first conceived this book, it was nothing more than an idea. The first steps toward realizing the idea were to write down a title and a brief abstract describing the idea. Next I produced an outline and a rough estimate of the number of words and illustrations that would be required. At this point I had to do some hard thinking about the final format of the book for the first time. I did this hard thinking in collaboration with my colleagues in the Printing Industry Center and RIT Cary Graphic Arts Press.

As an author, I would prefer to see my work printed on the finest paper, with the entire rainbow of available colors, gilded on the edges, and bound in hand-tooled leather. A beautiful leather slipcase and a satin pillow on which to display the open book would also be nice. I estimated the unit cost for doing the book this way to be around $1,000. This would have limited the market for the book to exactly one copy. I would have bought it for myself.

So we knew from the beginning that we had to get the unit cost down. This is where we enter the labyrinth of marketing. At this point in the narrative, I do not want to take you into the labyrinth, so we'll just stand at the doorway and talk about what happened in there when we were planning this particular book. Later, in the chapter on publishing in Part Two, we'll take a closer look at what's inside.

Our goal was to produce a book that would reach the largest readership among selected academic and industry audiences. We wanted to price the book so that it would be affordable to students and teachers, and would be attractive to corporate customers who wished to buy the book in quantity. Because the book contains many photographs and illustrations, the quality of print and paper had to meet certain minimum standards. The book was also intended to be used in two ways: as a narrative text to be read from cover to cover, and as a reference.

The most difficult decision we had to make was whether to print the book in color or black and white. We also looked at the option of printing a small section (a single signature) of the book in color. We rejected this last possibility because it would force us to organize content awkwardly and it would generally give the book a stale 20th century appearance. So it was either going to be all or nothing with regard to color pages. With most books this would be a simple yes/no decision. However, this book, if you haven't already realized it, is different. Most books, like most good companions, do not shamelessly talk about themselves the way this book does. Most books look outward and never call attention to themselves as books. But this book is similar to a song that a songwriter writes about writing songs. Or a play about a playwright writing plays. It's a book. But it's also a meta-book, constantly gazing into its own navel and struggling to explain the meaning of its own existence.

Given this extraordinary mission, there can be no doubt that color on every page would be desirable, since color is a common feature in many kinds of books today. But full color also costs considerably more than black and white. The premium cost of color would force us to price the book such that we would lose some of the audience. Yet color would make the book appeal to some potential buyers who would be more than willing to pay the extra price, but who would not buy the book if it were not printed in color.

We also wanted to make it possible for this book to be printed on demand using digital color printing technology so that it could be used to demonstrate the capabilities of the technology. This led us to conclude that we needed to produce content that would work in black-and-white as well as in full-color versions of the book. We told ourselves calmly, "If we're going to be in the business of publishing a meta-book, we're going to have to work harder than do the mere publishers of books."

The simplest way to accomplish this would be to prepare all of the content for color reproduction and then automatically convert to single color for black-and-white printing when needed. The only weakness with this approach is that black-and-white renderings of color images and illustrations do not always work well graphically. When you take away the color, some of the visual clarity often goes away with it. The designer of this book worked within these constraints to produce graphics that work well when printed either way. A single master file for this book is therefore used for volume offset production of the book, as well as both the full-color and black-and-white versions of the book that are digitally printed on demand.

CHAPTER SIX

PRINT DISTRIBUTION

N OW IT IS TIME TO FOLLOW THE VARIOUS PATHS that printed products take from manufacturing plant to end user. Some products leave the plant in final form and take a direct route through the postal system to the consumer mailbox. Others are routed to manufacturing facilities where they are combined with other product components and shipped through a private distribution system. In most cases, there are critical timing and coordination issues that arise from the communication function of printed products.

The distribution of printed products must also often be coordinated with the timing of broadcast events. The successful launch of a new product into the marketplace requires a precisely choreographed set of actions and events that work together to maximize the volume of sales. The more timely the messaging carried by the print, the more critical the timing of deliveries must be. The clearest illustration of this principle is the timing of the delivery of the morning newspaper. Most daily newspapers must be delivered within a narrow window of an hour or two to succeed. If the paper is delivered late, the consumer will go to an alternative medium for local news (radio, TV) and never open the paper at all. An unread newspaper is as effective an advertising medium as a radio without electricity.

POSTAL DISTRIBUTION

In his autobiography, Benjamin Franklin explains how his publishing business changed for the better when he was appointed postmaster of Philadelphia in 1737. The previous postmaster, Andrew Bradford, had been a formidable business rival of Franklin's up to that point.

Franklin well understood the value of the appointment.

> I accepted it readily, and found it of great Advantage; for tho'
> the Salary was small, it facilitated the Correspondence that
> improv'd my Newspaper, increas'd the Number demanded,
> as well as the Advertisements to be inserted, so that it came
> to afford me a very considerable Income. My old Competi-
> tor's Newspaper declin'd proportionably, and I was satisfied
> without retaliating his Refusal, while Postmaster, to permit
> my Papers being carried by the Riders.[10]

Bradford had corruptly used his power as postmaster to inhibit
Franklin's ability to circulate his newspapers. Fortunately for Franklin, Bradford was removed from office for other corrupt practices
and barred from using the postal service himself. Thus his publishing business declined and Franklin's flourished.

Franklin understood the critical dependency of publishing on
a reliable distribution system. He had spent many years prior to his
appointment to the office of postmaster developing his capabilities
as a writer and printer. But his fortune was made only when he se-
cured the capability to deliver his content to the intended audience.
He prospered by gaining control of all three components of the publishing enterprise: content, medium, and delivery channel. Today,
more than three centuries after his birth, the formula for success
remains the same.

The U.S. Postal Service (USPS) today is a direct outgrowth of
the colonial postal service of Franklin's time. Employing more than
700,000 people, the USPS delivers more than 200 billion pieces of
mail a year. This equates to an average of five pieces of mail to over
140 million addresses each day. Some other facts and figures about
the USPS are:

- 300,000 mail carriers
- 1.8 million new addresses each year
- delivers 46 percent of world's mail volume
- maintains 37,579 retail outlets serving 7 million people
  each day

The USPS has an annual operating revenue of $68.5 billion. Most of this revenue comes from six product lines:[11]

1.	Correspondence and transactions	$37.0 billion
2.	Business advertising	$17.2 billion
3.	Expedited delivery	$5.4 billion
4.	Publications delivery	$2.2 billion
5.	Standard package delivery	$2.2 billion
6.	International mail	$1.5 billion

The USPS is required by law to offer the same level of service to every postal address regardless of geographic location. Its stated mission is clear: "The Postal Service delivers everywhere, every day, to everyone."

The realities associated with this mission are more complex than Ben Franklin could have possibly imagined. The sheer geographic magnitude of the job is one factor. Current law requires that first class mail rates are the same regardless of distance. If I mail a letter from my home in Rochester, NY, to my next door neighbor, it will cost me the same as if I send it to San Francisco. But the real cost to transport the letter across the continent is much greater than to keep it in the neighborhood. So my letters to California are subsidized in part by my more localized first class mail.

Most of the printed matter that moves through the postal system takes advantage of bulk mailing rates and special legislated privileges that have been in place since Franklin's time. Unlike first class mail, distance is factored into these rates. Periodicals are a separate class of mail encompassing newspapers, magazines, and other periodical publications whose primary purpose is transmitting information to an established list of subscribers or requesters. This is an important qualification. To receive the lower periodical rates, the USPS requires that the recipient asks to receive the information from the sender. The justification for this is that the postal service is charged by the government to subsidize the transmission of useful information. The test of usefulness is whether or not the information is requested. Unsolicited transmission of information does not qualify, even if it takes the outward form of a periodical. The USPS establishes the following additional qualifications: "Periodicals must be published at regular intervals, at least four times a year from a known office of publication, and be formed of printed sheets. There are specific standards for circulation, record keeping, and advertising limits. There are special lower postage rates for Nonprofit and Classroom Periodicals."[12]

The USPS developed a system that enables the calculation of postal rates for bulk mailing based on weight and distance. There are nine distance zones in the system. Unlike fixed geographic zones, postal zones are determined in relationship to the point of origination. So each zip code in the country has a different zone map. A given address in zone 1 on my map may be in zone 6 on yours.

Bulk mailers qualify for a discounted price for presorting before mailing. There are several presort levels (first three digits of ZIP, five digits of ZIP, carrier route, etc.). More complete presorting lowers the bulk rate. Most printed matter that is sent through the mail today is presorted to the highest degree possible before leaving the printing plant.

The USPS maintains numerous Bulk Mail Centers around the country. These are highly automated mail-processing plants designed especially to handle bulk mail. For many high-volume publishing applications, the bulk mailing center resides in the printing plant itself. A subscription copy of *Time* magazine, for example, enters the U.S. postal system before it leaves the print production facility. The dependency of print media on reliable distribution channels is as much a reality today as in Benjamin Franklin's time. A modern printing plant that shares a roof with the USPS would make all the sense in the world to Dr. Franklin, were he to visit today.

Mailing directly from the print production facility makes it possible to take full advantage of the power of computing to optimize for the lowest possible mailing rates. The general rule governing bulk mailing rates is that the less work the postal service has to do to deliver a piece of mail to its intended recipient, the lower the rate will be.

Most of the printed matter that moves through the postal system is the result of communication between an organization and a list of recipients who are geographically dispersed. However, it is sometimes desirable to be able to distribute printed information to every address within a certain zip code. The postal service offers a special unaddressed piece rate for this purpose. The USPS delivers nearly 14 billion pieces of unaddressed mail each year to household addresses.[13] This is a small percentage of the total volume of mail delivered to households. In 2003, the postal service delivered more than 140 billion pieces of addressed mail to more than 100 million households. These households, in turn, sent more than 22 billion pieces of mail. The breakdown by class of mail looks like this:[14]

MAIL CLASSIFICATION	RECEIVED BY HOUSEHOLDS	SENT BY HOUSEHOLDS
FIRST CLASS	58.8	22.3
BULK RATE	61.8	—
NONPROFIT	12.4	—
PERIODICALS	6.9	—
PACKAGES	2.0	0.4
EXPEDITED	0.4	0.1
TOTAL (IN BILLIONS)	142.3	22.8

With the technology that sits on my notebook computer I can access all of the capabilities of the modern postal distribution system without ever having to get up out of my chair. I need two ingredients, both in digital form, to make this happen: a mailing list and a document. Digital formats suitable for mailing lists include Excel spreadsheets and database files such as those generated by Microsoft Access or FileMaker Pro. I can upload a PDF document file and a separate file containing mailing addresses to my web server, and send the Internet address to a company equipped to produce and mail one copy of the document for each address in my mailing list. Such a company typically has both digital and offset print production systems and can effectively print runs in any number from one to millions of copies. For documents that will be mailed without envelopes they use two technologies for applying the mailing addresses. If the piece is digitally printed, they merge the mailing data with the content to form a composite graphic file. If the piece is printed by offset lithography, they print all of the copies unaddressed and then use high-speed inkjet technology to add the addresses.

When my son Roger was a toddler, he was obsessed with cars. He had piles of little metal Hot Wheels and Matchbox cars that were so numerous that they could be poured like a liquid from one bucket to another. He had a tattered book about cars that he demanded be read to him many times each day. He would walk through parking lots pointing to each car and asking what kind of car it was. I thought that, at the respectable age of two, he had reached a point where he might appreciate a subscription to a car magazine. So I sent in a subscription card to *Motor Trend* in his name. About six weeks later, the first issue arrived, and it turned out to be a big hit. I showed him how he could cut out the pictures of the cars, and paste them to cardboard to make tokens that could be collected and traded like wampum. For the next few years, these car tokens proliferated throughout the house.

A few months after his first issue arrived, he started to receive direct mail from companies trying to sell car-related products and services. So here's a two-year-old boy getting letters inviting him to purchase NASCAR vacation packages, visit Oldsmobile showrooms, and buy auto insurance. He also started receiving a stream of credit card offers. With my help, he probably could have purchased a real car for himself.

This story illuminates one of the hidden reasons why the subscription price to a magazine like *Motor Trend* is so low. When you subscribe to a special interest magazine, you are freely giving the publisher something far more valuable than the annual subscription fee. You are giving the publisher your name.

With his subscription to *Motor Trend*, my son's name and address were added to its list of subscribers. If you were trying to sell premium car care products by direct mail solicitation, the *Motor Trend* list would be of great value. Fortunately, you can buy the list from the publisher. There are thousands upon thousands of lists for sale in the world, and the science of list creation is making great strides as print and the Internet combine forces.

The *Motor Trend* subscription list is crude by comparison to the most sophisticated lists in existence today. The inclusion of a name on a magazine subscription list only positively indicates one fact: this person subscribes to this magazine. The fact that the person may be two years old is not considered. The list doesn't tell you whether the subscriber has purchased anything other than the subscription. So using this kind of list is like panning for gold. You have to sift through a lot of sand to find the nuggets. The most successful use of such a list is by the publisher itself to sell the next round of subscriptions. All of the people on the list have purchased a subscription, so it is a safe bet that a good percentage will want to do it again. However, it is riskier to assume that the subscribers to *Motor Trend* will want to order a Dale Earnhardt glow-in-the-dark commemorative pencil sharpener.

So lists come with risks. In many cases, a return of one or two percent on a direct mail solicitation sent to a list is all that is needed for a profitable business. Imagine, then, what a return of 20 percent, or 40 percent would mean. The quest for the perfect list is unending. I will return to this topic in the next section of this book where we will learn how the most sophisticated list-generation techniques are used to dramatically increase the effectiveness of direct mail.

CUSTOMER SUPPLY CHAIN MANAGEMENT

Most printed products that do not travel directly through the mail to the end user are part of an input supply chain. As such, the manufacturers of those products have the opportunity to also manage the supply chain on behalf of their customers. Let me give a concrete example of how this works.

A major food company manufactures several hundred different kinds of canned vegetables and fruits in one of its plants. Each variety requires a unique label and it is critical that during a run of canned asparagus, for example, the supply of labels is adequate to fulfill the requirements for that run. If a canning line has to be shut down because the supply of labels is exhausted, the cost to the company will be astronomical.

Let's say the responsibility for making sure that this never happened was entrusted to a department of three full-time people. This department made forecasts of production volumes expected on a quarterly basis, and managed the procurement of labels from three suppliers. They rarely made the mistake of coming up short. They did this by always maintaining large inventories of labels as a safety buffer. The penalty for running out of labels was much higher than the less visible problems of high inventory values and spoilage.

When the company adopted an enterprise resource planning (ERP) system that made it possible for the first time to use data generated as raw materials were procured to schedule production far more accurately and further into the future, the more precise and digitally-accessible production schedule made it possible to think in new ways about the label procurement operation. But it wasn't the people in label procurement who thought in new ways. They were content to keep doing things the way they had always done them and to stay employed in the process.

One of the companies that had been a longtime supplier of labels makes a daring proposal to the upper management of the food company. "If we can have access to your production scheduling database, we will be able to replace your current label procurement system with a system that we will manage for you. We will guarantee that you will always have exactly what you need when you need it, and you will not purchase anything from us until you have removed it from inventory and released it for production. We will do all of this for 60 percent of what we estimate you are currently spending on label procurement without raising our unit prices."

This company is awarded an exclusive contract to supply labels on a one-year trial, after which time the food company assesses its savings and decides to continue the relationship. The two junior people who had been responsible for label procurement are redeployed within the company. The manager of the department retires gracefully after thirty-five years of service to the company.

The moral of this story is this: Print procured the old-fashioned way can never be more than a mere commodity. As such, print is subject to the same kind of competitive pressures and price wars as other commodities. To escape this fate, a print supplier must develop a profound understanding of the real value of print to his customer's business, and then devote his entire mission to improving the value proposition.

In this case, the label supplier understood that the label procurement function was a necessary evil for the food company. The supplier was struggling to compete for price with other suppliers bidding on the same business. The procurement department was only interested in getting the lowest price, and in ensuring that the supply chain was never empty. Upper management was not aware of alternatives to the existing system. The print supplier took advantage of the opportunity presented by the new ERP system to propose a sweeping change. By putting the procurement department out of work, the print supplier eliminated the root cause of its own commoditization and replaced it with a system that yielded it a bigger piece of the total value pie (which in this example is baked exclusively with canned fruits and vegetables).

THE EMERGING PRINTING INDUSTRY

The 1980s and 1990s were decades of accelerating development of constantly improving digital technology for the printing industry. The pace of change in the middle 1990s was so frenetic that it felt like the proverbial ride on the mechanical bull for companies that were trying to stay technologically competitive. The ride was particularly brutal for smaller companies that did not have the resources to invest in new technology that would quickly become obsolete and thus have to be depreciated in only a few short years. Before the beginning of the digital age, the printing industry was largely a collection of tens of thousands of small companies serving local markets. Today, the industry is increasingly dominated by a smaller number of larger companies serving broader geographic markets. As large multinational printing companies such as RR Donnelley, Quebecor World, Quad Graphics, and others become increasingly adept at serving smaller customers in local markets throughout the world, they will consolidate the printing industry in the same way that Barnes & Noble and Borders consolidated the book retailing industry. In ten years the printing industry will likely consist of a handful of multinationals that account for most of the industry's global revenues, and a diverse selection of smaller companies that serve highly specialized vertical niches. In the case of the latter, we may not even think of them as part of the printing industry, but as unique business categories unto themselves.

The core competencies of the large multinational printing companies are threefold. First, they are all very good at processing disparate streams of data—including text, graphics, and databases of all kinds—and transforming them into structured streams that can drive complex graphic production and distribution processes.

RR Donnelley, for example, publishes thousands of different magazine titles, from mass circulation magazines such as *Time* down to small special-interest magazines such as *Bowhunter* and *Dirt Wheels*. The most complex jobs involve merging graphic and distribution data from a multitude of sources, including the publisher and numerous individual advertisers, and producing thousands of different versions of a single magazine title. The versions are assembled and addressed in the bindery. This enables a publisher to send one version of a magazine to you, and a different version of the same magazine to your next-door neighbor. The versions may differ in editorial or advertising content, depending on specific knowledge that the publisher has about individual subscribers.

The second core competency of the large multinational printing companies is the ability to manage large complex manufacturing facilities with great efficiency. They harness the power of automated digital imaging and printing, workflow management, and enterprise resource planning to continuously reduce or eliminate costs that do not contribute to the value of the products and services they sell. They also use the power of the global network to move certain tasks offshore where they can be performed at lower cost. Customer files, for example, may be transferred from a plant located in North America to a facility in India or China, where they are processed by lower-wage operators, and then shipped back the next morning. The time difference between North America and Asia makes this work particularly well. When the day is ending in New York, the new day is beginning in Shanghai.

The third core competency of the large multinational printing companies is the ability to get the final product from the manufacturing plant to the end user through the major channels of distribution in the most timely and cost-effective way possible. RR Donnelley knows more about the USPS than any other company in the world. This is because Donnelley is one of the largest commercial customers of the U.S. Postal Service, accounting for approximately 15 percent of the total volume of U.S. mail (by pieces). Donnelley "annually direct[s] the distribution of more than 20 billion print and mail pieces through our 'pipeline-to-the-home' delivery network, as well as six million expedited shipments of time-critical and confidential materials."[15]

Distribution costs are a significant expense for magazine and catalog publishers. Donnelley is constantly looking for ways to improve the economics of postal delivery for its customers. They do this by using methods such as *co-palletization, dynamic entry,* and *drop-shipping.* Co-palletization combines magazines from different publishers on the same pallet, allowing smaller customers to gain the same postal rate savings as larger customers. Dynamic entry performs a complex analysis of each mailing to optimize postal discounts, entry points into the postal stream, and mailing schedules. Drop-shipping moves publications closer to their destination before inserting them into the postal stream to reduce mailing costs and delivery times.[16]

In addition to the postal channel, large multinational printing companies are also committed to making the other two major distribution channels, retail sales and newspaper inserts, work ever more efficiently for their customers. The retail channel is particularly challenging, because of the high percentage of products that spoil on the shelf before they can be sold. Magazines and newspapers are more perishable than most food products sold in supermarkets. Copies of *Time* magazine, for example, have less than a week to sell before they are out of date. The average spoilage rate for magazines in the retail channel is greater than 60 percent.[17] The daily newspaper spoils in less than 24 hours. Most packaged foods can stay on the shelf for much longer periods, thanks to the rapid improvement of the performance of packaging materials in recent years. Unfortunately, similar improvements in materials used to print magazines and newspapers cannot prevent their contents from spoiling once they reach their expiration date. The only way to reduce the spoilage of printed products in the retail channel is to make the distribution process smarter.

The greatest challenge in the next decade for the large multinational printing companies like Donnelley will be to continue to improve the value of print so that customers will continue to favor its use. There are still significant opportunities to reduce costs in the manufacturing process. However, the industry is already experiencing diminishing returns on these efforts. Far greater opportunities for increasing the value of print lie in improving the probability that each printed piece reaches its intended mark and exerts its intended influence. Today, a large percentage of printed products, whether distributed through retail channels, through the postal channel, or as newspaper inserts, are consigned to the landfill without ever having passed in front of anyone's eyeballs. This brings us to an updated version of a classic philosophical musing. If a television commercial plays in the forest and nobody is there to watch, the advertiser loses money on a wasted media buy. But at least the natural world is not harmed. However, if a print message fails to connect with its intended audience, trees will still fall in the forest.

An important pathway to increasing the value of print to its users is improving its ease of use. Today, commercial print production and distribution services are still very difficult to buy. As a result, print users spend a lot of money on the buying process. Printing companies also spend a lot of money on the selling process. Then a lot of money is spent on reconciling the capabilities of the production process with the promises that were made by the seller to the buyer. In the next decade much of this cost must also be eliminated. Rapidly multiplying legions of potential print buyers now have at their fingertips powerful computers, intelligent graphic design tools, advanced database technologies, and high-speed Internet connections. They should be able to use these capabilities to purchase commercial print services over the Internet and connect with their audiences easily. In Part Two of this book we will turn our attention to the diversity of emerging customer demands driving the creation of new print communication services.

At this point you have a good overview of the technologies and processes that are used to transform ideas and impressions into physical information products that people can hold in their hands. You also realize that physical products must be efficiently transported from their point of manufacture to their point of consumption in order to serve their function. We will now embark on a survey of the various ways that people put these technologies to work to fulfill a variety of communication needs. In each of the following chapters, we will explore current practices and discover key needs and wants that are beginning to be addressed by emerging Internet-enabled print manufacturing and fulfillment solutions.

PART TWO
THE USES OF PRINT

Now that you have a good understanding of the various means of production and distribution of printed products, we are ready to embark on the main mission of this book: to explore how print is used and what its real value is in the world.

Until the advent of electronic media in the 20th century, print lived what the ancient Greek philosopher Socrates described as the "unexamined life." Before radio, print was the sole medium of mass communication. The only alternative to print was to stand in front of an audience and shout. Print enjoyed a complete monopoly of broadcast communication that went beyond earshot. As in the case of all monopolies, print never saw the need to explain or question its value in the world. Printers only had to worry about competition from other printers driving prices down. This was kept in check for hundreds of years in Europe by legislated rules and licensing practices that restricted access to the industry. In America, the First Amendment to the Constitution guaranteeing freedom of political speech makes it difficult to justify these kinds of restrictions. Try to take away the God-given right to print, and you will find out how deeply Americans value this fundamental freedom as you are handed your head on a platter.

But enough political talk. This is more about the mindset of an industry that does not acknowledge the need to question its own value. The value is taken for granted. This leads to a "product out" view of the world. We produce a fixed assortment of printed products. We seek customers who want to buy the products we make. We sell the products to the customers. What could be simpler?

Life was also simple for the buyers of print when print was all there was. If you wanted to communicate with an audience at a distance, you did it with print. Having no choices makes choosing easy.

With the coming of radio and television, people were confronted for the first time with a question that they had never had to ask before: What is the best mix of media choices to deliver my message to my audience? During most of the 20th century, advertising agencies answered this question with a simple wink and wave of the hand. They bought print space from publishers and air time from broadcasters and then sold it to their clients for a higher price. The standard markup was fifteen percent.[18] The agencies would produce the print or broadcast messages for their clients, and run them in the spaces and slots they sold to them. Every time an ad ran in a magazine or on TV, the cash register would ring up a fifteen percent commission for the agency. Picture the happy advertising executive of the 1950s, highball in hand, hearing this sweet sound every time he opened a magazine or newspaper, or turned on the TV and saw one of his ads. It was a great time to be alive and in the ad business.

Even though the broadcast media of radio and television were seen at first as competition for print, they were never able to do what print could do. They could not carry the written word in its native format. They were fleeting, not persistent. They were time-specific or *synchronous*. They required electronic technology to be usable. Print transcends all of these shortcomings. It carries written language in a persistent, *asynchronous* format that does not require technology to be readable.

The Internet challenges print directly in three of these four dimensions. The Internet carries the written word, is persistent, and is asynchronous. The Internet is also electronically searchable. The only exclusive attribute left to print is the lack of need for electronic technology to decode it. The following chart provides a comparison of the four major media: radio, television, print, and Internet.

MEDIUM	GRAPHICS	TEXT	PERSISTENT	ASYNCHRONOUS	TECHNOLOGY-FREE	ELECTRONICALLY SEARCHABLE
RADIO	NO	NO	NO	NO	NO	NO
TELEVISION	YES	SOME	NO	NO	NO	NO
PRINT	YES	YES	YES	YES	YES	NO
INTERNET	YES	YES	YES	YES	NO	YES

From this chart, it is clear that the Internet presents more direct competition to print than the broadcast media. The chart also indicates that the enduring value of print, in relation to the Internet, is somehow tied to its materiality. I will return to this discussion in a while. But first I would like to present a model that will help us to better understand the value of print.

CHAPTER SEVEN

THE VALUE OF PRINT

THE WALLS IN THE FRONT LOBBY OF most commercial printing companies are covered with awards and certificates of all kinds. These are prominently displayed as an implied guarantee to customers that they are doing business with a company that has a track record of quality. But what do most of these awards really mean? For the most part awards are the result of a competition where samples of jobs are submitted for judging by panels of experts. The physical appearance of each entry is the sole criterion for judgment in many such competitions. No other information about the entries is available to the judges. For example, was the job delivered on time? Was the customer pleased with the service? Did the product deliver the anticipated value to the customer? Was the job profitable for the printer? Did the job lead to an expansion of business opportunity?

The point of all of these questions is not to diminish the importance of print and product quality. In most cases today, high product quality is assumed. All printed products must be of high quality. As a point of competition, quality was once a measure of the prowess of a company's craftsmanship. Every move of every craftsman in the company contributed to the overall quality of the final product. When reproduction copy was photographed with process cameras, films were assembled on light tables, and the sharpness of razor blades and steadiness of hands could all be detected in the finished product, a contest that focused on print quality was meaningful. But this is not true any more.

Today product quality is more a direct function of design than of production. Contests that focus solely on the appearance and physical characteristics of the entries, without reference to any of the invisible characteristics mentioned above, are therefore meaningless. Limited to these criteria, it is possible that a winner could have failed in all the important invisible dimensions and that a loser could have succeeded in the same. The "loser" could have been delivered on time, delighted the customer, and returned more than was anticipated on the customer's investment, while the "winner" could have been late, and as a result lost the customer the total cost of the job and then some. Except for the fact that the winner appeared better to a panel of "experts" who were given nothing beyond the physical sample itself as a basis for judgment.

The printing competitions that generate all of the thousands of awards that grace the lobbies of printing companies throughout the U.S. are relics of the age of craftsmanship. Most printing companies know this. But awards make for good decor in a place where customers begin to form their opinions of a company. So common and expected are they, that a front lobby devoid of awards would sow the seeds of doubt about the wisdom of doing business with the company, even in the mind of this skeptical author.

The above argument is not intended to suggest that the industry abandon print contests. The awards undoubtedly help companies market their services, and are therefore considered to be worth the time and effort. However, the idea of quality that is implied by contests masks a number of far more important contributors to the quality of most of the products of the industry. Everyone in the printing business knows that product quality alone is not sufficient for success. Good service is also critical. But quality and service are viewed as independent requirements. One must produce high quality products. One must also provide customers with excellent service. But what if product quality and service are not independent? Furthermore, what if the success of a product is inversely related to quality?

All of this leads to a common misunderstanding among print services providers about the real value of the products and services they offer their customers. This misunderstanding is rooted in the long history and rich culture of the industry. The myopic focus on the material attributes of the manufactured product is a natural consequence of craft-based thinking. However, printed products that are primarily channels of communication between organizations and populations find their ultimate value in the effectiveness of the communication. The value of a catalog, for example, is ultimately a direct function of the volume and distribution of sales that it generates. The physical attributes of the product are only part of the value formula.

All forms of media-based communication are modeled on basic human interactions that have been happening since Adam and Eve had their fateful discussions in the Garden of Eden. Every utterance is accompanied by an evaluation: how was the message received? How should I change the message to get a better response? In Eden the serpent probably chose Eve over Adam because she seemed to be better able to listen and act upon the forbidden instructions.

When print primarily serves as a medium of communication, its value is determined largely by human response. In some cases this response can be directly measured. For example, if I mail out a catalog, I can measure the number of orders that are generated. Catalogs and direct mail are the easiest forms of print media to evaluate. If I run an advertisement in a magazine for a product that is available through a large number of retail outlets, it is harder to determine the actual impact of the ad on sales. This is complicated even further by the fact that print ads are often running in parallel with broadcast ads. Rather than try to establish the exact return on the investment in a specific ad, companies typically settle for a loose cause and effect between total advertising expenditures and total sales volumes.

The more directly measurable the response to a message, the easier it is to evaluate. This is one area where the Internet really shines. The link between a specific ad placement and an ensuing sales transaction can be positively established. Thus the Internet provides for the same kind of direct evaluation as direct mail and catalogs, with two added benefits: the evaluation cycle is much faster and a direct electronic connection with the buyer is established.

CATEGORIES OF VALUE

The North American Industrial Classification System (NAICS) developed by the U.S. Department of Commerce defines three broad categories of value created by industry, and classifies industries accordingly.[19] The three categories are products, services, and information. Prior to the adoption of this new classification system in the mid 1990s, the Standard Industrial Code (SIC) defined only two categories: products and services. Printing and publishing were grouped together as products. With the adoption of NAICS, printing is in the product sector, and publishing has been moved to the newly-defined information sector. This underscores the fact that publishing is no longer married to print as it was in the days before the Internet existed.

Even though print is categorized as part of the product sector of the economy, the value produced by the printing industry is not simply a function of its "product-ness." Without the services that accompany the printed product, such as the timely delivery of the product to the end user, the product by itself has little value. And if the information content is not accurate, the product can actually have negative value. Thus most printed products have a high service and information value as well.

If we compare print to other manufactured products, we begin to understand that any classification system that forces print into only one category distorts our understanding of the true value of print as an industrial output. Most industries produce value in more than one of the three broad categories of product, service, and information. However, print is rather unique in that it carries high value in all three categories. The following chart compares four common industrial outputs in terms of value created.

	AUTO-MOBILE	TELEVISION SET	TAX SERVICE	PRINT CATALOG
PRODUCT	**HIGH**	**HIGH**	LOW	**HIGH**
SERVICE	MEDIUM	LOW	**HIGH**	**HIGH**
INFORMATION	LOW	LOW	MEDIUM	**HIGH**

Because print is typically highly valued as a product, as a service, and as a source of information, the industry has a three-dimensional challenge as it strives to increase the value that it delivers to its customers and end-users. To increase the value of the product, the industry must continually strive to improve the precision and efficiency of the manufacturing processes that are used to produce printed products. This requires continual investment in new generations of production equipment that deliver improved product quality. To increase the value of the service and information, the industry must continually work to improve its responsiveness to its customers and the accuracy and relevance of the information delivered. This requires continual investment in improved information systems and re-engineered manufacturing and logistical workflows. The ultimate goal toward which the industry must continually strive is to deliver high-quality products carrying the right information to the right audiences at the right time. No other industry has such a complex and interesting mix of challenges.

SIX VECTORS OF PRINT VALUE

The ultimate value of any printed product is determined by summing value contributions in six discrete dimensions. These six dimensions are described as follows:

1. **Informative.** The ability of the product to convey information from sender to receiver. A newspaper has high informative value.
2. **Instructive (directive).** The ability of the product to convey instructions or directions from sender to receiver. A recipe book has high instructive value.
3. **Persuasive.** The ability of the product to persuade the receiver to take some course of thought or action. A sales brochure has high persuasive value.
4. **Evocative.** The ability of the product to induce an intended emotion in the receiver. A book of poetry has high evocative value.
5. **Decorative.** The ability of the product to favorably alter the appearance of an environment. Wallpaper has high decorative value.
6. **Operative.** The ability of the product to enable actions or transactions to take place. A passport has high operative value.

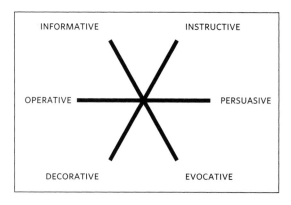

Six vectors of print.

A diagram showing all six of these value vectors is useful for graphically depicting the discrete value components of any printed product.

Let's use this diagram to depict the value of some common printed products. We can start with this book. Hopefully the book has high informative value. This is the dominant value component. But it is not the only one. The book also has some instructive value. For example, an earlier chapter explains how to make paper in your kitchen. So while the book has high informative value, it also has a moderate amount of instructive value. At specific points in the text, I am also trying to persuade you to think or act in a certain way. At the very least the book needs to persuade you to buy the book.

This book has high informative value, medium instructive value, and some degree of persuasive value. What about the other three dimensions? Does the book have any evocative value? Has any part of this book thrilled you, made you laugh out loud, or brought you to tears? If so, then the book has some evocative value. If not, perhaps I need to find a different career. Does it have any decorative value? Well, unless you plan to leave this book casually lying on a table to impress visitors with your fine taste in books, probably not. Lastly, does the book have any operative value? Does it enable actions or transactions? Again, this is not a big contributor to the value of the book.

So this book is valued primarily because it is informative, and to a lesser extent because it is instructive, persuasive, and evocative.

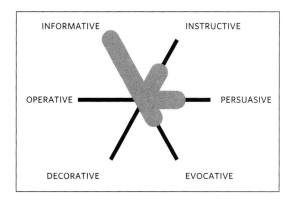

Value vectors for this book.

It is not much valued for decorative or operative purposes.

We can produce a diagram of this type for any print product. A novel, for example, would have a high evocative value, but relatively low instructive and persuasive values. Some novels may have higher informative value than others. For example, I learned all I know about 19th century whaling by reading *Moby Dick*. A novel has little decorative or operative value.

The *Handbook of Origami* has high instructive value, medium informative value, and little persuasive, evocative, decorative, or operative value. A stock certificate has high operative value, some informative value, and almost no other kind of value. A food package

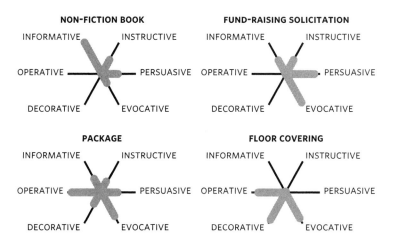

has high operative, informative, persuasive, and evocative value. A political advertisement has high evocative and persuasive value, but little informative, instructive, operative, or decorative value.

We can also use this device to diagram the value of various capabilities of print media. For example, design novelty has high persuasive, evocative, and decorative value. Content accuracy has high informative, instructive, and operative value. Reduced time to market and more accurate targeting of audience both have high value in all six dimensions. New technologies and practices that reduce the time required to produce and distribute a printed product have great value across the entire spectrum of print. Likewise, technologies and practices that improve the accuracy of audience targeting are of great value.

If we overlay the value vectors for any given product on top of the value vectors for any given capability, we can identify opportunities for enhancing the value of printed products by improving capabilities. If, for example, we overlay the value vectors for a direct mail fund-raising solicitation on top of the value vectors for a capability such as personalization, we can clearly see that the greatest opportunity for value enhancement of a fund raising solicitation through personalization is along the persuasive value vector. This makes a lot of sense. If a solicitation is informed by specific knowledge about an individual and appeals to specific personal concerns, it is more likely to receive a positive response.

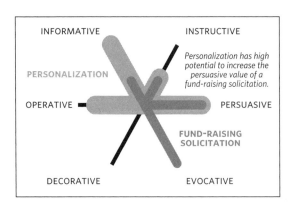

Personalization has high potential to increase the persuasive value of a fund-raising solicitation.

THE VALUE OF MATERIALITY

Print is the only material medium of mass communication. It is entirely made of atoms and molecules, not electrons and bits. If the power goes out, print remains "on." It can lie in the bottom of a drawer for a century, all the while remaining instantly accessible. The materiality of print makes it the ideal medium for storing dormant information in its final presentation format. I sometimes think of print as "freeze-dried information."

Materiality also allows print to reference the material world more literally than any other medium. This has great value in many marketing applications. Print has a high "drool factor" that is especially helpful in the marketing of expensive luxury goods. You can see this best in magazine advertisements for outrageously expensive wristwatches or clothes, or brochures for absurdly expensive luxury automobiles. The images of the objects of desire are reproduced with such clarity that the real things pale by comparison. But by then you've already spent your money and you're too preoccupied with buyer's remorse to notice.

Print can participate in the material world even more literally than this. Wallpaper, floor coverings, printed textiles, and packages all incorporate printed graphics. In these applications, print is part of the products themselves. Printed surfaces can mimic the appearance of wood, stone, fabric, and other natural materials. The manufactured housing industry would not exist were it not for printed surfaces of this kind. The next time you're in a mobile home or RV, try to find a real wooden or stone surface. You will not succeed.

Print works well as a channel of visual communication because it is matched perfectly to the requirements of the visual system. Humans have been perfecting the channel for the last couple thousand years. Because it is a long-established channel that works perfectly, it is inconceivable that people will give it up. Imagine, for a moment, a world where all of the print was removed. Now ponder the following question: What would be the most powerful channel of visual communication in such a world? The answer is, of course, print! In a world saturated with electronic media, the material medium of print has the potential to gain power for itself. Our challenge is to figure out how to effectively use the powerful medium of print for new purposes.

CHAPTER EIGHT

PUBLISHING

Print was invented to serve publishing. In the broadest sense, publishing is the making public of information and ideas through the use of media of any kind. Radio and television broadcasts are a form of publishing, although we normally do not think of them as such. The classical definition of publishing usually implies a non-interactive, one-to-many, formal communication through printed text and graphics. When we use the word casually, people automatically think of books, magazines, and newspapers. But we also commonly talk about "catalog publishing" and even "software publishing."

How small can the audience be before we start to strain the definition of publishing? We typically do not describe the act of writing a personal letter as publishing, although the same letter written to the editor of the newspaper is clearly so. Until the advent of digital printing and the Internet, this discussion would have been unnecessary. Publishing was the exclusive domain of organizations that had the means to purchase ink by the barrel and paper by the truckload. Today, publishing is possible by anyone with access to a copying machine, a digital printer, or the Internet.

BOOK PUBLISHING

The simplest and purest form of publishing is also the oldest. Johannes Gutenberg published his edition of the Bible in Latin in the 1450s. With funding from his business partner, Johann Fust, he produced fewer than 200 copies of the book.[20] Most of these were printed on paper. A small number of copies were printed on thin animal skin sheets called *vellum* to produce a deluxe edition.

The business plan was exceedingly simple:

Step 1: Produce books at a certain unit cost.

Step 2: Sell them for more.

Step 3: Pocket the difference.

Gutenberg ran into problems with Step 2. He was unable to sell the edition in time to pay back his creditor and Gutenberg ended up embroiled in a contentious lawsuit.

At the moment I am feeling a special kinship with Gutenberg. Before we committed the resources to producing a first edition of this book we attempted to estimate the potential demand. Based on that estimate, we established a budget for production of the content. If I were a scandalized celebrity or former politician, I might have been able to command an up-front payment from the publisher simply for writing the book. Even if the book bombed, I would still be able to keep the money. But I will only receive royalties based on actual sales of the book. If nobody buys it, I will have nothing to show for my work except an embarrassing sense of fruitless accomplishment.

Other contributors to the content of this book, including the designer, illustrator, copy editor, and proofreader received payment for services rendered up front. The publisher paid them by the hour for their work. They do not share the author's risk, but neither will they receive royalties based on the sale of the book. The publisher also needed to pay up front for the printing. The unit cost is linked to the number of copies printed. The more printed, the lower the unit cost.

Based on a crude assessment of the potential market for the first edition of this book, the publisher decided to order 5,000 copies at a unit cost of $1.44.

The retail price you pay for any book includes the markup from the wholesale price. Typically, the publisher will sell the book to the retailer for 50-60 percent of the suggested retail price. The most powerful retailers (e.g. Barnes & Noble, Amazon, Wal-Mart) command the largest discounts. These retailers can then turn around and discount the price. So the publisher of a book that lists for $20 will sell it to the retailer for $10-12. The retailer can discount the book 30 percent and sell the book for $14. This still leaves a healthy profit for the retailer, assuming all unsold copies can be

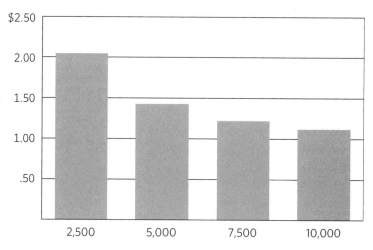

Unit cost and run length.

returned to the publisher for full credit.

The economics of this type of publishing are not significantly different from any mass marketing and production of other consumer products. Manufacturing unit costs drop with increased volumes of production. Marketing departments attempt to predict and create demand for the product. Success is determined by how close the predicted market comes to the actual market. Profits come out of the differential between total cost of production and distribution and total retail sales.

This book was designed by a professional designer using Adobe Photoshop, Illustrator, InDesign, and Acrobat to create the files that were transmitted to the printer. These Adobe tools have been refined to the point where they allow the graphic designer complete freedom of expression.[21] However, they are complex and difficult to master and not suited for casual use. The designer of this book invested many years learning how to design for print using them.

While the Adobe tools are essential for the creation of original print designs, many of the new opportunities for print in the future will need to circumvent the manual design process altogether. The key to making this work is a meta-design or template. In theory, as templates become increasingly sophisticated, they offer greater design freedom with fewer constraints. The ultimate template would allow for all of the freedom available from the Adobe tool set, but disallow errors by the designer. These capabilities are gradually finding their way into the design software. However, the best template-based applications still impose formidable constraints on the design process.

DIVERSITY OF BOOK TYPES

Not all books are created equal. There is a spectrum of complexity from simple text-only books in standardized formats to custom-designed books with complex graphics and geometry. On the simple end of the spectrum you will find books like series romance novels. In some series, there are hundreds of titles that all share the same basic structure. The typography and design are standardized. You can well imagine that once the standard design is set, it does not take much creative design work to produce subsequent books in the series. In fact, many book publishing applications of this kind lend themselves perfectly to template-based solutions.

On the other end of the spectrum are books that are so complex that they could only be manually designed by an expert designer using all of the power of the Adobe tool set. My favorite examples are children's pop-up books that present elaborate three-dimensional artwork on each page. Some of these books are marvels of mechanical engineering and design that demand a level of respect that no child is capable of giving them. When my children were young, I remember the painful experience of allowing them to destroy some of the most incredible books I had ever seen. If I had it to do over, I would have confiscated many of those pop-up books long before they had the chance to put their slimy little hands on them.

On the spectrum of books from the simplest romance novel to the most complex pop-up book, the likelihood that the book is manufactured in the U.S. steadily decreases.[22] Almost all pop-up books, for example, are manufactured overseas in places like China and Thailand. On the other hand, the great majority of text-only hardcover and paperback books sold in the U.S. are produced domestically. This has to do with the amount of craftwork and manual labor required in the manufacturing process. This book was printed by RR Donnelley in their Harrisonburg, Virginia, book production plant. If we had decided to produce a full color, three-dimensional, multimedia, pop-up extravaganza, we would have been compelled to print overseas—most likely in China.

Another important dimension to book publishing is the shelf life of the product. Here we can also imagine a spectrum from very brief to very long. On the brief end of the spectrum are books that are produced to exploit a fleeting market opportunity such as a celebrity murder trial, political scandal, sports championship, or unexpected death of a famous person. News organizations are especially adept at this form of book publishing because they have two advantages over other publishers: authoring and production systems in place that allow them to get to print quickly. Newspaper and magazine writers are especially skilled at cranking out text on very short deadlines. They also own a lot of relevant content that they can use without having to ask anyone's permission. A good news organization can produce what will pass for a book on almost any subject that has been well reported in a matter of days. Speed is of the essence because the demand for books of this kind falls off precipitously once the story has been resolved.

On the other end of this spectrum are books of enduring value that have a shelf life measured in years. A leather-bound edition of the King James Bible is the best example I can give. The value of the product does not decrease significantly over time. Publishers of these kinds of books attempt to strike a balance between the economies of scale offered by longer production runs with the cost of maintaining inventories over time. Typically they will produce enough units to supply the distribution channel for a period of a few years.

When yearly demand for a book falls below a certain threshold, publishers will allow the book to go out of print. This threshold should be the point where inventory costs offset anticipated profits to the extent that the next production cycle becomes a poor investment. Digital printing processes have changed this equation somewhat by allowing publishers to produce smaller runs of books at lower unit costs than conventional offset printing.

Some experts have even suggested that digital printing technology will ultimately end the need for a book to ever go out of print. The reasoning here is fairly simple. Almost all books are produced with software applications that can easily generate electronic versions in Adobe PDF format. These electronic files can be stored in a

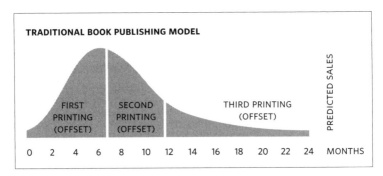

TRADITIONAL BOOK PUBLISHING MODEL

FIRST PRINTING (OFFSET)

SECOND PRINTING (OFFSET)

THIRD PRINTING (OFFSET)

PREDICTED SALES

0 2 4 6 8 10 12 14 16 18 20 22 24   MONTHS

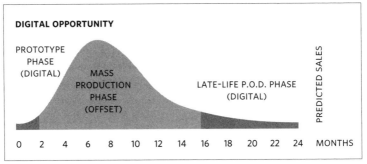

DIGITAL OPPORTUNITY

PROTOTYPE PHASE (DIGITAL)

MASS PRODUCTION PHASE (OFFSET)

LATE-LIFE P.O.D. PHASE (DIGITAL)

PREDICTED SALES

0 2 4 6 8 10 12 14 16 18 20 22 24   MONTHS

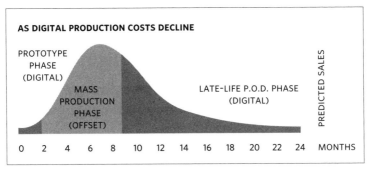

AS DIGITAL PRODUCTION COSTS DECLINE

PROTOTYPE PHASE (DIGITAL)

MASS PRODUCTION PHASE (OFFSET)

LATE-LIFE P.O.D. PHASE (DIGITAL)

PREDICTED SALES

0 2 4 6 8 10 12 14 16 18 20 22 24   MONTHS

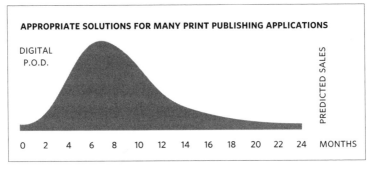

APPROPRIATE SOLUTIONS FOR MANY PRINT PUBLISHING APPLICATIONS

DIGITAL P.O.D.

PREDICTED SALES

0 2 4 6 8 10 12 14 16 18 20 22 24   MONTHS

database and retrieved on demand. When someone wishes to purchase a book, the PDF file can be used to digitally print one copy of the book on demand.

This zero-inventory approach to publishing also enables publishing on a scale never before possible. That book you have always wanted to publish of dinner recipes obtained during your recent abduction by aliens can now become a reality. There's more to it than this, however. Digital print production technology has the potential to totally eliminate the set-up costs that have made it heretofore impractical to publish books in small editions.

Digital print production coupled with Internet-based template-driven design tools make print publishing available to everyone, regardless of scale. Two pioneering companies worthy of recognition in this new field are Lightning Source and MyPublisher. Lightning Source (*lightningsource.com*) provides publishers with book design and on-demand production of digitally printed books. The most common format is 6 by 9 inches paperbound. Books are printed on high-speed monochrome laser printers. The print quality for text-only books matches offset quality. Images are reproduced with slightly lesser quality than offset, but not objectionably so. A finished Lightning Source book comes very close to that of a conventionally produced book—so much so that most casual users would not detect any difference.

Once the book is "in print," publishers can order any quantity of books from Lightning Source at a fixed unit cost. The unit cost will typically break even with traditionally offset monochrome printing somewhere between 500 and 1,000 copies of a 200-page book. For quantities below approximately 500, the unit cost is less than the same book produced by offset.

For small publishers, the ability to order low quantities at reasonable unit costs is the first step toward successful book pub-

[LEFT] *Digital print production enables the inexpensive creation of prototypes of new publications as well as the capability of keeping books in print long after the economics of mass production fail. As the variable costs of digital print decrease, production on demand can be implemented earlier in the life cycle. For publications that are expected to sell in low volumes over long periods, digital production on demand replaces mass production entirely.*

lishing. But how do you distribute a book once it has been produced? Until recently, the only option was direct distribution. Traditionally small publishers had no way to distribute through bookstores.

For some titles, direct distribution can be very profitable. Books that focus on passionate interests shared by fanatical subcultures lacking in formal documentation are good candidates. The key to this kind of publishing is the ability to reach the targeted audience through some advertising channel. Former RIT color printing researcher Zenon Elyjiw sold thousands of copies of his beautifully illustrated book about decorated Ukrainian Easter eggs by placing a small advertisement in the *Ukrainian Weekly* magazine. If you are the first person to write a book about a hobby that has a small but devoted following, and you can reach the target population easily, you are almost guaranteed a success. My next book is going to be *The Pez Candy Dispenser Collector's Bible*, if someone doesn't beat me to it.

If you publish a book that is competing with other similar publications, the direct marketing approach will not work as well. This is where you will need help with distribution. Lightning Source has agreements with major on-line bookstores such as Amazon and Barnes & Noble, and wholesale distributors like Ingram Book Group.

More consumer-oriented print fulfillment services are offered by companies like MyPublisher and Kodak EasyShare Gallery. These companies started as Internet-based digital photo processing labs serving the growing number of consumers possessing both digital cameras and high-speed Internet connections. Their first offerings were digital print services that mimicked traditional photofinishing. The basic product was a stack of four-by-six-inch borderless glossy photo prints in an envelope—essentially the same product that people purchased from the local drug store in the middle of the last century.

But electronic submission of digital picture files over the Internet began to open up the floodgates of new possibilities for personal publishing starting at the beginning of the present century. With digital customer content in hand, digital photofinishers were positioned to begin offering services that went far beyond the traditional stack of curled photo prints.

One useful way to view this convergence of photofinishing with print publishing is to re-examine with new eyes the photofinishing industry that was started by George Eastman in the 1880s.

Eastman's first commercial product was a simple box camera loaded with his newly-invented roll film. The camera was sealed and contained enough film for approximately 100 exposures. The user neither saw nor had to handle the film. The camera was a "black box" both literally and figuratively.

The real genius of Eastman's invention was the elaborate system of manufacturing and service that he built to support this simple product. The system was totally invisible to the user of the camera. Eastman's marketing slogan, "You push the button and we do the rest," perfectly expressed Eastman Kodak's vision of how technology could be made to serve the needs of non-technical users.

Before Kodak, photography was the exclusive domain of professionals who had to spend years learning how to master their difficult and technically challenging craft. Eastman removed all of the technical difficulty and created an industry that enabled casual users to produce their own photographs. Viewed from a contemporary perspective, Eastman launched the first revolution in "personal publishing." By using Kodak's system, one could produce a custom publication in the form of a family photo album. Kodak enabled every family to become a private publishing house.

Today Kodak's original product concept is alive and well in almost exactly the same form as the original. You can buy a single-use camera pre-loaded with film at any supermarket or drugstore. The camera works in the same way as the original Kodak camera. When you have made all of the exposures, you take the camera to the photofinisher and order prints. The photofinisher may have equipment for scanning and digitizing your developed film. In this case, the photofinisher can offer a number of new products and services that make use of your digitized images. They can be printed on a variety of substrates such as textiles and ceramics, or uploaded to a web server and made accessible to anyone with an Internet connection.

Film scanning thus provides a bridge from old to new, expanding the capabilities of the photofinishing industry to serve the personal publishing market. However, film scanning still requires a physical transfer of material from print buyer to print producer. With digital photography, this physical transfer of material is no longer necessary. Image content can be transferred over the Internet. And with the help of web-based software applications, text content can also be added.

MyPublisher has created a software application called *Bookmaker* that you can download from its Internet site (mypublisher.com). This application enables you to create a simple photo book complete with illustrated cover, title page, text introduction, and captions. The application offers a selection of style templates and page layout options. You can choose from a limited set of typefaces. The Bookmaker application makes it possible for a casual user to design a book and order multiple copies over the Internet.

Other Internet print providers offer addressing and mailing services as well. Kodak EasyShare Gallery (formerly Ofoto) will perform a mail merge of customer text and graphic content with a customer-supplied database of mailing addresses. You can design a custom greeting card and have Kodak print and mass mail it to everyone on your list. Internet services like Lightning Source, MyPublisher, and Kodak are pioneers in a publishing revolution that has the potential to transform any individual with a computer and an Internet connection into a publishing house.

At the end of this book, I will demonstrate a new suite of Internet services for publishers offered by a company called *Lulu*. Lulu has created a digital infrastructure that allows its customers to publish books at *no* cost. If you find this hard to believe, go to Lulu.com and search for this book. You can order the book from Lulu and they will produce the book, ship it to you, and send us a royalty payment. And we have never sent Lulu a dime! I will reveal how they do this in the last chapter of the book.

THE VALUE OF A BOOK

This brings me to one of the central themes of this book. I will illustrate my point by posing a simple question. Why were you willing to pay for this book? I'll give you a few clues to the answer. Experience tells us that you would not be willing to pay much at all for this exact same content in electronic form. I could easily place a PDF version of this book on the web and offer it for sale. However, you would expect this same content in that form to be free.

This has to do with the nature of the content itself. If this were the definitive industry newsletter about the futures market in pork bellies and you were in some pork-belly-related business, you would most likely be willing to pay a lot of money for access and you would prefer electronic access over paper.

But this book is different. It is not going to help you make a fortune by transmitting ultra time-sensitive information relevant to your business. Neither is it a voluminous body of critical reference material that you need to use on a regular basis for your business. The best example of such content that I can cite is an electronic law library. Law firms are willing to pay a lot of money for access to electronic databases like *Westlaw* and *LexisNexis*. Printed legal books, as a result, are in sharp decline.

So why does the trend to electronic substitution not also apply to this book? The reasons are twofold. First, this book enables direct communication between author and reader, and is intended to be read from beginning to end. Your expectation when you bought the book was that it would change the way you see the world. You expected to gain new perspective and understanding on many issues of common interest. You planned to spend a considerable amount of time with the book, and then to place it on your shelf as a permanent record of the communication that passed between us. The physical nature of the book enables the kind of relationship that you wish to have with me.

But just who am I anyway? What makes you value my ideas enough to actually pay money for them? Here's where we encounter the second reason why print is the preferred medium for a book of this type. One of the most important implicit messages of the print medium is that the content is somehow validated by the difficulty and expense of the medium itself. To quote Jethro Bodine, Jed Clampett's dimwitted nephew in the 1960s sitcom *The Beverly Hillbillies*, "They wouldn't print it in a comic book, if it weren't true!"

By this I do not mean to imply that your decision to buy this book was somehow evidence of weak-mindedness. Just that the mere fact of print lends to its credibility and value. Even if you had never heard my name before you picked up this book, you would probably think something along these lines: "Someone spent a lot of money producing and distributing this book. They wouldn't have made the investment if the author were some kind of crackpot. Therefore, I can buy it with some confidence that my money will not be wasted."

What will the impact of ubiquitous professional-quality printing have on this perceived value of content? The mere existence of a book is less impressive today than it was ten years ago. After all, you can go to MyPublisher.com or Lulu.com and publish one yourself. This is where branding becomes more important than ever. Do you recognize the publisher? Do you know the author? In many segments of book publishing, the author is the only significant contributor to the brand. Who cares, or even knows, what company published Hillary Clinton's autobiography? Hillary is one of the world's most recognizable brands. On the other hand, who cares or even knows who the author or publisher of *Book Publishing for Dummies* is? In this case the brand is entirely carried by one amusing word.

AMATEUR PUBLISHING: THE EMERGENCE OF A NEW MASS MARKET

Here are two interesting facts about the tools and equipment that have been used to produce graphics since the beginning of recorded history. First fact: All of the historical tools and processes that have ever been used are still being used somewhere, by somebody, to produce contemporary work. Somewhere today a person is carving a woodcut in one place, while someone else is etching a copper engraving with ferric chloride in another. Somewhere, someone is hand setting lead type in the same way that Gutenberg did more than five centuries ago. Somewhere, someone is coating a piece of paper with a light sensitive platinum salt, preparing to make a platinum print from a glass plate photographic negative. Somewhere, another person is sensitizing a silver daguerreotype plate by holding it over a bath of steaming iodine. I know that these things are happening because many of the people involved are personal friends and colleagues who devote themselves passionately to these pursuits.

Second fact: All of the printing technologies that are currently used by artists today to produce fine art prints were at one time important commercial processes used for the production of everyday printed products. Technologies cease to be commercially viable as soon as something faster, cheaper, and better comes along. But fine artists are more interested in the peculiar qualities of the print that can be obtained from a process than they are in the economics of the process. Furthermore, all of the obsolete technologies that today's fine art printmakers use are not ancient. There are contem-

The Kelmscott Press edition of Geoffrey Chaucer's works is considered one of the most beautiful books ever produced. Photo by ETC Photography at RIT.

porary artists using the original 1985 Apple Macintosh computers and laser printers to produce distinctive fine art pieces. Others use early models of Xerox copiers to produce prints that bear the distinctive artifacts of those devices that were likely viewed as defects when the devices were being used commercially.

This passing of technology from commercial users to fine artists has been going on since the first time new print technology replaced old. When Gutenberg put the scribes out of business, their tools passed into the hands of calligraphers. And so it has continued ever since. Up until the end of the 19th century, graphic arts technologies were almost exclusively in the hands of professionals, whether they were commercial printers or fine artists. At that point, a third party entered the scene. This was the amateur.

By this time commercial printing had become a true mass medium, ubiquitous and fleeting. The volume of commercially-produced print that washed past average people on a given day was immense. Print was an exclusively public medium in much the same way that television was an exclusively public medium in its early years before the advent of home video. A small number of amateur private printers began to construct print shops using commercially

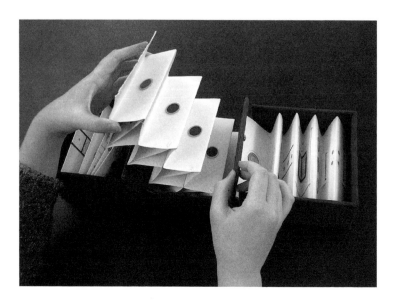

Bibles, Drums, and Bingo, *by book artist Gloria Helfgott, 1993.*

obsolete printing equipment and hand-set type to produce finely printed books in limited editions for the pure love of doing so. The patron saint of this movement was the Englishman William Morris, who named his private printing house the Kelmscott Press. His work is still considered to be among the most exquisite of the printing craft ever produced. Morris believed that he was returning to the quality standards that had been established by the first generations of European printers in the 15th century. But Morris also started a movement of amateur book printing that would grow into a fine art in its own right. He liberated the book from its singular function as a commercial vehicle for practical communication. The first and most powerful message that is delivered to the reader of a book from the Kelmscott Press is, "Look at me! I'm a beautiful book!"

Before Morris came along, books had become all but invisible as communications media. Readers did not see the physical aspects of the printed page any more than present-day television viewers see the camerawork and sound recording techniques used to produce a favorite program. Morris was correct to point out that books had become common objects that were largely taken for granted. However, the resulting movement to make the book visible to the reader had a negative side. If the book itself took center stage, the transparent connection between author and reader would be lost. The products of the Kelmscott Press are objects of unquestionable beauty. But they are not the kinds of books in which you can lose yourself, because the presentation constantly challenges the content for your attention.

This struggle between form and function has been going on for thousands of years and will likely never come to an end. Would you rather have a beautiful uncomfortable chair, or an ugly comfortable chair? OK, so you want a chair that is both beautiful and comfortable! That makes sense. But with media products, the relationship between form and function is more complicated. The credibility and authority of a book is also reinforced by its form because of expectations that people have for how a book should appear. Contemporary book artists who follow in the tradition of William Morris are always trying to make their work visible and profound by breaking away from established forms. But an uninformed person who happened upon an exhibition of contemporary book arts would probably not recognize any of the objects in the exhibition as books, and would certainly not be comfortable curling up with one of them in bed.

The idea of print as a transparent medium of communication that best serves its function if it remains completely invisible to the reader was articulated by Beatrice Warde, a type scholar and an employee of the British Monotype company, in a 1930 lecture that she gave to the British Typographer's Guild in London. Her lecture was later published as an essay entitled *The Crystal Goblet, or Printing Should Be Invisible*.[23] In the essay, Ms. Warde uses the metaphor of a wine glass to illustrate her idea of the proper relationship between printed media and the message conveyed. The role of a wine glass is to contain the wine and to display it in such a way that the glass itself disappears from view. The form of the glass is important, but its beauty is measured by how well it performs its function. The same is true for print. If print inserts itself between the author and the reader, it is not performing properly. This was not to argue against beauty and craftsmanship, but merely to assert the Modernist idea first articulated in 1896 by the American architect Louis Sullivan, that form should follow function, and that the function of print was to provide a transparent container for words and images to be trans-ported from author to reader.[24]

A few years back I found myself loudly pronouncing Beatrice Warde's argument when I confronted the editorial team of our week-ly campus student magazine, *Reporter*, with the fact that I could not read the articles in the magazine. The design had become so affect-ed in its avant-garde grunginess that it was no longer legible. This confrontation was precipitated by my unsuccessful attempt to read an article that one of my students had written on a campus political issue that was of great interest to me. The students responsible for the publication had allowed it to become a showpiece for experi-mental graphic design, and had forgotten that illegibility renders the best journalism pointless. They listened attentively and assured me that they understood the need to strike a balance between legibility and visual appeal to young, jaded, media-saturated techno-zombies. To their credit, the design of the magazine changed much for the better after our encounter.

Until the invention of sound recording technology at the end of the 19th century, there was no other way to externalize a thought but to write or print it out on paper. Now we have many ways to externalize our ideas. I could just as easily be sitting here in front of a video camera instead of at my computer keyboard. But then I would have to shave and get dressed. Today hundreds of millions of people in the world have the means to acquire devices that enable them to produce externalized records of their thoughts and experi-ences. Digital devices that produce simple discrete records of visual or audio experience like photography, sound recording, and video recording are all very simple to use. All you need to do to create a record is to press a button. The technology is so easy to use that every other parent of every other child in my daughter's junior high school class can make the same technical quality video of the holi-day concert that I can. And, believe me when I say that mine will be no more watchable than any of theirs!

All of these digital media have a fundamental weakness that limits their power to communicate. Every parent with a video cam-era knows that the audience for the video produced will most likely be restricted to members of the immediate family, and perhaps a weak-willed grandparent who cannot politely decline to watch.

Video and audio recordings are personal possessions, not appropriate for sharing with people outside of the immediate family. The reason for this is that recordings take the control of time away from the viewer or listener.

When people surrender their control of time they have very high expectations of the mediated experience they will have in exchange for their temporal freedom. These high expectations are set by the multi-million dollar production values of the major commercial media producers. When the Disney people take an hour of your life from you, they know that they have to replace it with something very good, or incur your wrath. Very few producers of home video would dare ask anyone outside of the family to sit through an amateur video production. One of the most powerful stereotypes of social boorishness in American culture is the dim-witted male who forces his dinner guests to watch home movies after dessert.

We can now clearly see that media take two distinct and dramatically different forms, depending on who is in control of time. With broadcast and recorded media, the producer is in control of time. With print, the consumer is in control of time. This is a useful way of grouping all media into two categories.

1. **Producer-timed media.** Television, radio, film, sound recording, video.
2. **Consumer-timed media.** Print, Internet.

The only socially acceptable media formats for sharing experience beyond the boundaries of the nuclear family are consumer-timed. Only print and the Internet, to the extent that it behaves like print, are able to do this. It is important to remember that watching a video on the Internet is no different than watching it on television or in a theatre. So the Internet swings both ways. To accommodate the reluctance of viewers to relinquish their control of time, producer-timed Internet presentations nearly always include a little button in the corner that allows the viewer to skip ahead. If a website takes exclusive control of time for even a few seconds, consumers get angry. So even though the Internet accommodates both producer-timed and consumer-timed content, the medium itself is clearly consumer-timed.

This distinction between producer-timed and consumer-timed media explains why an album of family photographs is a gracious medium for sharing family experiences with guests while the showing of video will often trigger a feigned seizure or migraine. Print media always leave the consumer in complete control of time. Of course, an obnoxious host who insists on providing a monologue to describe the context of each picture in an album can turn the viewing of an album of photographs into a producer-timed nightmare. The same would be true if Bill Clinton insisted on coming to your house to read you his 1,000-page autobiography. Consumer-timed media presentations make no guarantee that the producer won't still feel compelled to steal back your control of time. A boor is a boor, after all.

I PRINT, THEREFORE I AM

Because print is a purely consumer-timed medium, and because it can be made to last for hundreds of years, most people understand that print is the preferred medium for preserving personal experience and family history. They instinctively know that the photo album they produce now will still be easily accessible by their great grandchildren. The piles of video tapes of their children's holiday concerts will probably not live past the current generation of technology, because they won't be viewable.

The family photo album has one weakness, however. Usually, there is only one album with a certain collection of photographs in it. If you want to guarantee that a photo album will be accessible by all of your great grandchildren (assuming a normal replacement birthrate of two children per family, your great grandchildren will number eight), you will need eight copies. If your family culture favors lots of children, this number could be much larger.

The Latter Day Saints church encourages large families and also recommends each family to record its history in printed form. Brigham Young University in Salt Lake City runs a printing plant that provides digital print services for the University as well as book production services for families who wish to publish their family histories. If you want to make a copy of your family history available to every one of your great grandchildren, you can use the following table to determine how many copies you will need to print:

AVERAGE NUMBER OF CHILDREN	GREAT GRANDCHILDREN	GREAT GREAT GREAT GRANDCHILDREN
2	8	32
3	27	243
4	64	1,024
5	125	3,125
6	216	7,776
7	343	16,807

Now you can see how Abraham could have been promised "more descendents than there are stars in the sky." Even with only two children per family, you will end up with a thousand descendents in ten generations. But will any of them really care to know about your experience at your daughter's holiday concert? The answer is a resounding *yes*.

I have a few photographs of my great grandparents, and only one from the generation before theirs. She is my mother's mother's mother's mother. Her name was Caliroy Christopoulos Panos. She was born in 1840 in Tripolis, a city near the ancient city of Sparta, in Greece. Beyond these few facts, this picture is all I know about her.

I once used her photograph in a lecture that I gave to a class of first-year students. The class was about basic digital imaging concepts, and I used the photograph to demonstrate some forgotten characteristic of a scanned photographic image. After class ended a student came up to the front of the room and asked me whether I was related to the woman in the picture. I asked her why she had asked that question. She responded, "Because she looks just like you." At that moment I realized that the only information I would ever have about this person who was responsible for my very existence was contained in that one photograph, and that I would have given a lot of money for even one more image, let alone an album or a journal.

Looking forward, we are fortunate to live at a time when the medium of print, in the same forms that have served commercial markets for centuries, is becoming accessible to everyone with a computer and an Internet connection. We can speak through the medium with increasing ease, publishing beyond the boundaries of the family both *horizontally* and *vertically* in time. A good example of a horizontal opportunity is the publishing of a personalized book of selected photographs from a wedding that is sent to every guest who attended, along with a personal note of thanks from the bride and groom. The family histories that Brigham Young University produces are examples of vertical publishing opportunities.

ADVERTISING-DRIVEN PUBLISHING

One thing you will not find in this book is advertising. If you turned the next page and stumbled upon a full-page ad for Kodak thermal offset plates or RR Donnelley's book manufacturing division, you would be shocked and perhaps even angered. You would probably feel that a trust had somehow been broken between the publisher and you.

When you buy a book, you enter into a covenant with the author and publisher. The terms of this covenant are clear and rooted in a tradition that goes back more than half a millennium. You purchase access to content produced by an identified source that is uncompromised by external influences. A book serves as a fully transparent medium of communication from author to reader. The price of the book reflects the full value of the content to the reader.

For the price you pay for this or any other book, an advertisement on the next page would be unacceptable. The most the publisher might get away with would be a page or two at the end of the book suggesting, "If you liked this book here are some other titles of interest that we also publish."

In Benjamin Franklin's day, almost all publishing was like book publishing. Colonial newspapers were priced to reflect the perceived value of the content. Franklin made his fortune by selling his publications for profit. His readers were willing to pay for the full cost of production and distribution, and then some. Because Franklin acted as author, publisher, and printer, nearly all of the profits went into his pocket. Today, for the most part, these roles are all played by different parties. However, the Internet-based print fulfillment and distribution services offered by companies like Lightning Source, described previously, are enabling a new generation of self-published authors to capture more of the publishing value chain for themselves. (Every author's dream is to cut the publisher out of the deal entirely. I am no different, as much as I dearly love my publisher.) For most books other than mass-market titles authored by famous people, the author receives a royalty of approximately 10-15 percent of the selling price. So, if you paid $15.00 for this book, I will receive $1.50. The publisher makes a lot more on each sale than the author.

Once there is an established channel of communication between publisher and reader, advertising becomes possible. Allow me again to use this book to illustrate my point. Your eyeballs are currently focused on this sentence. What better place to deliver an advertising message than a few inches away from where we know you will be looking? It is also very helpful to know that you are here because you have a specific interest in the subject matter of this book. So it is a good bet that an advertisement for some product or service related to printing or publishing would draw your attention.

Advertisements began to appear in American newspapers at the beginning of the 18th century. However, they were almost an afterthought and they did not significantly impact the nature of the content or price of the newspaper until the fourth decade of the 19th century. In 1833, the publisher of the *New York Sun*, Benjamin Day, created a new business model for publishing by subsidizing most of the cost of production through the sale of a percentage of the print space to advertisers. Day is credited with the creation of what came to be called the *penny press*. Nearly everyone who could read could afford to purchase a newspaper for a penny. The *New York Sun* was the first newspaper to achieve the status of a mass medium.[25]

Day also set in motion a complex dynamic between editorial and advertising content that continues to the present. Before 1833, the readership of newspapers was restricted to a small minority of people who could afford the purchase price. When newspapers became affordable by everyone, publishers had to broaden the appeal of the content. The size of the readership determined the rates that could be charged for advertising. Because advertisers were paying for most of the cost of production and distribution, they had an increasing influence on the nature of the content. In earlier newspapers, content primarily served the interests of publishers to communicate political ideas to select readerships. Now content served the interests of advertisers to communicate their messages to large mass audiences. The temptation to embellish content to increase its mass appeal was very great.

A newspaper devoid of content and containing only advertising would have limited appeal. Newspaper content also needs to be credible. But how much credible content can there be? And how interesting is reality, really? If newspapers were restricted to objective documentary work periodically reporting on what was happening in the world, there would be little guarantee that the world would comply with the need to be continuously interesting enough to draw and hold the attention of a mass readership day after day.

So newspapers have had to invent all kinds of creative ways to find interesting stories on which to report and comment. They have been so successful in this endeavor that most people today believe that "news" is something that happens naturally and constantly. People believe that newspapers passively dip into the current of news on a regular basis to reveal to their readers what is actually happening in the world. Newspapers, however, play a far more active role in determining what the news will be than you may realize. The publisher of a leading daily metropolitan newspaper once told me, "There's not a lot really interesting happening in the world every day. We are in the business of transforming some of it into news."

Few subjects have inspired more scholarly research or had more written about them than the inner workings of newspaper journalism. For our purposes we can identify a few simple requirements that have driven the evolution of newspaper journalism from Benjamin Day's time to our own.

1. Content secures a readership.
2. A steady stream of content is necessary to create a stable vehicle for advertising.
3. Advertising-subsidized publications use a variety of creative techniques to produce and deliver content that is credible, interesting, and steady.
4. There are numerous temptations to embellish or compromise the integrity of content to create a better platform for advertising.
5. If readers lose confidence or interest in content, they will stop reading and become unreachable by the advertising.

These principles hold true for all advertising-supported publishing, from general interest newspapers and magazines to highly focused specialty publications. Each publication embodies a channel of communication for advertisers to reach audiences. *Time* and *Newsweek* reach large general audiences. *Cat Fancy* and *Climbing* magazine reach very specific audiences of people who share common interests or engage in common activities. If you want to advertise your new electric bicycle seat warmer, *Cycling* magazine provides an appropriately targeted audience.

Wouldn't it also be nice if your bicycle seat warmer ad were accompanied by an article about possible performance improvements that might derive from the controlled application of heat to the rider's posterior? What would make it even better would be a glowing testimonial from a Tour de France winner. That could probably be arranged. This is where the publisher needs to exercise caution. If the article crosses over the line from credible to incredible, the reader's trust will be lost. Perhaps it would be better to run an article about performance-enhancing innovations and include a discussion of the bum-warming seat along with other novelties. This would reduce the reader's suspicion that editorial integrity was being compromised by advertising. In special interest magazines, it is far more difficult for the publisher to maintain the integrity and independence of editorial content than for general interest, mass-circulation magazines. Advertisers in those magazines do not look to editorial to help make the sales pitch. Editorial exists only as the Trojan horse that gets the advertising in front of as many pairs of eyeballs as possible. An automobile manufacturer like Ford Motor Company has entirely different expectations of *Time* magazine than of *Motor Trend* in this regard. Still, it would be helpful if next week's celebrity profile of Tiger Woods featured a nice photograph of him with his new teal green Ford Thunderbird.

The delicate relationship between advertising and editorial has become a real Pandora's Box in recent years with the conglomeration that has been happening in the media industry. The temptation for a news publishing arm of a large media conglomerate to run a cover story about the new blockbuster movie offered by the entertainment arm of the same company is great. When the weekly news magazine is perceived primarily as an advertising brochure for its parent company's product line, readers may lose interest and circulation may fall off.

Although we may be tempted to think that the threat to journalistic integrity posed by powerful commercial forces is growing, business necessities have always exerted pressures on the editorial enterprise. Sensational stories full of amplification and embellishment were used to increase the sale of newspapers during the age of yellow journalism. Respectable people all across America were simultaneously outraged and titillated when they first encountered a Hearst newspaper a century ago; much the same kind of reaction that their descendents have had to the advent of "shock radio" in recent times.

All of this highlights the central truth of publishing, past, present, and future: content is king. Without compelling content, publishing cannot work. So the struggle to procure content is the central activity of the publishing enterprise. This struggle takes different forms in different segments of the industry. Daily newspapers employ reporters and writers to gather news and write stories of local interest. They also tap into the wire services for content from the larger world. In pre-Internet times, access to these services required elaborate and expensive connections to private networks. The Associated Press, United Press International, and Reuters news services served the newspaper publishing industry exclusively. Today, these services are accessible directly by anyone with Internet access. By the time a wire service story appears in print in your local paper, you have probably seen it long before on the Internet. This is especially true of big stories that spread like wildfire on the web. The growing worldwide network of Internet bloggers can surface and distribute a story faster than a traditional newspaper editor can sharpen a pencil.

This has led to a lot of speculation in the newspaper publishing industry about the enduring value of the medium. There is an emerging consensus among people in the business that the value of national and international content from the wire services is falling. Some voices in the industry advocate the reduction of wire service content in favor of more local coverage. I, for one, would value my local paper more if it stopped pretending to know anything about the world beyond our metro area and dug deeper into the local dirt.

Print publications that are intended for general mass audiences must provide content that will attract and hold the attention of the largest number of people possible. The proliferation of news and general interest outlets in print, broadcast, and on the Internet fragments the market and reduces the size of audiences. The major television networks have all seen their audiences dwindle as cable and satellite drained off viewers. The top ten mass circulation magazines have also experienced significant declines in readership over the past decade.[26] At the same time, the growth side of the broadcast and publishing industries is on the special interest side.

One of the rapidly growing industries that I have been watching for the past couple of years is the *scrapbooking* industry. Scrapbooking is an activity that is practiced by people who wish to create permanent records of the history and accomplishments of their families. A scrapbook is a hybrid between a craft project and a photo album. Thus scrapbooking can be seen as a part of the emerging *personal publishing industry*. This industry includes amateur arts, crafts, photography, photofinishing, photo albums, blank books, journals, and web-based print fulfillment services.

The segment of the population that engages in scrapbooking

is clearly defined by a common set of interests. The demographics of the population are fairly well known to the businesses that serve it. For example, nearly all members of the population are female and have children. The average amount of money that an individual spends on the scrapbooking hobby annually is also known. The market for scrapbooking products and services is large enough and well enough defined that it now merits its own "Dummies" book.[27] As you can imagine, there are magazines that target this market. Two monthly magazines directly relevant are *Memory Maker* magazine and *PaperKuts*. The readership of each of these magazines multiplied by its average annual spending gives a good estimate of the total size of the market for products advertised in the magazine.

If you manufacture a product for the scrapbooking community, you must have some idea of the size of the market for your product, as well as the competitive landscape. From this information you can estimate sales and revenues that may derive from advertising in a given publication. The pricing of advertising is strongly correlated to circulation and the size of a particular market. The price of an ad will also depend on the size, placement, and number of colors in the ad, and whether the advertiser buys space in a single issue or multiple issues. For magazine advertising to make sense, the return on the advertising investment has to be positive.

There are also alternatives to advertising in special interest magazines. The advertiser can purchase the subscriber list from the publisher and send direct mail solicitations. This provides a significant additional source of revenue to the publisher. Lists are sold with various stipulations. The number of times that a list can be used is one of them. One-time use is less expensive than multiple or unlimited use. In some cases it may be possible to buy geographically-focused subsets of a list.

Advertisers also have electronic choices. Cable television provides access to hundreds of target audiences defined by sets of common interests. If you want to sell things like fishing lures, golf clubs, boats, or bullets, there are special interest cable programs that will deliver the appropriate audience for your pitch. The Internet provides an even greater variety of special interest websites that can connect you to your target audience. The Internet also enables manufacturers of specialty products to create their own websites that contain editorial content and advertising. These are often designed to work in tandem with print advertising. If you look through a special interest magazine like *Vintage Guitar*, you will find hundreds of small ads containing little more information than the name of the company, a graphic illustrating a product, and a web address. The magazine ad is nothing more than a pointer to the website.

This symbiotic relationship between print and web advertising is becoming increasingly common. It is almost a marriage made in heaven. A typical issue of *Vintage Guitar* magazine can illustrate this discussion. We often use the metaphor of real estate when we talk about print. An advertisement is said to take up a certain amount of real estate. Ad space is priced accordingly. The basic unit of space is the page. In *Vintage Guitar* magazine, you can buy ad space in units of full page, ¾, ½, ¼, ⅛, and ¹/₁₆ of a page. The price per square inch decreases slightly as the amount of space purchased increases. Still, doubling the size of an ad nearly doubles the price.

Vintage Guitar also charges more for some locations than others. The back cover is the most expensive space. The inside front cover is slightly less expensive. The inside back cover comes next and the first inside page comes after that. Space on page 113 is least expensive. Color printing is also more expensive than black and white. In the case of *Vintage Guitar*, color ads cost almost twice as much as black-and-white ads on average. Thus print advertising space is priced much like real estate. A color ad on the back cover is a luxury condo on ocean-front property in Santa Cruz. A small black-and-white ad at the bottom of page 113 is my house. (Someday I dream of living on a nice half-page color ad at the top of page 5.)

This real estate metaphor does not apply to the web. The cost of a website is not strongly tied to the amount of space or information it contains. It is, however, very strongly correlated to the number of people who can access the information on the site at the same time. If you want to enable thousands of simultaneous visitors to your site, you will have to invest in a lot of expensive equipment to handle the traffic. If only a few people at any one time are expected, the cost will be much less.

So it makes sense for manufacturers of specialty products that appeal to narrow markets to invest in a small amount of print real estate where they can put up a modest sign to draw potential customers to a website, where they can then present detailed product information. The material nature of print advertising in a magazine like *Vintage Guitar* almost guarantees that an ad placed in the magazine will at one point fall under the eye of a reader. The editor's job is to weave enough high quality content through the magazine to improve the chances that readers will visit and dwell long enough on every page. I selected *Vintage Guitar* for this example because I believe that the current editor of the magazine accomplishes this mission successfully.

Special interest magazines aimed at consumers are sold to them either by subscription or on the newsstand. The subscription price is usually much lower per issue than the cover price. In addition, if a magazine subscription is sold through a third-party agent, the publisher must pay a percentage of the subscription price to the agent. If a magazine is sold on a newsstand, a percentage of the cover price goes to the seller. If copies are not sold by the time the next issue of a magazine arrives, the covers are torn off and returned to the publisher for credit. The revenues that flow to the publisher as a result of magazine sales through retail and subscription sales account for only a small percentage of total revenues. The bottom line is that magazines without advertising are not viable. The few exceptions, like *Ms.* magazine, are supported by foundation grants, society membership fees, and other sources of philanthropy.

Many magazines geared toward business audiences are distributed to qualified subscribers for free. These *trade publications* are aimed at readers in specific industries who constitute markets for specific products and services. For the printing and communication services industries that I study, there are a large number of such publications. Some of the standards are *Graphic Arts Monthly*, *Printing Impressions*, and *American Printer*. To subscribe to these kinds of publications, money is not the ticket. You must be "qualified" by the publisher. This means that you must fit a profile that the publisher establishes for the readership. This profile has nothing to do with race, gender, ethnic origins, or sexual preferences. It does, however, have to do with how much potential influence the publisher thinks you have over the purchase of the type of products that are likely to be advertised in the magazine.

For example, a magazine that targets computer network administrators will qualify subscribers who are believed to influence the purchase of more than a certain dollar amount of computer network products on an annual basis. I use the phrase "are believed to influence" for good reason. The only way publishers can realistically know whether you really possess this kind of power is for you to tell them that you do. They don't have the resources to hire special investigators the way the Secret Service does when you apply for the job as the president's official food taster. So they have no choice but to accept your word that you are responsible for personally signing the checks for a million dollars worth of new hardware each year.

If everyone who applies for a free subscription to a trade magazine of this type told nothing but the truth on the application form, the list of subscribers would be worth a lot more than it really is. Everyone assumes that there is some amount of exaggeration going on. However, if your mailing address is a legitimate business address, the assumption is that you would probably not bother to answer all of the questions on the form if you were not somehow involved in influencing purchasing decisions relevant to the advertisers.

Some publications are more careful than others in screening subscribers. The more rigorous the qualification process, the more potential advertisers will trust the claims of the circulation department. The ultimate dream of any advertiser is to know everything that can possibly be known about the composition of the target audience. Who are they? What do they want? How much are they willing to spend?

CHAPTER NINE

MARKETING COMMUNICATIONS

THERE ARE MANY ALTERNATIVES TO ADVERTISING in content-driven media for communicating a marketing message to an audience. In this chapter we will turn our attention to direct forms of marketing through print that do not piggyback on editorial content.

Just as advertising can exert subtle influences on many types of editorial content, pure marketing often adopts the look and feel of editorial to gain credibility and influence over the consumer. The term "advertorial" is sometimes used to describe marketing pitches that are dressed up to look like editorial content. This is rarely done with malicious intent to deceive. However, the general perception among people of good breeding when they encounter advertising that acts like editorial content is that, although it is not against the law, they would prefer not to live next door to the people who produce it. They constitute a kind of untouchable class that does not have a place in the refined company of genuine journalists or advertising professionals.

These attitudes cannot stop progress, however. Effective marketing sometimes requires a sincere dedication to fact-finding and truth-telling. It all depends on the expectations of the customer. If you are in the business of marketing quack cures for arthritis to people in pain and desperate for the slightest relief, your marketing message may not be subjected to the most rigorous verification. If, on the other hand, you are marketing expensive lab instruments to engineers and research scientists, your marketing messages will likely be held to a higher standard.

If you want to communicate a marketing message to your customers, there are many possible approaches you can take. Whether you are a small one-person business or a large multinational corporation, you will probably perform some of the work yourself and hire outside services for the rest. Most companies, regardless of size, will purchase print production and distribution services from outside vendors. Many companies rely exclusively on outside vendors for creative services.

The relationship between players responsible for developing marketing strategies and messages and those responsible for creating the actual media products that communicate these messages is complex. The development of a new product or service concept is guided by marketing. Marketing is responsible for defining the nature of the potential demand. Marketing guides the communication processes by which potential customers are informed about new products or services. Marketing takes credit for successes and blame for failures. Thus marketing cannot stand aloof from the creative processes that craft these messages.

In the traditional use of print, messages are developed in relation to anticipated response. Anticipated response is predicted by marketers based on research. The most expensive research employs focus groups scientifically selected to represent the larger population. These groups are presented with alternative messages and then evaluated for their responses. But the crafting of alternative messages is still largely an art form and even the best research leaves room for error. Traditional print marketing communication is to some extent a game of chance. Messages will be lost on some, offend some, amuse but not convince some, and hopefully hit the mark with a large enough percentage of the target audience to subsidize the entire enterprise and produce a positive return on the investment.

The Internet and digital print have given birth to a fully interactive new world of marketing communications. The production of printed marketing communication pieces can now be the consequence of rich interaction between an organization and its individual customers. This defines an entirely new role for print in marketing communications. With the Internet, print can break free of the need to anticipate a response. Print can answer real questions rather than try to anticipate the questions in advance.

THE DIRECT AGE

If there is a single word that describes the age that began with the commercialization of the Internet in the mid-1990s, it would be the word *direct*. In this word we can find the root causes of both the wild optimism, and the fear and trembling of the present age.

Before we tackle the meaning and significance of the word direct, let's first consider its opposite. Indirect implies the existence of some intermediary or intermediate step. For example, I am taking an indirect approach to this discussion of the word direct. If I communicate indirectly to you, the implication is that there are other parties responsible for conveying my voice to you. The publisher and distributor of this book do that. I really don't know who you are, or how to find you. If I did, I might be tempted to try to communicate directly with you. Then I could cut the publisher out of the deal, lower the price of the book, and still make more money per copy sold.

The appeal of direct communication is great. The dot-com bubble of the last few years of the second millennium was built on this appeal. Indirection was considered a necessary evil. Messages get garbled and profits get taken. If you can sell a product directly to your customer, you don't have to share profits with distributors and retailers. The dot-com bust happened not because these assumptions turned out to be false, but because the relatively small share of margins taken by distributors and retailers didn't add up to enough money to keep the massive bubble inflated once people started really thinking about it.

Direct marketing and sales enjoyed a long and successful history before the Internet came along. The progenitor of the entire direct marketing industry was the Sears and Roebuck catalog. Daniel Boorstin, in the third volume of his superb historical trilogy, *The Americans*, recounts the foundation story of this ground-breaking American business enterprise.[28] Sears and Roebuck bought products from workshops and manufacturing companies throughout the world. They sold these products directly to consumers through a voluminous catalog that became an icon of late 19th-century American culture. One could buy almost any manufactured product that existed at the time directly from Sears. If you were looking for an Italian mandolin, a windmill, a pair of eyeglasses, or even a house in kit form, you could find it in the Sears catalog.

Sears, and the printing company that produced the catalog, RR Donnelley, were both headquartered in Chicago, the ideal location for companies that use the postal system to reach a geographically dispersed population of customers. Most of the largest print communication services companies maintain major facilities in the region surrounding Chicago and Milwaukee for this reason. As discussed in Chapter 6, the total cost of bulk mailing a catalog from Chicago to several million households nationwide is considerably less than mailing the catalog to the same list of addresses from Miami or Seattle. First class mailing costs do not vary with distance, so there is no cost advantage to centrally locating. However, distance does still determine how long it will take for mail to travel from origination to destination. Therefore, mailing from Chicago will take less time on average than mailing from the edges of the country.

Catalogs have come a long way since the early days of Sears and Roebuck and the settling of the "Wild West." The basic mechanism for transactions between a catalog company and its customers is simple. When you see something you want to buy in a catalog, you dial a toll-free phone number and interact with a live person who will take your order. You supply your mailing and credit card information and the coded numbers for the items you wish to purchase. The person taking the order is seated at a computer terminal in a call center located somewhere in the world. This somewhere doesn't have to be anywhere near the catalog company itself. The company headquarters may be located in Boston, the distribution center in Chicago, and the call center in Bangalore.

When your call is completed, your order has been entered into a database where it will be processed by an order-fulfillment system. The most sophisticated order-fulfillment systems rely on robots to *pick and pack* orders in meticulously organized automated warehouses that may contain tens of thousands of individual items. Items are stored in bins or stacked on shelves in the warehouse. The computer system that controls the warehouse knows precisely where each bin or stack of items is located. Orders are assembled and then packed for shipment. In most cases this process is optimized to reduce the volume and weight of the package to a minimum to save on transportation and mailing costs.

Most catalog companies offer a choice of shipping services ranging from slow surface shipment to fast next-day air shipment. The larger companies integrate the order tracking services offered by the major package shipping companies with their customer service system. When you order from one of these companies, you can log onto the company's website and watch your order as it makes its way across the country from the warehouse to you.

Most print catalogs today are mirrored by parallel websites that replace the printed catalog and call center with a web server. Orders generated by the web server can be indistinguishable from those generated by a call center. Once the order has entered the system, the fulfillment operation looks the same. The user interface is different, but what goes on "under the hood" is the same.

There are three obvious advantages to the web interface versus the catalog/call center interface. These are:

1. No need for a printed catalog. Elimination of catalog mailing costs. Ability to *scale* (increase the capacity of the system) according to volume of traffic.
2. Unmanned server replaces manned call center. No restrooms or cafeterias needed.
3. Ability to change content of the "catalog" instantaneously to reflect price fluctuations, changes in product specifications, and product availability.

The cost of printing and mailing a catalog is partially offset by the need for an ongoing website maintenance effort. The design and production of a printed catalog is very labor-intensive. But once the catalog is printed and mailed, it does not need to be regularly maintained like a website.

A conventional printed catalog, however, does not have the scalability of a website. To get the best economies of scale from a catalog, the catalog company mails to the largest population of potential customers that it can. (Remember that the production cost per unit of printed products decreases significantly as the run length increases.) Catalogers know a lot about their customers, especially the ones who regularly do business with them. Some will cull inactive customers from their list and stop sending catalogs to them. I recently received a catalog with an inkjet printed personalized message on the cover saying, "Frank Cost, we haven't heard from you in a while. This will be your last catalog from us unless you order something." This is one approach to improving the yield on a mailed catalog. Only send mail to people who maintain a steady track record of business with you. Some companies even charge their customers for their printed catalogs. They frequently offer a discount from the first purchase as reimbursement. If people actually pay for catalogs, chances are very good that they will end up purchasing something from the company.

These techniques for improving the yield of a catalog are limited to certain markets where customers are willing to spend time and money to continue receiving the catalog. This will not work for general consumer catalogs that compete for business with other catalogs and retailers. How much of an effort would you be willing to make to ensure that you continued to receive most of the catalogs you receive in the mail? Not much, most likely. So catalogers play a low-yield game of chance. They know that most of the catalogs they mail fall into that largest category of print known as "direct-to-landfill" printing. (I am not sure who coined this expression because it has been so widely quoted.)

Mass market catalogers such as JCPenney have also improved the yield per pound of print by publishing a larger variety of lower page-count catalogs that contain selected offerings. This is particularly interesting because JCPenney is the last mass merchandising firm to also publish an omnibus catalog in the spirit of the original Sears catalog. (Sears ceased publishing its big catalog in 1994.) This catalog is not distributed free through the mail, but sold or distributed in exchange for mailed coupons in JCPenney stores. JCPenney has integrated its retail, catalog, and Internet operations to create a nearly seamless capability to serve individual customers in the way that works best for them. One can purchase products from JCPenney through web, phone, or retail interaction, and choose to pick up in the store or receive shipment at home.

Because JCPenney has a large network of retail outlets, its primary purpose for print advertising is to motivate people to come into the store. To achieve this, a mailed catalog is not the most effective print medium available. For lower cost per piece, JCPenney and other international retailers make use of another distribution channel that competes with the postal system: the local newspaper. In the next section we will turn our attention to the newspaper insert business. But first, I would like to address a critical question about the future of printed catalogs.

If the Internet eliminates the costs of print production, mail distribution, and maintaining a large call center (even a low-cost overseas call center), how can the printed catalog possibly compete? An Internet-based catalog has the added benefit of instantaneous universal access plus scalability to accommodate any volume of customers simultaneously. It might appear at first glance that the printed catalog is a walking candidate for extinction.

However, the catalog has a few advantages of its own. The first advantage is that it arrives in the mailbox in the form of a book, and forces itself upon the person going through the daily mail. People are trained from infancy to automatically consume the content of books when they have them in hand. (I can close my eyes and see my daughter, at five months, lying in her crib and sucking on her favorite book.) If you hand a book to anyone in the world who is five months old or older, the response is almost universal. They will open the book and look inside. So, if you place a catalog in someone's hand, there is a good chance that they will do the same.

The other advantage is that print allows instant access without hassle or threat. The medium itself cannot be offensive (although the message surely can be). People may call it "junk mail," but more out of disrespect than anger. There is little risk that you will offend or anger a potential customer with print. By contrast, the most innocuous email solicitation has the power to convert the majority of your prospects into a raging, torch-bearing mob screaming for your blood, if they could only discover how to find you.

This formula changes somewhat once you have an established relationship with a potential customer. If I have recently bought a Sony product from Sony's website or mailed back a Sony warranty card, I am much less likely to be offended by an email message from Sony informing me of a new product or service. The email may still be annoying, but it won't elicit the same kind of impotent, frustrated, angry reaction as the five hundredth email offer for Viagra I've received this month.

I can't resist adding a personal note here. Electronic solicitations from reputable companies that I have come to trust have the effect of lowering my esteem for the company. It's as though I found the jeweler from whom I had recently bought an expensive watch hawking ten-dollar replicas on the street corner. Paper-based solicitations seem to possess a quiet dignity and somehow don't leave the same bad taste.

Having said all of that, I think that it is likely that the long-term cultural advantages of print will disappear over time. The percentage of the American population who read literature is in accelerating decline, according to a study entitled "Reading at Risk: A Survey of Literary Reading in America" published in 2004 by the National Endowment for the Arts.[29] The NEA takes a grim view of these trends and suggests that the decline in literary reading will lead to a degradation of civil society and democratic institutions. It is always worth reminding ourselves that authors of studies conducted by government agencies and funded by legislatures may be tempted to spin their findings in ways that will lead to continued funding of their work in the future. Nonetheless, the statistics contained in the study indicate a downward trend in literary reading that may contribute to the erosion of the authority of print as a medium over time.

Here's why I think it is safe to make the connection between the habit of literary reading and the authority of print. Literary reading is different from other forms of reading in that it requires a reader to begin at the beginning and follow a linear argument all the way through to the end. Other forms of reading, newspaper or magazine reading for example, allow the reader to jump around, choosing to read some items, and not to read others. What this means for civilization and the future of democracy remains unclear. But what is clear is that people who do not acquire the disciplined habit of reading books are less likely to develop the automatic responses to print that contribute to the power of the medium. If you are not a reader, it is less likely that you will open a catalog that appears in your mailbox.

Print does not have to take this trend lying down. Print technology and graphic design evolve steadily to accommodate changing reading habits and expectations. Graphic design is very similar to fashion design in this regard. Graphic designers continually strive to balance design novelty with the need for clear communication of the message, just as fashion designers strive to create novel designs that are also wearable. If designers place too much emphasis on design novelty to the detriment of usability, the enhanced initial attention of the reader may be compromised by an unclear message. The ghost of Beatrice Warde may also return to raise objections. Digital printing technology offers new capabilities that can be harnessed to increase the effectiveness of print. It is possible to customize or personalize the messaging in printed matter to make it more relevant to the individual.

NEWSPAPER INSERTS

The only practical alternative to the postal system for economical distribution of stand-alone printed advertising is to include it as an insert in a newspaper. Daily newspapers rely on advertising inserts for a significant percentage of their total advertising revenues. Preprinted inserts are supplied by the advertiser. The newspaper takes no responsibility for the production of the inserts, just the insertion into the paper and distribution. The advertiser pays a piece rate based primarily on the weight of the insert. Inserts are produced in specialized plants.

Newspaper inserts have some distinct advantages and a few disadvantages when compared to postal delivery. The primary advantage is that the delivery cost per inserted piece is significantly lower than the cost to mail the same piece. The primary disadvantage is related to the targeting precision of the delivery mechanism. Newspaper inserts will only reach those households and individuals that either subscribe to the paper or purchase it from a newsstand. In smaller metropolitan areas such as my home town, Rochester, New York, the ratio of subscribers to newsstand purchasers is higher than in a big city like New York or Chicago, where people are more likely to buy the paper on the street. Another significant trend in all markets is toward fewer competing newspapers. In Rochester, a metropolitan area of more than a million people, we have exactly one paper, the *Democrat and Chronicle*. At one time, in the early 20th century, Rochester had as many as five independent competing newspapers. The trend toward consolidation has proceeded steadily since then.[30]

The existence of only one daily paper makes it easy for advertisers to decide who will distribute their inserts in Rochester. This could lead to the kinds of difficulties that are normally associated with monopolies. However there is enough indirect competition from television, radio, and mail-distributed advertising to keep the potential monopolist somewhat in check.

With the insert business the newspaper also offers something that the electronic media cannot. For advertising that is integral to the newspaper itself (so-called *run-of-paper* or ROP advertising), an advertiser purchases ad space in every copy of the paper distributed. Inserts, on the other hand, can be selectively included in some copies, and not in others. The newspaper publisher divides the metropolitan area into geographic *zones*. Each zone represents a grouping of households that are assumed to possess common demographic characteristics. Daily newspapers make it their business to know a lot about their communities. The single most important piece of knowledge one can have about a household is its total income. Only the government has the power to obtain this information coercively. (Try saying no to the IRS.) Everyone else must ask politely or try to infer how much money you make. The simplest and crudest inferential methodology is to assume a simple correlation between property value and income. If you live in a house worth X dollars, you have to make at least Y dollars per year. During the past few decades, newspapers have been refining their zoning methodologies using their intimate knowledge of the communities they serve. More sophisticated zoning leads to more effective targeting opportunities for advertisers.

This trend toward more intelligent zoning is countered by other trends that diminish the effectiveness of newspaper insert advertising. The percentage of households in most metropolitan markets subscribing to a daily newspaper has been in steady decline over the past two decades. Evening newspapers are fast becoming extinct. The average amount of time that people spend with the newspaper each day is also declining sharply. Sunday subscriptions, where most insert advertising is concentrated, have suffered the most in many markets. Sunday is not the quiet Sabbath that it once was. The frenzy of the work week spills over into the weekend, robbing people of the long lazy stretches of time that once accommodated a relaxed reading of the Sunday paper.

These readership trends have inspired much soul-searching and creative thinking among newspaper executives. Two major areas of speculation that have emerged in the past few years have to do with the unique and enduring mission of the daily newspaper in an Internet-saturated world, and new business models that will improve the ability of the newspaper to deliver targeted eyeballs to advertisers.

If news directly from the wire services is freely available to anyone with Internet access, why bother with the local paper? Ten years ago, when the Internet began to take off, the consensus answer to this question was that the Internet was a raw feed and that people needed the newspaper to filter and prioritize the raw news—to decide, in the famous language of the *New York Times*, what news is "fit to print." Without the help of the wise people who decided what was important, ordinary people would be unable to make sense of daily events. In other words, they were unfit to decide what was fit. I remember attending many conferences during the early days of the Internet revolution and hearing this message played over and over again. The great unwashed masses would never be able to get along without the help of the professionals.

What these early prognosticators failed to foresee was the inevitable emergence of a new decentralized system of information dissemination made possible in a networked world. A global web of tens of thousands of bloggers is rapidly self-organizing into an entirely new news-gathering species. The so-called *blogosphere* is organized like a community of interconnected news-gathering organisms that criticize and reinforce each other to collectively expose the truth about what is happening in the world by processing and cross-checking inputs from millions of individual sources. The emergence of the blogosphere, with its power to enable millions of people to interactively find, report, and verify the news, presents a significant challenge to the traditional news gathering organization. Who are you more likely to believe about what is actually happening in the streets of a strife-torn city: a lone reporter staked out in the bar of a luxury hotel, or hundreds of independent bloggers reporting from their neighborhoods spread throughout the city?

Where the major international news outlets and the blogosphere fall short is in the coverage of local news. Here is where the daily metro newspaper still serves a unique and important function. James Lileks, a pioneer blogger from Fargo, North Dakota, publishes a daily blog called *The Bleat*. Lileks makes this prediction about the future of the daily newspaper:

> In the future, I think, newspapers will become almost entirely devoted to local news and happy fluff, like me. I depend on my paper for local news, because I don't watch TV news... That's the niche that waits for them. The Internet will swamp [the newspapers'] ability to sum up the daily state of the world, because a) there's so much available on the net from the big dogs, and b) small little-noted institutional biases in the paper's selection of news stories will kill their credibility with those who sample from many sources.[31]

If local news is the strength of the daily newspaper, we should expect to see more and newer varieties of local coverage at the expense of national and international news in the future. But will this be enough to stop or reverse the downward trends in circulation and readership? What other options are available to newspaper publishers?

You will recall from an earlier chapter on newspaper publishing that the modern daily newspaper is built on a business model that was first created by Benjamin Day back in the 1830s. Day lowered the price of the paper to a penny and subsidized its production with advertising. In recent years, there has been mounting evidence that this model may be reaching the end of its 170-year run. The fifty cents that I currently pay for my local paper probably has less real value than a penny in Benjamin Day's time. In general, the real price of a paper has been dropping. When I first started working in the newspaper industry in the 1970s, the basic rule of thumb about pricing was that a newspaper should cost the same as a cup of coffee. Today you can buy copies of your local paper, *USA Today*, the *New York Times*, and the *Wall Street Journal*, all for the price of a medium cappuccino at Starbucks. This either means that the paper is a real bargain or that Starbucks has very special coffee.

If we graph the real price to the consumer of the average daily newspaper over the past ten years, we will see a clear downward trend. This trend is accelerated by the free distribution of papers in hotels, schools, on the airlines, and in other similar venues. Even with declining prices, circulations are still trending downward. Most daily newspapers derive a far greater percentage of revenues from advertising than from circulation. If circulation declines, ad revenues also decline. Thus newspapers are tempted to lower prices to stem the loss of readership.

If current pricing trends continue, at some point in the near future, prices will approach zero. Some in the industry have begun to speculate on the possible merits of a quick leap to free universal distribution as a way of fast forwarding to a new business model without suffering through the slow, painful death of the old one.[32]

The distribution system necessary to support such a move already exists. If half of the households in your city subscribe to the daily newspaper, even if you don't subscribe, it is almost guaranteed that a delivery route driver is already passing your house. The incremental cost of delivering to every house (rather than every other house) would be relatively small. All of the cost associated with subscription advertising, sales, and account maintenance would disappear with free universal distribution. A universally-distributed daily newspaper that offered enhanced local coverage combined with more sophisticated zoning options would present advertisers with better access to their potential customers. Currently, the only way an advertiser can distribute a piece to every address in a given geographic area is to use the postal system.

Even with improvements in the reach and sophistication of the newspaper distribution channel, what kind of future is in store for the newspaper insert? How vulnerable is it to replacement by Internet-based advertising? There appears to be a natural symbiotic relationship developing between newspaper inserts and the Internet. This relationship with the Internet exists for other forms of print advertising as well.

Vertis, Inc., a major communication services company and one of the leading newspaper insert producers, conducts extensive surveys of consumers to better understand how they use print advertising and the Internet when making purchasing decisions. From this research Vertis has been able to develop a clear picture of the role that print advertising plays in influencing consumer behavior. Its most interesting finding is that consumers typically use both print and electronic media together to decide what to buy. I'll give an example of how this works.

Imagine that you are planning to purchase a new high-definition television set. You have some idea of what is available because you have been drawn to it like a moth to a flame every time you walk through a consumer electronics store. You know vaguely that there are different technologies: plasma, CRT, LCD, flat screen, projection, etc. You know also that the prices range from many hundreds to many thousands of dollars, and that there are several leading manufacturers. You wonder whether the Koreans are as good as the Japanese. You wonder whether the trees surrounding your house will interfere with satellite reception. You wonder whether the time is right to announce your intention to buy a giant television to your family. You wonder whether this is a foolish indulgence that will turn your entire family into a quivering pile of mindless lard.

In other words, you have many questions that need to be addressed before you will be ready to make a choice and hand over your credit card number. Your first move will probably be to go to Best Buy or Circuit City to look at what's currently available. You may then go onto the Internet to study the various technology options in greater depth and see what people are saying about various products. You will begin to narrow your choices based on price ranges, features, manufacturers, and consumer reviews. At some point you will be ready to act.

It is at this point that the newspaper insert plays its vital role. The Sunday newspaper contains inserts from all of the major consumer electronics stores in your area. You collect all of these and sit at the kitchen table and go through each one looking for products that meet your criteria. You may find that several of the stores offer some of the same products at comparable prices. You also know that most of these stores will bargain prices if you show them a lower price advertised by a competitor. You now must decide which store to visit first. The newspaper insert has a very strong influence on this decision. If one of the major stores were to somehow miss having their advertising insert in this Sunday's newspaper, all of the people like you who are ready to embark on a purchasing expedition would be more likely to visit a competitor first.

The important thing to realize is that much of the advertising in newspaper inserts relies on the support of the Internet and broadcast media to work its magic. Television commercials build brand awareness for the companies that make products and the retailers that sell them. The Internet provides detailed product information and a place for consumers to look for advice from other people who have gone before them. The newspaper insert has the effect of steering the consumer to a particular store once the decision to buy has been made.

This power of a newspaper insert to influence the consumer's choice of retailer is true for less complex purchasing decisions as well. Have you ever wondered why a supermarket would spend a lot of money advertising bananas for 29 cents a pound on the cover of a newspaper insert? How could they possibly sell enough bananas to justify the cost of advertising them? The answer is that selling bananas is never the main reason for advertising bananas. Cheap bananas, or toilet paper, or blueberries, are a lure to get shoppers into the store. Once inside, they will most likely do all of their shopping there.

A proper understanding of how print influences the real behavior of consumers leads to an important revelation about the value of printed advertising. It's not quantity, but quality that matters most. The only purpose of an advertising insert is to entice people into a store. Once they are inside, the responsibility for converting them into customers rests with the retailer. So the choice of which products to feature in an insert is critically important. The goal is to reduce the volume of content in the insert while increasing the number of people who are influenced by it. The intelligent selection of featured products, sale pricing, and use of zoned distribution are all factors that determine the effectiveness of an advertising insert. Companies like Vertis are constantly working to improve the performance of print advertising. In the words of Don Roland, CEO of Vertis,

> The way to get rid of wasted advertising is to not print that which will fall on deaf ears. We can target as finely as the

distribution method allows. In the United States over the last twenty years, newspapers have added more and more delivery zones. They slice their distribution into smaller and smaller pieces. If they can zone it, we can produce it. Targeting is the key to making the medium more effective. People are increasingly likely to get information about what they are actually interested in buying, so there is less clutter. They then rely on that medium more because they know it is relevant to them.[33]

DIRECT MAIL

Direct marketers use the mail to solicit business directly from consumers and businesses. In Chapter 6 we looked at how mailing lists are created and refined, and how they are used by direct marketers. You should know by now that any list of people who share common interests or attitudes has potential value, and that the buying and selling of lists is big business. You should also know that a list only reveals facts about the past behavior of the people on it. Lists make no claims about their future behavior. Just because everyone on a list has a subscription to *Gourmet* magazine doesn't mean that anyone on the list will be interested in purchasing your deluxe electronic spatula. As Jesse Jackson might say, before selling you his list of donors, "You must take a risk, if you intend to use my list."

The new frontier of direct mail is being pioneered by companies that are harnessing the power of the Internet to give birth to a new kind of list and then using digital print production to communicate more effectively with the people on the list. Here's how it works.

The Internet provides the infrastructure to support complex interactions among large numbers of globally dispersed individuals who share common interests. A website can be configured as an engine that dynamically generates leads as people interact with it. The interaction may take any form. The simplest and least sophisticated form is where the lead is generated when someone asks directly for information. The most sophisticated lead generation may happen as the result of someone playing a game. When people identify themselves as good prospects by volunteering information about themselves they are said to be "raising their hand," and a direct marketing program based on this kind of lead generation is known as a *hand-raiser* program.

Unlike the traditional list of prospects obtained from a special interest magazine publisher or member-supported organization, a list generated by a hand-raiser program has some predictive claim on the future. Prospective customers tell you that they want more information about specific products. They may also tell you things that enable you to respond to individual prospects in a personalized way. For example, you may be interested in getting more information about a dark red Ford Mustang convertible with a white leather interior and magnesium alloy wheels. If you visit the Ford website, you can raise your hand and tell them all of these things. They will mail you a custom-printed brochure with graphics and information that exactly match your personal interest. The customer-specific information gathered on the Ford website is used to produce custom printed one-to-one direct mail pieces. This information-driven digital printing operation was designed by Vertis for Ford.

PSYCHOLOGICAL OPERATIONS

Thus far we have considered the use of print as a largely benign medium that seeks to influence behaviors by presenting the positive consequences of following the suggestions offered. If you buy this car, you will be dating women who look like this. If you brush your teeth with this toothpaste, you will be dating men who look like this. If you kill your crabgrass with this chemical, you will go forth and multiply and your descendants will number more than all the stars in the sky. And so forth.

Commercial messages tend to emphasize positive benefits because people know instinctively that failure to heed a particular commercial suggestion will have no negative consequences. Failure to buy this car or use that toothpaste will not destroy a person's chances for true love. We all know this. Most commercial advertising therefore plays on our hopes, not on our fears.

However, fear can be a great motivator. Thus it makes sense that, in some cases, marketing communication messages play on fear more than on hope. As I write this paragraph we are nearing the end of a U.S. presidential election campaign. The messaging coming out of all of the political camps is dominated by warnings of the dangers associated with the intentions of the other camps. Vote for us, because the consequences of letting our opponents win are too horrible to contemplate. The economy will collapse. Grass will grow in the streets. Neighbor will rise against neighbor. Our descendents will be hairy troglodytes who live underground and eat each other's children. Pretty scary stuff!

The form of communication that appeals most directly to fear is the messaging issued by combatants during wartime. Print plays a critical role, because it is often the only medium that works in a battlefield situation. Leaflets dropped from the sky or fired from artillery carry simple messages intended to persuade enemy combatants or civilians caught in the line of fire to take specific actions.

The branch of the U.S. military that is responsible for creating all of the media products that are used overseas during military operations is the United States Army Civil Affairs and Psychological Operations (PSYOP) Command. This branch of the U.S. Army is headquartered at Fort Bragg in Fayetteville, North Carolina. It defines its mission as follows:

> PSYOP are planned operations that convey selected information to foreign target audiences to influence their emotions, motives, objective reasoning, and ultimately, the behavior of foreign governments, organizations, groups, and individuals. The purpose of all PSYOP is to create in neutral, friendly, or hostile foreign groups the emotions, attitudes, or desired behavior that support the achievement of U.S. national objectives and the military mission. In doing so, PSYOP influence not only policy and decisions, but also the ability to govern, the ability to command, the will to fight, the will to obey, and the will to support. The combination of PSYOP products and actions creates in the selected target audiences a behavior that supports U.S. national policy objectives and the theater commander's intentions at the strategic, operational, and tactical levels.[34]

The Psychological Operations Command functions on behalf of the U.S. government in the same way that an advertising agency functions on behalf of a commercial client. The consequences of failure, however, can be far graver than anything that the most fearful civilian

PSYOP field print unit.

advertising executive could possibly imagine. In the PSYOP world, success and failure are measured in stark terms of life and death.

To serve the needs of their military and civilian clients throughout the world for print communication products, PSYOP maintains different kinds of print production facilities. Fixed facilities, equipped with direct imaging offset presses, are located at Fort Bragg, and are used to produce print communication products in high volumes and with the longest lead times. Mobile facilities containing smaller offset and digital printers are used in the field. The most mobile printing facility currently operated by the army is housed in a domed tent deployed from a trailer dragged by a specially-equipped Humvee.

The print communication needs served by PSYOP span the broadest range imaginable. Some of these needs can be serviced adequately by conventional print production technologies and delivery systems. The key factor is lead time. In some parts of the world, PSYOP products support long-term objectives such as promoting positive perceptions of U.S. military or civilian authorities through the dissemination of public service information. A good example of this is a poster or picture book that teaches children how to identify land mines, a publication that teaches people how to remove bacterial contaminants from drinking water, or perhaps even a soccer ball or Frisbee imprinted with a logo associating the gift with the U.S. government.

*PSYOP poster warning civilians not to handle landmines
and unexploded munitions.*

Some products have a much shorter lead time, however. A field commander involved in a firefight who wishes to use a printed leaflet to deliver a message to an opponent needs almost instantaneous print order fulfillment. To accommodate this level of need, the army envisions print production and distribution systems that make extensive use of network-based image asset management, automated graphic design, field-based digital printing, and robotic airborne drones for physical delivery.

CHAPTER TEN

LARGE FORMAT AND OUTDOOR ADVERTISING

THUS FAR I HAVE BEEN TALKING ABOUT ADVERTISING that must somehow enter your personal space before it has an opportunity to influence you. It must come into your possession or enter your home. Once it crosses this threshold it also risks being ignored or destroyed. You can toss away newspaper inserts and direct mail before you ever look at them. You can ignore the ads in a newspaper or magazine. You can TiVo your way past television ads or switch off the set. The advertising industry expends a lot of effort trying to assess the effectiveness of various forms of advertising.

When an ad is placed in a magazine or newspaper, the only concrete information available to the advertiser is the number of copies of the publication that were distributed through subscription and newsstand sales. These numbers are reported by publishers on a regular basis and are assumed to be accurate. As I write this paragraph in mid-2004, there is a story emerging on the web about a number of publishers that are being accused of inflating their circulation numbers. This story is only the latest in a long history of disputes between advertisers and publishers over the veracity of reported circulation numbers. A story once circulated in Rochester of complaints by municipal authorities that large quantities of undelivered free advertisers were routinely being dropped into the Genesee River and were clogging up the free flow of the waterway.[35] Although unverified, this story has a ring of truth to it. I once stumbled on a number of discarded bales of similar publications as I walked through a field near my home. Papers dumped into the river or discarded in a field under cover of darkness would most likely still be counted by the publisher in the circulation numbers reported to advertisers.

If reported circulation numbers are assumed to be accurate, the next logical question is related to how many people will read the publication and have the potential to see your ad. This number is assumed to be some multiple of the circulation number. When a magazine enters a household or a place of business such as a doctor's office, more than one person on average will read it. The magazine may also be given away after the subscriber has finished reading it. This *passalong* factor is supported by assumptions based on census demographics and occasional supplementary research. The total number of potential exposures to a printed advertisement in a given publication is thereby established and the cost per exposure for an advertisement can then be calculated. Because this cost is very small for most forms of advertising, the industry uses cost per thousand (CPM) as a standard metric to obtain numbers that are easier to compare.

What is the exact relationship between the number of people exposed to an advertisement in a given publication and the resulting sales increases of the product or service advertised? This is nearly impossible to answer in most cases because advertisements in one publication rarely stand on their own. Advertising strategies seek to maximize the overall return on the advertising dollar invested by selecting a mix of media placements that all work together toward a common goal. When you enter a Ford dealership with the intent to purchase a Mustang convertible, there is really no way that Ford or its agency can tie your decision to a specific magazine, television, radio, or outdoor ad. The success of the overall strategy is all that really matters. The advertising agency is responsible to produce an increase or *lift* in sales through whatever means.

The process used by agencies to determine the right mix of media advertising was once fairly intuitive and unscientific. Now the process is more rational. Media planning and placement is a formalized discipline that is supported by a growing body of research about how advertising really influences the decisions that people make. Some of this research is based on surveys. Some is based on high-tech scientific methodologies that use sophisticated instrumentation to measure squirm rates and eyeball movements of people exposed to various graphic stimuli.

We now turn our attention to print advertising that is placed in public spaces outside of the home and away from the personal control of the individual consumer. The Outdoor Advertising Association of America, Inc. (OAAA) identifies four distinct categories of public advertising:[36]

1. **Billboards.**
2. **Street furniture:** Advertising space on displays positioned at close proximity to pedestrians and shoppers for eye-level viewing, or at curbside to influence vehicular traffic. (Includes bus shelters, bus benches, newsstands, newsracks, kiosks, public telephones, shopping mall displays, in-store displays, and convenience store displays.)
3. **Transit advertising:** Advertising space on displays affixed to moving vehicles or positioned in the common areas of transit stations, terminals and airports. (Includes transit advertising, mobile billboard displays, bus displays, rail displays, airport displays, taxi displays and auto wraps.)
4. **Alternative outdoor media advertising:** Advertising space on non-traditional locations outside the home intended to reach a more localized target. (Includes stadium, airborne, marine vessel, beach, ski resort, golf course, rest area, bicycle rack panels, fuel pump panels, and parking meter panels among others).

In 2003, advertisers spent approximately $5.5 billion on outdoor advertising in the U.S. Approximately $3.5 billion of this was for billboard advertising. The balance, about $2 billion, was for street furniture, transit, and alternative outdoor media. Sales of outdoor advertising has been growing at an average of greater than nine percent annually for the past thirty years. During the past three decades there has been a creative explosion of alternatives to the classic billboard. In 1970, billboards accounted for nearly 80 percent of all outdoor advertising. By 2003, billboards accounted for about 62 percent.[37] Many of these alternatives have been enabled by new materials and large-format digital printing technologies.

The industry sometimes refers to outdoor advertising as

A ubiquitous genre of outdoor advertising in Rochester, NY.

out-of-home advertising to underscore its public nature and its transcendence over the power of the consumer to turn it on and off or throw it into the trash. The industry is quick to point out the indisputable fact that publicly displayed ads are difficult to ignore. If you drive through my hometown on the expressway, you will be left with two overwhelming impressions. The first is that you should probably stop at the next convenience store you pass to purchase a New York State Lottery ticket. The jackpot is getting huge and, well, you never know. The second is that if you are involved in an auto accident during your visit to Rochester, you will be able to choose from a broad selection of personal injury law firms should you decide to sue. (I wonder if anyone will ever sue a personal injury law firm for becoming distracted while driving by its billboard and losing control of the car?)

If you look closely at the billboards you pass on your next drive, you will notice that most of them have the name of the outdoor advertising company at the bottom. A few of the largest companies are Viacom, Clear Channel, Lamar, and Adams. These companies maintain billboards in metropolitan areas and along interstates and major highways throughout the country. They often rent space from private property owners who are passive partners in the outdoor advertising business. They typically sell advertising placements on a contract basis for a specified period of time.

The cost of renting the space depends largely on the frequency with which people in the relevant demographic are expected to view the ad. This is all based on data collected and reported by the outdoor advertising industry. They make extensive use of government-generated data such as the Federal Highway Administration's advanced Highway Performance Monitoring System (HPMS). HPMS is a database containing monthly updated information about traffic density used by the federal government to gauge roadway usage levels. The system covers highways and major city arterials nationwide. This data is useful for generating circulation numbers for all forms of outdoor advertising intended to be viewed from vehicles.

In 1999 the OAAA commissioned Perception Research Services to conduct a series of studies to measure how consumers observe and react to outdoor advertising. In regards to billboard advertising, they concluded that passengers examine about 70 percent of the billboards in their field of vision and are likely to read more than 60 percent of them.[38] These findings were based on an analysis of eye movements of groups of test subjects wearing special eye-tracking glasses as they drove past outdoor advertising posted in three major metropolitan areas, New York City, Los Angeles, and Minneapolis. A quarter of the people surveyed during these studies claimed that reading a billboard would have some influence over their purchase decision. By combining this type of information with traffic density information provided by government sources, the value of an ad placed in a given location can be determined.

A billboard presents a stationary message that derives its power from the flow of people who pass it. Other stationary forms of out-of-home advertising operate on the same principle. An ad placed in a bus shelter, in a shopping mall, on a public telephone, or on a kiosk all depend on moving pedestrian traffic. But why must a posted message just sit patiently waiting for people to walk by? Rather than the people coming to the billboard, why not have the billboard go to the people?

Fortunately there are millions of potential moving billboards out there. A semi-trailer is a good candidate for a moving billboard. But semi-trailers are usually moving at high speed down the interstate and do not spend a lot of time weaving through heavily traf-

Full bus wrap of the Statue of Liberty.
Photo courtesy of 3M Commercial Graphics Division.

ficked areas at a slow enough speed to allow people to absorb advertising messages that may be written on the side. The exceptions are trailers that belong to the major retailers in a metropolitan area that spend a lot of time making local deliveries. Furniture stores and food retailers are good candidates.

The next best moving surfaces in larger urban areas are city buses. The challenge with a city bus is that a large percentage of the area on the side of the bus is taken up by windows. A real breakthrough occurred when it became possible to apply graphics to all of the surface area of the bus, windows included. High precision wide-format digital printing technology is used to apply graphics to transparent film preprinted with a special screen pattern. The screen allows people inside the bus to see out of the windows, even though they appear from the outside to be completely obscured by graphics.

The idea of wrapping objects with printed advertising has expanded rapidly into other types of vehicles. In some of the larger cities it is even possible to sell advertising space on your personal car. This affords a wonderful way to offset the burdens of the payment book for people who are not concerned with the stigma that this might carry in some social circles.

The purest form of mobile advertising relies on a specially-designed flat-panel campaign truck that carries large billboards on the

The entire block-long façade of the New York Historical Society on Central Park West in Manhattan, decorated by a single graphic advertising a show commemorating the life of Alexander Hamilton. Photo by Roger Cost.

bed and follows programmed routes selected by clients to circulate their advertising messages. Campaign trucks are dedicated to the advertising function and do not typically carry third-party cargo or freight. They are often used by advertisers to publicize special events such as sporting events, conventions, and grand openings. The contract for a mobile display may be as short as one day or as long as a week.

Digital technologies have made the changeover from one advertisement to the next generally quicker and less expensive than in the past. Most out-of-home advertising graphics today are produced on large-format inkjet printers that apply durable inks to plastic substrates in widths up to five meters. For standard-sized billboards (approximately 15 by 48 feet), the largest billboard printers can produce the entire image on a single sheet of plastic. These can be installed and removed rapidly, reducing the amount of dead time during changeover.

In some of the largest cities in the world, outdoor advertising can reach mammoth dimensions, sometimes covering the entire face of a building. The largest outdoor advertisements I have seen in recent times were in the city of Moscow, where gigantic graphics once promoted the authority of the state. Today, in the city where giant portraits of Lenin and Stalin once dominated the skyline, block-long images of fashion models now recline in expensive designer underwear.

The rapid growth of outdoor advertising over the past three decades has not happened without some conflict. Try putting up a big billboard on your front lawn to get a first-hand taste of what the outdoor advertising industry has been facing since Lady Bird Johnson decided to dedicate her energy as First Lady of the U.S. to highway beautification back in the mid-1960s. Highway beautification was a euphemism for "getting rid of all those ugly billboards."

Since that time, the outdoor advertising industry has had to become very active in local, state, and national politics. Because visibility is the most important attribute of outdoor advertising, it lives in the gray space between public and private. A billboard may sit squarely on private property, but it almost always directs its message toward public space. This legitimizes the exercise of public authority to regulate the content and placement of outdoor displays. The public reserves the right to prevent certain kinds of speech expressed through the medium, and to decide where it is inappropriate for the medium to operate altogether. Without this kind of regulation rooted in public interest, every schoolyard in America would likely be surrounded by billboards extolling the romance and coolness of cigarette smoking and other expensive vices expressly designed to appeal to young people.

The outdoor advertising industry actively supports the First Amendment right of advertisers to freely promote legal products and services, while embracing practical restrictions designed to protect community interests. These include exclusionary zones that "prohibit outdoor advertisements of products illegal for sale to minors that are intended to be read from, or within 500 feet of, elementary and secondary schools, public playgrounds, and established places of worship."[39] The industry also voluntarily supports limits on the total number of outdoor displays in a given market that advertise such products, and asserts its right to reject advertising that is untruthful, or incompatible with individual community standards. This line is sometimes difficult to define and requires some form of public debate. What appears to one person as a legitimate ad for designer underwear may appear to others as pornography. The advertising

industry often walks the thin line between acceptable and unacceptable to test where those limits might be. This is almost always the case when the product makes some claim to enhance sexual appeal or performance. In a nation that is home to many people who are Puritans by day and something else entirely by night, the public debate over decency can be very entertaining at times.

American society has devised a form of penance for its oversized appetites in the form of public service advertising. Advertisers who use public air waves or encroach on public spaces are required to devote a small percentage of their time and resources to the production of advertisements that explicitly promote the common good. Smokey the Bear is the patron saint of public service advertising. When I was growing up in the 1960s, I truly believed that I had a personal obligation to prevent forest fires, even though I didn't live within a hundred miles of anything resembling a forest. Forest fires were as frightening for a little boy to contemplate as nuclear war. (Smokey the Bear reminded us that only we could prevent forest fires, in the same way that Khrushchev the Bear reminded us that only we could prevent nuclear wars.)

Public service advertising is at its most penitential in the form of ads paid for by the tobacco industry, boldly proclaiming the wickedness of tobacco. Still, the penitent is spared complete humiliation. The largest outdoor ad currently adorning the main expressway through the center of Rochester exclaims in massive red lettering, "Tobacco Lies!" The terms of the historic tobacco settlement apparently do not require the tobacco companies to flat out admit that they themselves lie. Rather, tobacco is responsible for its own misstatements. Clever little dodge!

From the perspective of the printing industry, the trade-off of public service advertising for better access to public spaces for commercial advertising is a win-win situation. Money is made, debts to society are paid off, and the total volume of outdoor print just keeps on growing.

SELF-PRINTING BILLBOARDS

The high cost of changing the graphics on a billboard places practical restrictions on the minimum length of time that an advertiser can purchase. Given the current technology for off-line production and manual mounting of billboard graphics, it is not possible to purchase a day, or even a week of advertising in most cases.

Billboard-size electronic displays are becoming commonplace in the highest traffic volume locations in the world such as Times Square in New York, Ginza in Tokyo, and Piccadilly Circus in London. The great advantage of these displays is that the messaging can change instantaneously, allowing much smaller increments of advertising space/time to be sold. However, these large electronic displays are still too expensive for use in most existing billboard locations. There simply isn't enough traffic to justify the rates that would be necessary to make such a display profitable.

One ingenious idea for bridging the gap between static printed billboards and dynamic electronic billboards is being developed by VaryFrame Technologies Ltd., an Israeli company. Rather than print the billboard off-line and then mount it manually on site, this invention incorporates a digital printer into the billboard itself. New imagery can be transmitted to the billboard via the Internet. The self-writing billboard erases the previously written image from a reusable substrate, and then prints the new image in its place. The re-imaging cycle takes less than a minute and produces graphics that are indistinguishable from conventional printed billboards. By reducing the labor, downtime, and substrate cost associated with changing over conventional printed billboards, this technology has the potential to enable outdoor advertising companies to sell much finer slices of advertising space/time to their clients.

CHAPTER ELEVEN

ADVERTISING AT THE POINT OF PURCHASE

THUS FAR I HAVE LIMITED MY ATTENTION TO out-of-home advertising that seeks to influence decisions that will be made at a later time. In some cases an advertisement is intended to influence behavior soon after the driver passes the billboard. McDonalds, the top user of outdoor advertising in 2003, uses billboards along interstates and expressways to inform drivers that Big Macs are available if they exit at a specified location on the road ahead. In other cases, an advertisement intends to make an impression that will influence less immediate behavior. I am not about to hire a personal injury law firm or purchase auto insurance at the next expressway exit. I will at least wait until I get home. In truth, I will most likely need to be impressed by a few hundred billboards, radio commercials, television commercials, magazine ads, and perhaps even a message or two written in the sky, before I will be sufficiently motivated to find out whether I can really save fifteen percent on my auto insurance by switching to Geico.

Some forms of out-of-home advertising seek to influence immediate behavior. These appear in two broad categories: *point-of-purchase* advertising and *packaging*.

As you move closer to actual physical contact with a product you are intending to buy, the role of advertising changes dramatically. Before you enter the store, advertising builds brand awareness, connects product to lifestyle and self-image, conveys information about product specifications and capabilities, and addresses issues of pricing and competition. These are all abstract ideas that are communicated by print media through image and text. The appeal is to your heart and mind to build desire and promote the intention to spend money.

When you enter the store, advertising must communicate more directly with your lower brain. You have already thought as much as you are likely to think about your purchasing decisions. You know the type of product you want to buy. But perhaps you haven't made up your mind about the exact brand or model. At this point you are driven mostly by pure instinct, like a female peacock looking for the most colorful and appealing set of tail feathers she can find. The competition is ferocious. Vibrant color, rich texture, glitter, and sparkle are all fair game for competing products that are trying to win your affections and end up in your shopping cart. Movement, sound, and flashing lights are also allowed. For these reasons, print advertising at the point of purchase must come closer to a simulation of reality than any other form of print media.

If we trace the consumer's path from the point of first contact with the idea of a product all the way to the point of purchase, the demands on the advertising medium to flaunt its material qualities increase. Your first contact may not even involve material communications. You may hear a radio commercial or see a television commercial and begin to form an impression of the product before anything physical enters your possession. Your first impressions may be from print in the form of a printed advertisement in a magazine or newspaper, or in a catalog. The graphics are printed in black and white or four-color process and they serve the purpose of moving you forward on the road to becoming a customer. Your next move may be directly to a purchase via Internet or toll-free telephone call. More often it will be a trip to a retailer, where you will encounter the last and most materially-inviting forms of advertising.

Advertising at the point of purchase often relies on print media production capabilities that greatly expand the available options for form and appearance. Up until this point in advertising, print serves mostly as a transparent window that is used to communicate information about a product. At the point of purchase, print is part of the product itself. When you look at a magazine or a catalog, if the print is doing its job properly, it should be as invisible to you as the glass surface of your television screen. But when you enter the store to look for the advertised product, print must be almost hypervisible for you to see it.

The techniques for creating visually attractive and differentiated designs fall into four broad categories.

1. **Surface qualities.** Departure from the confines of four-color process printing. These include inks with an extended range of colors, light reflectance properties such as metallic and pearlescent, foil stamping and embossing.
2. **Shape.** Departure from the confines of the rectangular window that predominates in most forms of advertising that precede the point of purchase.
3. **Dimensionality.** Departure from the confines of two-dimensional space.
4. **Movement.** Departure from the confines of static graphic design. This is accomplished with motorized mechanisms and microprocessor-controlled light emitting diodes.

Some of the most innovative uses of the print medium can be seen in retail point-of-purchase displays. Some of the most dramatic examples are the life-size stand-up displays that grace the lobbies of movie theaters. If you take a walk through your local supermarket or building supply store, you will encounter a broad spectrum of stand-alone point-of-purchase displays that greatly increase the visibility of the products they display. Most of these are constructed of corrugated board laminated with offset-printed graphics, and are produced by commercial printing companies that specialize in their manufacture. Some point-of-purchase displays employ complex die-cutting and folding to achieve the desired appearance.

PACKAGING

If you walk down the aisle at Wal-Mart, you will encounter two distinctly different types of packaging. *Primary packaging* is what you place in your shopping cart. *Secondary packaging* normally takes the form of corrugated boxes that contain multiple primary packages for transport from distributor to retailer. Most corrugated boxes are marked with printed graphics and text to allow for easy identification of the contents during shipment. High-speed industrial inkjet print heads are used to apply bar coding that is used to track packages throughout the distribution cycle. Wal-Mart has mandated that all secondary packages that enter its distribution system also include Radio Frequency Identification (RFID) tags that will enable cartons to be scanned by radio signal transmission. For a more detailed description of RFID technology, turn to Chapter 15.

Primary packaging presents the last opportunity to influence consumer buying decisions. In the supermarket, consumers often make these decisions in a few moments while standing in the aisle. When we try to analyze the psychological forces at play in such a decision, we begin to appreciate the importance of the various forms of advertising to the final sale. The role of the package is to attract the eye and identify the product inside. Once a consumer recognizes a product, he or she will automatically recollect previous impressions from television and radio commercials, print, and Internet advertising. When finally reaching for a particular brand of product, all of the advertising impressions the consumer has experienced up to that point will influence the final choice.

Because the messages communicated by packages are designed to work in concert with all of the other forms of advertising, the pressure is on the package printing industry to speed up the production of new package designs. A printed food package enables the manufacturer to communicate with potential consumers walking down the supermarket aisle. The communication is effective if the consumer purchases the product.

The key to rapid service is a smooth workflow from package design to production that enables the designer to clearly specify the exact appearance of the final package as it sits on the store shelf. This is easier said than done. In magazines, newspaper inserts, catalogs, and outdoor displays, four-color process printing is the rule. Designers of these products are able to visualize their final appearance using color-managed computer displays or four-color proofing systems that are capable of rendering near perfect facsimiles of the final product.

Packaging does not live within the same boundaries as other forms of print. Many appearance attributes of packaging cannot be simulated with a simple four-color proofing process. An HP desktop inkjet printer can easily reproduce the entire range of colors printable by four-color publication printing processes such as lithography or gravure. But no four-color digital proofing technology can simulate a metallic, pearlescent, or fluorescent surface. The best they can provide is a good picture of the final product, not a facsimile of it. Thus it is common in packaging for new designs to be approved for production only after production has begun. The printer pulls samples at the beginning of the production run and shows them to the buyer. If the sample meets the expectations of the buyer, approval is given to complete the run. If the sample does not meet with the buyer's approval, the printer goes to work feverishly adjusting the process. This adjustment can sometimes go on for hours, or even days, and requires the physical presence of the buyer on site at the production facilities. Keeping a customer properly fed and watered during these times requires significant investment and ongoing effort by the printing company. The customer accommodations maintained by the best package printing companies have an ambiance similar to a well-appointed private airline club, complete with food, drink, and media entertainment.

If the buyer can visualize the final product without having to be on site during the first part of the production run, the time that elapses between final design approval and production run can be shortened. Package designers have access to a growing number of special visualization tools that enable them to evaluate designs long before they exist in their final physical form. These tools produce three-dimensional computer models of package designs that can be manipulated and viewed from various angles and lighting conditions. The designer can also evaluate how multiple units of the package will appear stacked on the store shelf. Often a design that works well for a single unit will present undesirable visual effects when grouped together. Using a combination of software visualization tools, color management, and physical swatch books of inks and surfaces that cannot be simulated with process color proofs or on a computer monitor, the package designer can get a good sense of how the final package will appear long before the production process begins. Because packages are three-dimensional objects, it is often desirable for a designer or product manager to evaluate a three-dimensional proof. Most packages will pass their final test when held in the hand of the consumer. The feel of the package in the hand can be as important to the sale as the graphics.

Rigid packaging includes all types of primary packaging that have a fixed form, independent of the contents. These include corrugated boxes, setup boxes, folding cartons, metal containers and cans, glass and plastic bottles. A walk through your local supermarket will help you to grasp the variety of different types of rigid packaging currently available. In some cases, rigid packages are hybrids. Aluminum beer cans are packaged in a folded paper carton, for example.

The design of rigid packages involves a lot of complex mechanical engineering, in addition to the graphic design. Package designs must satisfy a number of requirements that are not always complementary. The first requirement of a package design is that it must work perfectly in the manufacturing facility. Most rigid packages are filled with product in automated machines. If a package fails to perform properly on the production line, the result can be disastrous.

Corrugated boxes are one of the cornerstones of modern manufacturing and distribution. All kinds of products, from toothpaste tubes to refrigerators, are shipped in corrugated boxes. In some cases corrugated boxes serve as primary packaging. When you open a corrugated box containing a refrigerator or a television set, you don't find another, prettier, box inside. But most consumer products are shipped from the factory in corrugated boxes that contain folding cartons or flexible packages that serve as the primary packaging on the store shelf. The corrugated box is considered secondary packaging in this case. It carries the printed brand and product identification on the outside, but is not intended to sell the product to the consumer.

Corrugated board is made in special machines that laminate three or five layers of a material. The outside layers are called *linerboard*, and are made of heavy unbleached groundwood paper—the familiar brown material on the outside of a corrugated box. Corrugated board can also be made with a bleached outer layer that appears white and is suitable for higher quality multi-color printing. The actual corrugated core of the board is made by crimping rolls of rough unbleached board. This is glued to the liner to form the board. Five-layer corrugated board has three liner layers and two corrugated layers. Corrugated board is available in different grades and strengths depending on the final application. A refrigerator box has different structural requirements than a carton filled with potato chip bags.

There are three basic levels of print quality available on products made from corrugated board. The lowest quality graphics are printed by flexography directly onto the brown liner. The machines used for direct printing on corrugated combine flexographic printing, die-cutting, folding, and gluing in one in-line process. These machines produce finished boxes folded flat and ready to ship to the manufacturer.

For higher print quality, the linerboard can be preprinted in large multi-color flexographic presses and then fed into the laminating machine that forms the corrugated board. The highest quality printing on corrugated is obtained by printing with sheet-fed offset on separate sheets of paper and then laminating these to the finished board. You can easily see the structural difference between directly printed liner board and laminated offset print. Because of great strides in the technology of flexography over the past few decades, the quality of graphics on printed bleached linerboard is approaching the highest quality offset printing.

Corrugated board is used extensively in point-of-purchase displays as well as boxes. Graphic quality is of critical importance here, for obvious reasons. Multicolor printed bleached or coated linerboard serves some markets well. I was recently walking through one of our local building supply stores and most of the free-standing point-of-purchase displays that I saw were decorated with graphics that were printed directly on the bleached linerboard. The quality of the graphics seemed to fit perfectly with the industrial décor and lighting. The graphics on many of the corrugated point-of-purchase displays in our most upscale local supermarket are more likely to be decorated with laminated offset printing.

FOLDING CARTONS

Although corrugated boxes are technically folding cartons, the term is reserved for packages that are constructed from printed paperboard. This heavy material comes in a number of different grades and varieties. The most familiar type is something called *solid bleached sulfate*, a heavy white groundwood paper, usually clay-coated on one side to provide a smooth surface for printing. The best common example of this material is a Crest or Colgate toothpaste box. In addition to bleached boards, there are unbleached and recycled grades. This material can be printed by sheet-fed offset lithography, web offset lithography, gravure, or flexography. It is often difficult to tell which printing process was used until you examine the graphics under magnification. The differences in graphic quality among offset and gravure printed board are subtle.

Folding cartons are printed in sheet or roll form. Roll-fed processes such as gravure, flexography, and web offset are more productive than sheet-fed offset printing, so the trend is in this direction. In some cases coatings, laminations, or foil stampings are applied. This is followed by die-cutting, folding, application of adhesives, and gluing. In some applications, thermal-setting adhesives are applied to flaps that will be used to seal the carton after it is filled with the product in the manufacturing facility. Stacks of finished folding cartons are shipped flat to the customer where they are loaded into automated packaging machines.

Related to folding cartons are *blister packs* that combine a flat printed, die-cut, paperboard base with a vacuum-molded clear plastic enclosure that traps and seals the product. Blister pack bases are shipped ready to load into the packaging machinery at the manufacturing plant. The blister can be either pre-molded to the shape of the product, or heat-formed over the product during the packaging operation.

METAL CONTAINERS AND CANS

A sheet-fed offset lithographic press can be used to print beautiful color graphics directly onto sheets of steel that have been coated with a thin layer of lacquer or enamel. These printed sheets are then die cut and formed into cans or boxes. The inks used are designed to be very flexible, allowing for the stresses of the fabrication process. In some cases the graphics are pre-distorted so that they assume the correct geometry when the metal is shaped into a three-dimensional container.

Other metal containers are printed after they are formed into their final shape. The most common of these are two-piece aluminum soda and beer cans. The two pieces that make the can are the body and the lid. The bodies are manufactured in dedicated factories that extrude the cans from circular blanks punched from sheet aluminum and then coat and print the surface of the cans in offset letterpress decorators at high speed. The decorated can bodies are then shipped to the filling plant where they are filled and sealed with a lid. One of the shortcomings of the printing method is the inability to apply more than one layer of any particular color ink to the can. So the graphics must remain quite rudimentary. If you inspect the graphics under magnification, you will clearly see that there is a small gap between areas of different color, and that the colors never overlap.

An interesting approach to printing photo-quality color images on two-piece aluminum cans was developed in England during the 1980s. This involves using offset lithography to print color images with dye sublimation inks on paper sleeves. These sleeves are then wrapped tightly around aluminum cans that have been coated on the outside with a layer of white polyester-based lacquer. The wrapped cans are then passed quickly through an oven that rapidly heats up the dyes and causes them to vaporize and transfer to the polyester coating on the can. The result is a photo-quality color image on an ordinary two-piece can. The process is more expensive per unit than offset letterpress printing directly onto the aluminum, but for certain premium beverages and food products, the higher cost is well justified. (You can read about other interesting applications that use sublimation inks in Chapter 14.)

BOTTLES

Whether made of glass or plastic, there are essentially two ways to apply graphics to the surface of a bottle. Graphics can be screen printed directly onto the bottle. Specially-designed screen printing machines are able to print with precision on cylindrical surfaces. The graphic effect can be very clean and elegant. A thick layer of screen printed ink fused directly to a glass or plastic surface has a relief texture that you can feel.

Most bottles are decorated with labels or wraps that take a growing variety of forms. The simple unassuming paper label is being eclipsed by newer and more attractive alternatives. Plastic labels take many forms, from simple replacements for paper labels to

Rapidly advancing material sciences enable new applications for flexible packaging.

full shrink-wrapped enclosures that cover the entire bottle. Shrink-wrapping turns a plain white polyethylene bottle into a magnificent colorful billboard for the product. Unlike conventional wrap-around labels, shrink-wrapping is able to cover the entire surface of the bottle. This eliminates dead space and the disruption of the package design that this dead space causes. The net effect is that the perceived value of the contents can be more easily manipulated by the package designer. I recently paid two dollars for a measly eight ounces of some mystery beverage because the shrink-wrapped bottle hypnotized me. After I finished drinking (in two easy swigs) I came out of my hypnotic trance and felt like a sucker. I asked myself: "How could I have paid so much for so little?" My sad answer: "It's the packaging, dummy!"

FLEXIBLE PACKAGING

The basic concept of flexible packaging has existed for thousands of years. The first flexible packages were animal skins or bladders that were used to contain food and drink in a portable form. Plant leaves, textiles, and paper have all been used as packaging materials as well. Commercial flexible packages made of printed paper first appeared in the early 19th century. Multicolor printing on paper packages started to appear after the Civil War. In Rochester, the horticultural industry was at the forefront in the use of multicolor lithography for printing paper seed packets that featured illustrations of the mature flowers that could be expected if one planted and nurtured the seeds properly. Today, the majority of seed packets sold in the U.S. are still printed in Rochester by a single company, Hammer Lithograph.

Before the invention of plastics, paper flexible packages were restricted to containing dry products. Paper could be coated with waxes or varnishes and used to contain moist products or liquids, but only in rigid package forms like milk and juice cartons. The development of sophisticated multilayer polypropylene- and polycarbonate-based plastic films, along with a growing number of ingenious package designs, has led to an explosion of new flexible packaging applications in recent years.

Flexible packages enjoy two clear advantages over rigid packages. Flexible packages generally weigh much less than rigid packages that contain the same volume of product. Flexible packages also occupy much less volume when empty than rigid packages.

HOW FLEXIBLE PACKAGING WORKS

Before you continue to read, go to your nearest supermarket and take a walk down the salty snack food aisle. Find a bag of Lay's potato chips in a size and flavor that you like and buy it. When you arrive back at home, open the bag immediately and empty the contents into a large bowl set on the kitchen table. If you have children, the chips will disappear before the end of the day, and you will be left with the empty bag. If you are so inclined, eat a few of the chips yourself. Regardless of your taste in food, it is difficult to deny that the chips are crisp, attractive, and remarkably unbroken.

What is even more remarkable is the journey the potatoes made from the time they came out of the ground to their arrival on your table. The empty bag that you casually discard once you have eaten the chips is worthy of far more attention than you have given it up to now. The bag is central to the life of the modern potato chip and the key enabler for the marketing, manufacturing, and distribution systems that support it. Without the bag, we would be living back in the dark ages when potato chips were all made locally and potato chip delivery vans were a fixture of American suburban life.

A significant problem with potato chips is that they are perishable and they tend to spoil rapidly. The two primary causes of spoilage are exposure to oxygen and moisture. Left out on the table in a bowl, it doesn't take long for chips to lose the appeal they have when the bag is first opened. Moisture in the air robs the chips of their crispness, and oxygen reacts with the oils in the chips to form obnoxious compounds called aldehydes and ketones. So quickly do they spoil that once out of the bag it is even difficult to contemplate putting them back inside (unless, of course, they will only be used for the children's lunches).

Let's take a journey that starts when the potato is harvested and ends when the chips are sitting on the shelf at your local supermarket. Strictly speaking, potato chips can be made from any kind of potatoes. But a leading snack food manufacturer like Frito Lay does not take chances with its raw materials any more than it takes chances with other aspects of its business. The variety, taste, texture, and nutritional content of the potatoes that will be made into chips are rigorously specified by the manufacturer. The growers strive to meet these specifications.

Once potatoes are harvested, they are transported to the chip factory by rail car. Here they are unloaded onto huge conveyers and taken through a cleaning process where dirt and rocks are removed. The potatoes are then peeled, sliced, and washed to remove starches that would otherwise tend to glue the slices together as they move through the cooking process.

The washed slices then move on conveyers to the fryer where in a few short minutes they are transformed into potato chips. The term *fryer* may recall domestic images of frying pans on stovetops. But in a potato chip factory, the fryer is a massive piece of industrial equipment containing thousands of gallons of hot oil and a sophisticated conveyer system that moves the potato slices through at a precisely controlled rate. In the most sophisticated modern fryers, the cooking oil temperature can be varied from one end of the process to the other to fine tune the cooking process.

When they emerge from the fryer, the chips are transported through a large oxygen-free de-fatting chamber where pressurized steam is used to remove excess oil from the chips. The steam carries the oil away to another part of the factory where the oil is reclaimed for reuse in the frying process.

Once the chips emerge from this chamber, they are nearly ready to be packaged and shipped. But first there are some last minute operations that must be performed. The chips stream past an optical scanner where they are automatically checked for color. Individual chips falling outside of the desired color tolerances are mechanically ejected from the line and discarded. In this way, chips that end up over- or under-cooked do not make their way into the final packages.

The chips are then sorted roughly by size for the different bag sizes produced by the factory. The smaller chips go into the smaller bags and the larger chips into the larger bags. The chips then stream through devices that add seasoning and divide them into portions by weight. These machines are set up to portion the chips for specific bag sizes. The portioned chips are transported to the bag forming, filling, and sealing machines in individual metal trays.

The bag forming, filling, and sealing machine is where the finished food product meets the packaging material in a way that recalls the child's poem:

> Algie met a bear.
> The bear met Algie.
> The bear was bulgy.
> The bulge was Algie.

The bag forming, filling, and sealing machine is a mesmerizing marvel of modern engineering. Bags are formed by drawing a continuous roll of material over a steel collar. The collar forms a cylinder and the two edges of the roll are then welded to create the vertical seam that runs down the back of the bag. The top of each filled bag and the bottom of the next empty bag are sealed simultaneously. As soon as the bottom of a bag is sealed, the machine releases a preweighed cascade of potato chips into it through a chute. The top of the bag is then sealed along with the bottom of the next bag. The filled, sealed bag is cut loose and deposited on a conveyer. All of this happens in a fraction of a second. Filled bags emerge from the machine at a rate approaching 100 per minute.[40] Bags are then packed into cartons and stacked on pallets ready for shipping.

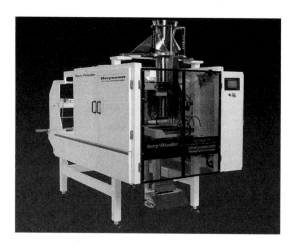

Bag forming, filling, and sealing machine.

Now that we have followed the potato on its journey from farm through the potato chip factory, we can take a closer look at some of the finer points of the package manufacturing process. The bag is made of a multilayer material that is printed and laminated in a single in-line operation, and is far more complex in structure than most people would ever imagine. The outside layer is a smooth clear plastic film called *polypropylene,* which can be printed by lithography, flexography, letterpress, or gravure. Nearly all potato chip bags and similar flexible packages are printed by either flexography or gravure. If you walk down the supermarket aisle, you will have a difficult time distinguishing among these two processes. Both are able to render sharp, colorful graphics on clear, white, or metalized polypropylene film.

The clear polypropylene film is composed of several layers that impart strength and barrier properties required for food packaging. The graphics are typically "back-printed" on the film. This means that you are looking through the clear film to see the printing ink underneath. The back-printed film is laminated with a second layer of polypropylene using either a cold contact or molten plastic adhesive, locking the printing ink and the adhesive between two layers of plastic. This second layer of film is often metalized to enhance its protective barrier properties. Laminated films that incorporate brilliant multicolor graphics are the basic building blocks of a rapidly

Nutrition Nutrition

Serving Size 1 oz. (28g/Ab Serving Size 2 cookies
Servings Per Container 16 Servings Per Containe

Flexography.   *Gravure.*

proliferating range of high-tech flexible containers for both solid and
liquid products.

Flexography is used to print the majority of flexible packaging materials produced in the U.S. Most other flexible packaging is
printed by gravure. In Europe and Japan, the gravure process dominates the market, with flexography accounting for a much smaller
percent than in the U.S. Why is the U.S. market so different from Europe and Japan? These factors have been cited by various experts.

- Europe and Japan have traditionally used the gravure process
  for shorter runs than the U.S., and have developed the supporting industries such as cylinder engraving to accommodate lower volumes with greater efficiency and lower prices
  than the same services in the U.S.
- Flexography was invented in the U.S. and most of the improvements in the technology have been the work of U.S.
  companies.
- Flexography works with water-based and ultraviolet-curable
  inks, and thus it is more compatible than gravure with strin-
  gent FDA regulations governing the properties of inks used
  in food packaging and the tort lawsuit-encouraging nature of
  the American legal system.

In many cases the differences between the U.S. and other major
markets are simply the result of different evolutionary paths that
cannot be explained with reference to a few simple causes. It is likely that the printing processes that currently dominate each market
will continue to do so, and that the qualitative differences between
gravure and flexography will continue to diminish. The truth today is
that only an expert eye aided by a magnifying glass can really tell the
difference between the two processes. The key is in the small type.

Small type printed by gravure has a *serrated* edge, whereas small type printed by flexography shows ink squeeze around the edges.

CHAPTER TWELVE

PRINTING IN
THE OFFICE

D URING THE DECADE OF THE 1950S, several technologies for making copies of documents were developed and marketed to business users. All of them employed some kind of chemical reaction to form an image on proprietary materials through photographic or thermal exposure. The Kodak *Verifax* used a dye-transfer method that required an intermediate negative, and a wet chemical process to transfer the positive image to a coated receiver paper. The *Thermofax* process developed by 3M employed a thermal-sensitive translucent paper that would turn black when exposed to heat reflected from the black ink on an original document.

When Xerox announced the 914 copier in 1959, it started a revolution in office printing that few people could foresee at the time. The machine was push-button simple to operate. One simply had to place an original document face down on a glass plate and push a button. Fifteen seconds later the first copy would emerge, dry and ready to use. Subsequent copies of the same original were delivered at the rate of one every seven seconds. An untrained operator could walk up to the machine, place an original on the glass, punch in the number of desired copies (up to a maximum of 15), and light up a Lucky Strike while the machine did all of the work.

The success of the 914 was the combined result of breakthrough technology along with a new business model invented by Xerox out of sheer necessity. The 914 was an extraordinarily expensive machine to manufacture. Xerox knew that it would not be able to convince businesses to spend thousands of dollars on a copying machine to replace the relatively inexpensive (hundreds of dollars)

Thermofax and Verifax machines that were currently available. So Xerox decided to lease the machines for a relatively low monthly fee ($95 originally) that covered the machine rental plus 2,000 copies per month. Beyond 2,000 copies Xerox charged four cents for each additional copy. Xerox also allowed customers to cancel the deal within fifteen days of receiving the machine, if they didn't like it. Thus, Xerox removed almost all of the risk that may have prevented a company from deciding to order the 914. Xerox based its business model on the prediction that once a company began to use the machine, it would become indispensable and that most users would end up far exceeding the lease allotment of 2,000 copies per month. This prediction came true beyond even Xerox's wildest imagination. By the mid-1960s, Xerox was recouping its expenses on the manufacture, advertising, and sales of each 914 copier in a year. Beyond that, the only expense was for service. Everything else was pure profit.[41]

The volume of business copying exploded during the 1960s because Xerox had broken through a barrier that previous copying technologies had not. The 914 copier was to office copying what the original Kodak roll film camera was to amateur photography. Kodak had designed a system to support a push-button simple user interface by locating all of the technology required to process and print film in a central manufacturing facility far removed from the customer. Eighty years later Xerox placed all of the technology required to make xerographic copies into a box under the direct control of the customer. Xerox also created a huge network of field service technicians who would respond rapidly to calls from customers whose machines had broken down. Even though the 914 was the most complex machine ever devised for the office, the user was able to approach it as a simple push-button appliance.

Ease of use is a *threshold function*. This means simply that until a technology crosses the line from "too difficult to use" to "easy enough to use," the majority of people will avoid using it. With the 914 copier Xerox crossed this threshold. Even though Xerox believed that copying volumes would increase substantially as a result of the ease of use of the new machine, it is nearly impossible to foresee what will really happen once a threshold is crossed. Up until the introduction of the 914, copying was used primarily as a substitute for carbon paper. Copies were made for distribution at the same time documents were originated. The Verifax and Thermofax machines produced additional legible copies of original typewritten documents. They were more expensive than carbon copies, but worth the premium in applications where maximum legibility of each copy was important. (Carbon paper copies degraded in quality from first to last. Carbon copies also had to be made simultaneous with typing the original, so mistakes were difficult to correct.)

Xerox copying technology precipitated a flood of new copying applications that had never before been contemplated. The 914 made it easy to copy existing printed information as a way of supporting discussion and decision-making. Before Xerox, the idea of copying a magazine or journal article for wide circulation among a team of co-workers did not exist. Previous copying technology was simply too cumbersome and time-consuming to consider such a use. But Xerox crossed the threshold and entered a new world where copying became a natural extension of expressing ideas within an organization. This opened the floodgates. In the mid-1950s, approximately twenty million machine copies were made in the U.S. annually. By 1966, the number had reached 14 billion, an increase of almost a thousand-fold. By the mid-1980s, the number of office copies made annually worldwide exceeded 700 billion.[42]

The desktop computing and printing revolution that began in the early 1980s was at first about replacing the typewriter for document creation. I remember the joy that I felt when I acquired my first personal computer. The backspace key alone was worthy of a book of love poetry. The first desktop digital printers were noisy devices that did not match the legibility of good typewritten copy. Apple's introduction of the Macintosh computer and the first desktop laser printer in the mid-1980s placed professional-quality typesetting in the hands of common, casual users. It would be several years before digital document production and printing became the standard method of document production, but smart investors began to steer clear of typewriter manufacturers and typesetting companies shortly after Apple introduced the Macintosh and Laserwriter.

Desktop publishing was first applied to document production. Laser printers were used to generate originals, and these would then be "Xeroxed" to produce multiple copies. One might occasionally be tempted to run off a few copies on the laser printer, especially if the copier had a long line in front of it or was waiting for service. But the significantly higher page cost and slower print speed argued against making this standard practice. I remember on more than one occasion having to use my desktop laser printer to run off multiple copies of documents because I found myself up against a deadline staring at a broken copier with the "service has been called" sign attached. On these occasions, I would close my office door and hope that one of our bean counters didn't intrude while I ran my expensive copies, riddled with guilt.

Even now, two decades after the introduction of the first desktop laser printer, the trade-off between cost and convenience in paper document production is still a dominant issue. I currently have many different options for making multiple copies of documents. I have a color inkjet printer and a black-and-white laser printer on my desk. I can send a document to a network laser printer down the hall that prints faster and at slightly lower cost than my desktop laser printer. I can also send a document to a centralized printing facility that is my lowest-cost option, and wait 24 to 36 hours for the copies to be delivered. When I do this, however, I pay for the service out of a different account than the one we use to buy consumables like toner and paper for internal use. In addition to digital print options, I also have two levels of photocopying available. I can make a photocopy on a small table-top copier in a nearby office, or I can send the job to be copied on a large high-speed production machine that serves our entire division. I have the option of using our departmental machine myself, but must submit work to be copied on the big machine.

My point in the above paragraph is not to suggest that there is anything special about our current print production infrastructure. On the contrary, I am faced with a typical range of print publishing choices for documents. The choice about which path to take is mine alone. I nearly always choose the path of greatest personal convenience. I am fully aware of the absolute differences in cost among the various paths available. But since there are no incentives to consider cost in my current work environment, it is easy to ignore. There are neither rewards for saving money nor punishments for losing it. There are few ways more effective than unregulated print production practices to squander an organization's money.

Fortunately, companies like Xerox, HP, IBM, and Standard Register have devoted a lot of hard thinking to the problem of creating rational cost-effective document production systems for organizations of all sizes. Today these systems encompass both paper and electronic publishing formats. The goal is to provide communication support services that will satisfy the needs of the various players in an organization while keeping costs as low as possible. This can get complicated. The optimal choice of publication path must satisfy a number of requirements that must often be traded off against one another. These include material qualities of the published document, production turnaround, distribution, and cost.

Since everyone in our organization has a high speed Internet connection and the ability to attach Microsoft Office and Adobe PDF documents to emails as well as upload them to our web server, all of the documents that we create can be distributed electronically. If the sole purposes of publishing in our organization were *informative* or *instructive*, we would be able to eliminate print as an option altogether. We rely almost entirely on electronic channels for informative and instructive internal communications. Print serves the internal communication needs of a completely wired organization like ours only when it plays an *operative* or *persuasive* role. I will elaborate on each one of these.

Print plays an *operative* role when it is used as a device to organize a group discussion. The distribution of printed copies of a document does not have the same operative effect as projecting the same document in electronic form onto a screen. The projected document establishes a different set of power relationships than a distributed printed document. The display of the projected document is under the control of the person running the meeting. By distributing printed copies, power is more democratically distributed among participants. The decision to print or not to print is more appropriately determined by these considerations than by differences in economics.

If print is the right medium, there are a number of qualitative attributes that come into play. The three that are most important are colorfulness, paper grade, and finishing. If the appropriate choice for a given situation is black and white on standard copy paper with a staple in the corner, the use of color print on an expensive paper with a more finished binding will communicate the wrong message. The more finished a document appears, the more the power relationship between author and reader shifts toward the author. A stapled black-and-white document on cheap paper marked DRAFT on every page invites a far different response than a spiral-bound color book printed on heavy glossy paper.

The qualitative attributes of print also help to establish its *persuasive* value. In my personal experience using print for the purposes of persuasion, I have found that the grade and type of paper can sometimes be a very significant factor. In my office, the standard grade of paper for use in our copiers and digital printers is close to being the cheapest paper money can buy. The paper is suitable for personal use. I often print a document so that I can review it away from the computer with pencil in hand. I have no reservations about using the paper if there is no possibility that the pathetic limpness of the cheap groundwood medium will undermine the authority of the message. For certain documents, the choice of paper adds significant persuasive value. I have a secret stash of very heavy watermarked 100-percent cotton bond paper for special occasions. The paper casts a subtle spell on anyone who touches it. This spell always seems to work in my favor.

With wireless mobile computing, the distribution of electronic documents among the participants of a meeting may substitute for print in some cases. The necessary condition for this to work is that all participants have personal reading devices. Today this can only be accomplished with notebook computers accessing and exchanging common document files over a network. Still, tools that support collaboration among individuals in a workgroup are most suitable for asynchronous interactions, and it is rare to find organizations using these same tools in face-to-face synchronous meetings.

The idea of a "paperless office of the future" was first introduced by Wang, one of the long gone early pioneers of word processing, back in the late 1970s. Since that time, advocates for print have referenced this prediction over and over again to deflate current arguments about the possibility that the latest generation of computer technology might finally deliver us to that promised land. My favorite comment along these lines was made by RIT professor Frank Romano, who said, "Wang's prediction of the paperless office hasn't yet come true. However, the Wangless office has."

If print only served informative and instructive needs, the paperless office could become a reality the moment everyone in an organization was connected to the Internet. The extent to which paper will disappear from the office really depends on the ability of electronic substitutions to support operative and persuasive needs. Wang did not identify or think hard enough about these other needs before predicting the paperless future. As computing becomes more pervasive and portable, there can be no doubt that electronic communication channels will replace an increasing number of operative and persuasive functions currently performed by print. It seems unlikely to me, however, that print will ever disappear entirely from the office. In the "paperless" office of the future, the uncommonness of print will only add to its power in those cases where it is used.

CHAPTER THIRTEEN

CURRENCY AND SECURITY DOCUMENTS

M ONEY IS NOT WHAT IT USED TO BE. When money was entirely in the form of metal coinage, the value of the coin was determined by the weight and purity of the metal itself. Coins provided a convenient way to meter and indicate the value of lumps of metal. The metal allowed for value to be transferred indirectly and made it possible for society to escape from the extreme limitations of direct barter.

Soon after the appearance of metal coinage came the idea of using a token to represent a promise to supply the metal coins at a later time. The token could be made out of any material that could be used to carry information that would retain credibility over time. The Babylonians used clay tablets impressed with symbols representing trade agreements and financial promises. Today we use printed paper. Up until the early part of the 20th century, people believed that the value of the paper could only be maintained if each note in circulation was directly exchangeable for precious metal of the value indicated on the note. This requirement maintained the value of currency independent of economic and political forces that might otherwise have undermined it. But it also put restrictions on the supply of available money to support future expansion of the economy.

The creation of the Federal Reserve System and the eventual end to the requirement that the paper money supply be backed by metal completed the evolution of U.S. currency to its present form. A paper Federal Reserve note represents nothing more than a promise that the note can be exchanged for goods or services of an equivalent value upon presentation. The Federal Reserve is responsible for ensuring that this promise is kept by regulating the amount of money in circulation with respect to the fluctuating value of goods and services in the economy. In my adult lifetime, starting in the early 1970s to the present, I have seen a dramatic improvement in the ability of the Federal Reserve board to regulate the value of money. The frightening combination of economic recession coupled with double-digit inflation that characterized much of the 1970s seems as far away in time as Leonid Brezhnev reviewing his intercontinental ballistic missiles and T-72 tanks from atop Lenin's tomb.

The only important attribute of paper currency is its authenticity. If it were easy to create copies of Federal Reserve notes that were indistinguishable from the real things, there would be no way to know whether a bill was authentic, and paper currency would not work. So paper currency is designed to be as difficult to duplicate as possible. The ultimate goal of government is to produce paper currency that clearly and unquestionably demonstrates its authenticity. Ideally, this should be evident to anyone using only the direct senses of sight, hearing, touch, and smell. Techniques that were first developed for ensuring the authenticity of printed paper currency are being applied to an ever-widening range of printed products that need to ensure their own authenticity.

You may be somewhat confused by my reference to the use of four of the five senses for determining the authenticity of a printed product in the above paragraph. (Taste is the only sense that does not apply.) Sight is easy to understand. Appearance is the most important characteristic of a bank note. There are many appearance features manufactured into currency that contribute to its ability to prove its authenticity. But features that appeal to the other senses are also deliberately built in to the paper product.

The paper used for U.S. currency is rigorously specified and manufactured by a single supplier (Crane). This ensures a consistent surface texture and feel. The paper is even expected to produce a signature sound when it is crinkled or snapped in the hand. This is a function of the composition of the paper fibers and the specifics of the manufacturing process. If a bill does not have the expected feel and emit the expected sound when you fondle it, you will take quick notice. Freshly printed paper currency also has a distinctive odor that is also expected. If the stack of twenty dollar bills that you obtain from the ATM has the odor of fresh lithographic ink instead of the expected odor of printed paper currency, you will probably take quick notice of that as well.

The distinctive appearance of a Federal Reserve note is the result of specific features of the papermaking and the printing processes. The papermaking process is responsible for the color and surface texture of the paper. If you look at an unprinted part of a note through a magnifier, you see small colored fibers randomly distributed on the surface. These are added to the paper during manufacture and are one of the first things that you would look for if you suspected that a note was not authentic. Another feature of the paper that is built in at the time of manufacture is the watermark that is visible on all U.S. currency at the extreme right-hand side of the note. You can only see the watermark if you view the note against a strong back light. The watermark on each denomination is a smaller version of the head and shoulders portrait in the center of the front side of the note.

The watermarks are produced by pressing a die into the wet paper pulp as it is formed during manufacture, and is very difficult to duplicate by other means. On some notes, other features such as holographically-imaged ribbons are built into the paper. Many of these same techniques for adding security features to the paper during manufacture are used in other security document applications such as passports and stock certificates. The importance of papermaking to the creation of security documents is best illustrated by the fact that intelligence agencies that seek to create forged security documents often maintain dedicated papermaking facilities to produce the required substrates.

A combination of printing processes is used to print most paper currency in the world today. U.S. currency is printed by a combination of three processes: intaglio, offset lithography and letterpress. Intaglio printing employs engraved steel cylinders that transfer a thick layer of paste ink directly to the paper surface. Most of the graphics on U.S. currency are intaglio printed. The ink layer is so thick that you can feel it when you rub your finger across the surface. The front side of U.S. notes is intaglio printed in black ink and the back side in dark green ink. If you observe the print through even a ten-power magnifier, you will clearly see the three-dimensional quality of the print. The intaglio process is also used to add decorative graphics rendered in metallic and color-changing inks to some denominations. The new twenty-dollar note, introduced in the fall of 2003, has a color-changing intaglio printed feature (the digits "20") in the lower right corner. Depending on the lighting and angle of view, the color of the ink appears either orange or green. This note also has lithographically-printed background features that are difficult to duplicate by alternative means. Each note has a unique serial number imprinted by letterpress in the upper left and the lower right quadrants of the front side. This is printed by special mechanical numbering print heads that advance after each impression.

The number of security features built into paper currency has steadily increased during the past twenty years. The most sophisticated paper money in the world today has so many built-in security features, that the technology required to create a perfect counterfeit would cost more than the value of the fake money that one could make with it. Hostile foreign governments are the only parties with the resources to create such undetectable counterfeits.

Unfortunately, the small-time counterfeiter does not need to produce perfectly undetectable fakes. All he has to do is to produce a "good enough" facsimile of the real thing to fool the typical convenience store cashier. The greatest gift to the small-time counterfeiter has been the desktop computer connected to a desktop color laser printer. The denomination of choice for people who prefer to make money this new-fashioned way is the twenty-dollar bill. That is why the U.S. government rolled out the newly-designed twenty with all of the new anti-counterfeiting features first. There is some irony in this. Andrew Jackson, who dedicated himself as president to destroying the first national bank of the United States, is now at the vanguard of protecting the value of the currency issued by its modern reincarnation, the Federal Reserve.

I should probably say a few words about the risks associated with trying to pass counterfeit notes as real. The federal government treats counterfeiting as a grave crime. The Secret Service is charged with enforcement of anti-counterfeiting laws. Those who try it and are caught in the act are guaranteed to spend many years locked up in a federal prison. When I first began to teach courses in graphic arts at RIT, I was informed by the administration of the school that it was my legal responsibility to inform the Secret Service if I discovered any of my students trying to scan or photograph U.S. currency. While I never caught anybody in that particular criminal act, I did once catch a student trying to produce a counterfeit handicapped parking pass.

SECURITY DOCUMENTS

The most common security documents serve to identify the people who carry them. I once discovered how dependent we are on such things when I lost my wallet in Los Angeles on a business trip. Getting home was not easy. I was able to borrow some cash from a colleague to cover my expenses while I stayed in town. Although I did not lose my airline tickets, I had no way of proving my identity at airline security. Fortunately I had left my passport at home, and through a series of phone calls and faxes, I was able to convince the airline that I was really the person whose name was on my ticket. At one time during this ordeal, I even contemplated a cross-country Greyhound bus ride. Now I wish that I had been forced to take that route, if only to make this story more amusing. I have since developed the habit of compulsively checking for my identification documents approximately once every five minutes while traveling by air.

Passports incorporate many printed security features similar to those used in paper currency. These include features that are added during the papermaking and printing processes. The technologies for producing security features that are nearly impossible to forge have improved dramatically in the past decade. For example, the first page of a U.S. passport that bears the photograph and personal information of the bearer is now created using a proprietary combination of digital print, holographic imaging and lamination that creates an appearance that cannot be duplicated by alternative means. The visa pages in current U.S. passports have watermarked and printed features that also defy attempts at forgery. These new features were added to the U.S. passport in 2002 as part of the effort to improve security at the borders. At the same time, the U.S. government no longer allowed passports to be issued by offices outside the country. The high-tech process of laminating a digitally-

Micrograph (inset) of microprinting on a passport visa page.

printed photo identification panel on the inside front cover can only be accomplished in dedicated facilities in the U.S. Unfortunately, many countries issuing passports in the world today still rely on antiquated methods to build security features into paper documents.

Passports are usually scrutinized carefully by trained passport control inspectors before the holder is allowed to pass. Whereas counterfeit currency only needs to be good enough to fool unsuspecting and often unobservant convenience store cashiers, counterfeit passports are guaranteed to be subjected to a more thorough visual and tactile examination. The act of creating a counterfeit passport is therefore usually perpetrated by agencies of governments, not criminals. It is a big-budget operation often requiring millions of dollars worth of specialized equipment and operated by a staff of technical and scientific experts who know how to replicate security documents such that they will pass for authentic ones.

Even if it were possible to produce a perfect counterfeit passport, there is another layer of security that is external to the physical document itself. Your passport identification number is used to query a database that is used to verify the information on the passport and alert the passport control official as to any special considerations that may be warranted. The information in the database is constantly being refined with increased cooperation among nations to share information that will hamper the movements of international criminals and terrorists.

The number of discrete security features built into a printed product to assist authentication generally increases with the risks associated with falsely authenticating a counterfeit. Passports and paper currency include many discrete security features because the potential risks of misidentification are so high. The goal is to use a combination of features that will make it extremely easy to authenticate a document while at the same time making it extremely difficult to counterfeit. Here is a partial list of common security features used in security documents today:

1. **Paper base composition.** The raw materials that constitute the pulp from which paper is cast give the paper its physical properties.
2. **Embedded fibers, planchettes, and ribbons.** *Planchettes* are tiny flakes of material that remain intact when they are added to the pulp. Fibers, planchettes, and ribbons added to the pulp are molded into the finished paper, where they remain visible. Counterfeits often feature printed reproductions that simulate the appearance of these embedded features.
3. **Paper finishing.** During the papermaking process the molded paper can be run through rollers that impart texture to the surface. *Calendering* employs steel rollers that make the surface smooth. Paper surface coatings are also applied online.
4. **Watermarks.** Genuine watermarks are pressed into the wet paper pulp before it dries, altering the concentration of fibers and the light-transmitting qualities of the finished paper.
5. **Fluorescent patterns.** Many security documents feature intricate patterns printed in clear fluorescent inks that can only be viewed under ultraviolet illumination. Passport examiners are equipped with small portable ultraviolet lamps that can be used to inspect suspect documents.
6. **Microprinting.** If you look closely at one of the visa pages in a U.S. passport, you will see that the page is divided into four quadrants separated by what appear to be very fine printed lines. When you inspect these lines under magnification, you will discover that they are actually very fine type spelling out the words "PASSPORT VISA PAGE" followed by the page number. These microscopic features, printed by lithography,

are impossible to reproduce by digital means.

7. **Color-changing inks.** In new issues of U.S. currency, inks that appear to change color depending on the angle of illumination and viewing are used to print discrete features on the notes. These features can only be reproduced with special inks that are formulated for the purpose. They cannot be counterfeited using digital means.

8. **Split-fountain printing.** By the controlled feeding of ink of different colors onto the ink rollers of an offset lithographic press, a printed background can be produced that gradually fades one color into the other. This feature is also very difficult to fake.

9. **Lamination.** Clear plastic films containing security features can be laminated with a printed image to produce a composite that has very distinctive visual characteristics that cannot be duplicated by other means.

10. **Foil stamping.** On packaging materials, foil stamping serves a decorative as well as an anti-counterfeiting function.

11. **Holograms.** The most common security hologram in current use is the familiar flying bird that is used on Visa cards.

12. **Water-soluble inks.** Some of the background features in passports are printed in water soluble inks that will run if an attempt is made to alter the information overprinted on them. Similar features are used on checks and other financial instruments to protect against tampering.

13. **Embedded electronics.** According to the U.S. Department of State, new U.S. passports will soon include embedded chips that will broadcast on command an individual's name, address and digital photo to a computerized reader. The chips will employ radio frequency identification (RFID) technology that will be discussed in more detail in Chapter 15.

COUNTERFEIT PACKAGING: A GROWING PROBLEM

Some of the same techniques for building security features into products such as paper currency and passports are used to assist authentication and prevent counterfeiting of an increasing variety of printed products. The most interesting of these is primary packaging for counterfeit consumer products. These include pharmaceuticals, over-the-counter health and beauty care products, electronics, and designer clothing and fashion accessories. If you purchase a tube of Crest tooth paste in China, a package of Viagra in Mexico, or a Canon rechargeable battery in France, there is a significant chance that you will end up with a counterfeit. If you purchase a Rolex watch on Canal Street in New York City for ten dollars, you are guaranteed to end up with a counterfeit.

Counterfeit products are often the work of international criminal organizations that operate in several countries, often with the tacit approval and assistance of government agencies. A counterfeit pharmaceutical may be sourced in one country, formulated into tablets or capsules in another, packaged in a third, and sold to the consumer in a fourth. In some cases, state-owned factories are employed in the manufacture of counterfeit products.[43] The two countries that receive mention in almost every article and discussion of consumer product counterfeiting that I have encountered are China and India. However, counterfeit manufacturing operations have been discovered in many other countries throughout the world, including the U.S. I have heard many first-hand accounts by colleagues from China and India, as well as from countries in Southeast Asia and South America, of counterfeit manufacturing facilities.

The key to passing counterfeit products for the real things is often the printed packaging, because packaging is the principal interface between the product and the consumer. It is a relatively simple process to reverse engineer the graphics on a package and produce a counterfeit. This has become easier as the print manufacturing technology base has been modernized throughout the world. The machinery and materials available in China today are the best available anywhere in the world. Print quality is no longer a barrier to the product counterfeiter. In China, the technical ability to create near perfect counterfeits is supported by a general lack of legal restraints. Americans have had more than two centuries of experience recognizing and enforcing intellectual property rights. This is regarded as a foreign idea in China. Although the Chinese government has been forced to agree to honor specific rights claimed by American companies, the recognition of these rights is not generally supported by the culture. Therefore, counterfeiting of products will likely continue to be a growth industry in China and, as China grows

I was surprised during a trip to Beijing a few years ago when a student approached me after a lecture and asked me to autograph her copy of my Pocket Guide to Digital Printing. *She then produced a Chinese language version of my book that I had not known existed. I was both flattered and disturbed at the same time. But after discovering that the book was selling for a little more than a dollar, and the royalty would have been less than a dime per book, I quickly decided to remain flattered and cease being disturbed.*

in power and influence, throughout the world.

How can legitimate consumer product companies protect their markets from this kind of profit-destroying activity? One answer is to try to build security features into the packaging materials that make it difficult to produce counterfeits. The most practical first step is to add a hologram to the package. Holograms provide a high level of security because they can be produced in the millions from a single master tool, are extremely difficult to reverse engineer, and provide an instant visual verification of the authenticity of the package. This can only work as a foil to counterfeiting if the consumer is vigilant and wishes to purchase authentic products. As counterfeit products approach the quality of genuine products, however, consumers may make a conscious choice to purchase the counterfeit at a significantly lower price than the genuine. At this point, counterfeits become "knock-offs" and both seller and buyer are accomplices in the violation of intellectual property rights. There is evidence all around us that the concept of intellectual property may someday be regarded as a quaint archaism that passed into history along with U.S. dominance of global culture.

In the meantime other methods of building security into packages are under exploration. One method that shows some promise is the incorporation of RFID tags on printed packages. Current technology allows for the printing of RFID antennas directly onto the surface of a package. A tiny chip is then attached to the antenna. The chip can be programmed with coded data to identify the package when queried by a special digital device.

CHAPTER FOURTEEN

APPAREL AND DECORATIVE PRODUCTS

P RINTING PROCESSES ARE EMPLOYED in the manufacture of many products that do not serve primarily as vehicles of communication. You are probably not aware of most of these, even though they are staring you in the face almost every waking moment of your life. The two largest categories are printed textiles and decorative surfaces.

TEXTILES

Printed textiles are used extensively in the garment and home furnishing industries. Apparel textile printing is the highest single value category of printed product worldwide.[44] Garments and other textile-based products can be fabricated from pre-printed materials, or graphics can be added to finished garments.

People have most likely been printing graphics on textiles for thousands of years. I was reminded of this recently as I walked through a small boutique on St. Mark's Place in the East Village in New York. The shop was full of Indian crafts and artifacts, both antique and modern. On one shelf was a pile of small wooden blocks that each bore an intricate pattern carved in relief on one side. The blocks were all about two inches thick and ranged in size from approximately one to three inches on a side. I recognized these blocks as hand-made stamps used to print repeated patterns on fabrics. They represent the earliest known method of textile printing, which is still practiced actively in some parts of the world. They are contemporary products of a traditional culture and are nearly indistinguishable from blocks that were produced many hundreds of years ago.

Indian wood block used for textile printing.

Modern industrial textile printing takes many different forms. Direct printing from a relief surface is still viable for some applications. But this works best with very smooth and closely woven fabrics. Porous and uneven surfaces require different approaches. Two processes account for the majority of contemporary textile printing: screen printing and transfer (sublimation) printing.

SCREEN PRINTED TEXTILES

Screen printing can be used to add graphics to textiles while they are being manufactured or to finished textile-based products afterwards. Rotary screen printing presses apply ink to a continuous roll of fabric by pushing it through a porous roller onto the fabric. Textiles can be decorated in large volumes by this method. The use of mechanical pressure to transfer ink through a cylindrical stencil allows this method to be used on a variety of surfaces. Contemporary textile designers use specialized digital design tools to create patterns that are transferred to the cylinder masters. A set of screen cylinders (one for each color in the design) is very expensive to manufacture, and therefore must be used to mass-produce printed textiles in high volumes. Discrepancies between real and projected market demand for a particular design account for a great deal of discounting in retail sales of textile-based products.

Screen printing is also used to add graphics to finished textile products. These include T-shirts, athletic wear, hats, bags, luggage, or practically any other product that you might find with printed graphics on it. Screen printing presses are available in formats to accommodate a broad range of applications. A major advantage of the process is its ability to apply graphics to non-flat surfaces. Low-end screen printing equipment is priced such that the barrier to enter the business is very low. Many of the printed T-shirts that you see are produced by "mom and pop" businesses operating out of residential basements and garages. Others are produced by large companies that specialize in printing graphics on apparel. Defects associated with setup and manufacturing errors result in significant numbers of printed products that can neither be sold to the original customer nor recycled for raw materials. One of the largest manufacturers of printed athletic apparel, Champion, addresses this problem with a network of retail stores that sell defective goods at deep discount prices.

TRANSFER PRINTING

Graphics that are applied to textiles add value to the finished product. However, this is only true if there is a buyer for the finished product. Overestimating the demand for a particular design or pattern can easily lead to overproduction and large inventories of unsold material. Viewed from this standpoint, printing graphics on textiles that cannot subsequently be sold actually destroys value. This is true of all printed materials, but most consequential when graphics are applied to expensive materials that are sold into markets heavily influenced by fashion trends.

Transfer printing provides a way to delay the binding of graphics to finished textiles and minimize the risks of overproduction. Transfer printing employs an inexpensive paper-based medium to store inventories of printed graphics that can then be subsequently transferred to the textile surface. If the demand for a particular design does not meet initial market projections, excess inventories of printed transfer paper represent only a fraction of the value of the equivalent volume of printed textile. In addition, the range of colors and graphic detail obtainable from transfer printing can far exceed that of direct screen printing.

The most common form of transfer printing uses special dye

colorants that will sublime when heated to a certain temperature. *Sublimation* is the physical change of a solid into a gas, or a gas into a solid, skipping the liquid phase. Sublimation is commonly observable in nature when dry ice evaporates directly into vapor, or water vapor crystallizes directly into frost, bypassing the liquid phase. Sublimation dyes are designed to turn from solid to gas instantly at a specific temperature. If a piece of paper coated with dye sublimation ink is pressed into direct contact with a polymer surface such as polyester and heated to the required temperature, the dye molecules will turn to gas and permeate the surface of the polymer where they will be trapped and become a permanent part of the plastic surface. Sublimation dyes generally work at temperatures above 180°C, but newer materials have been designed to work at temperatures as low as 160°C.

Sublimation inks are available for offset lithography, screen printing, and gravure, and have been used for decades for decorating textiles as well as a wide range of other manufactured products. There are specialized high volume applications of sublimation printing for decorating polymer floor tiles and two-piece aluminum beer cans. There are only two requirements for successful implementation of sublimation transfer printing. First, it must be possible to hold the printed transfer paper in direct contact with the surface that will receive the dyes. Sublimation does not work on surfaces that have compound curves that cannot make continuous contact with a flat sheet of paper. With textiles this is not a restriction. The transfer paper can be pressed against the textile surface in a specially designed flatbed or rotary press. The second requirement is that the surface must be a dye-sublimation-compatible polymer such as polyester. Sublimation does not work with natural fibers such as cotton or wool. However, special cotton/polyester layered materials are available that have a polyester outer layer and a cotton inner layer.

One of the great advantages of sublimation transfer is that the only material transferred to the textile surface is the dye itself. The purity of the color of the dye is not compromised by other materials such as varnishes or adhesives. A large palette of brilliant colors is therefore available to the textile designer. Furthermore, the use of high resolution printing processes such as lithography and gravure allow for photographic quality images to be printed and transferred to fabrics. Sublimation transfer represents a revolution in the graphic quality available to textile printing.

The latest development in textile printing has come with the use of inkjet printers to print the sublimation transfer paper. This makes it possible to print custom graphics on textiles and a wide range of other materials on demand. Digital printing allows the complete elimination of physical inventory of imaged materials. In addition to the printing of dye sublimation transfer paper, inkjet printing processes can also be used to print directly onto textiles with specially-coated surfaces, or onto heat transfer material that employs a layer of adhesive coated onto a silicone-coated release paper. But neither of these methods produces as high quality a graphic result as sublimation transfer.

One of the greatest benefits that has come from the use of inkjet printing processes to decorate textiles either directly or through a sublimation transfer process is the ability to produce proofs of new textile designs and ideas before they are put into mass production. Textile and clothing designers can determine how a new design will work in an actual product, rather than try to visualize how the design will work from a computer display or paper print. The closer a prototype comes to the final product, the better.

DECORATIVE AND FUNCTIONAL SURFACES

In addition to textiles, many of the interior surfaces that surround us in the home and workplace are decorated with printed graphics. These include floor and wall coverings as well as countertops and furniture.

To begin with, any surface that looks like wood, but is not really wood, is printed. My desk at work, for example, looks like fake mahogany. In any modern business organization, real wood surfaces are usually reserved for upper management. Presidents of large corporations often have office furniture made from the rarest exotic woods that are harvested from the darkest rainforests. The mass of lower level workers, of which I am one, have to settle for printed simulations.

Nearly all simulated wood surfaces are the product of gravure printing. Gravure has several attributes that make it ideal for this application. Gravure is capable of reproducing the subtle texture and detail of wood grain that makes it difficult to distinguish the printed surface from the real thing. Gravure can print on paper or plastic substrates with permanent inks in high volumes at low cost per unit area. Gravure can also print an uninterrupted pattern on rolls of material up to several meters wide. In some cases the printing is done on a paper substrate that is then laminated between plastic layers. In other cases, a clear plastic substrate is back-printed and then laminated with other materials to form the surface. Plastic laminates can also be molded to produce three-dimensional components such as simulated wood automobile dashboards and decorative panels on consumer electronic products.

PRINTED FLOOR COVERINGS

Gravure is also used to print the graphics on most of the resilient vinyl flooring materials made by companies such as Armstrong and Congoleum. The gravure presses used in these applications are among the largest printing devices in the world, enabling the manufacture of continuous rolls of vinyl flooring in widths up to 16 feet to provide for seamless installations. Multi-colored patterns are printed onto a thick paper-based substrate and then coated with a layer of polymer. A chemical agent is added to the polymer to form gas bubbles that expand its thickness and make it slightly compressible. To form simulated grout lines or impart natural textures to the surface, chemical inhibitors are printed in appropriate patterns on top of the graphics. These inhibitors prevent the polymer from expanding in the areas where they are printed. This polymer layer is then coated with another clear polymer layer that serves as the surface of the floor.

Different grades of printed vinyl flooring differ largely in the thickness of the topmost clear polymer layer. The most expensive grades have the thickest layer of polymer, and have the longest expected service life. The least expensive materials with the thinnest top layer are used in low-cost manufactured and modular housing units.

The high cost of manufacturing a set of gravure cylinders for a single new floor pattern can only be justified by high volume production. Large quantities of finished goods must be manufactured and kept in inventory for long periods of time. If the market for a particular pattern does not match the original market projections, the manufacturer may be left holding vast quantities of material that cannot be sold profitably. The high inventory costs and high risks associated with changing market demands have driven the major manufacturers to look for digital alternatives to gravure printing. Sublimation transfer printing has been successfully adapted to the production of floor tiles, but the size requirements for resilient flooring have thus far prohibited the use of sublimation processes. The ideal digital process to replace gravure would be a wide-format high-speed multicolor inkjet process. The widest format inkjet printers that are currently being used to print billboards cannot reproduce the necessary detail. (Billboards are meant to be viewed from distances of hundreds of feet, whereas floors are viewed from much closer distances.)

If a viable digital alternative to gravure were developed for this application, it would have a profound impact on the structure and operation of the industry. Rather than producing and warehousing large quantities of each pattern offered in the current catalog, and then waiting for orders to be generated by retailers or contractors, orders could be produced on demand. The variety of available designs would expand exponentially and the possibility of custom designs would become a reality. Physical inventories and the need to sell overproduced products at discount would be eliminated. If interior designers had the ability to offer their customers custom design services, flooring might even become a more changeable and disposable feature of everyday life. Imagine, for example, seasonal changes in the color and texture of your floors, or special promotional floor coverings. This is already becoming a reality with digitally-printed floor signs that can be applied to existing floor surfaces. Why not expand the concept to make the entire floor a sign?

Digital printing provides a clean and simple interface between the capital-intensive print manufacturing operation and any software-based design operations where new products are created. When manufacturing lines for decorated surfaces of all kinds are fitted with digital print engines in place of the traditional mechanical processes, the diversity of product designs that can be manufactured at a single plant becomes unlimited. This will enable one-person design firms to compete effectively in businesses that have historically been dominated by a handful of very large companies.

PRINTED WALL COVERINGS

People have been decorating walls with graphics for thousands of years. In the ruins of Pompeii, the famous Roman city that was buried by an eruption of Mt. Vesuvius in 79 A.D., there are many examples of wall decorations that included both paintings and mosaics. Some of the earliest examples were walls that were painted to look like imitation architectural elements such as moldings, archways, and columns. Later wall paintings depicted scenes from nature or everyday life among the common citizens of the city. Mosaics were used to create geometric patterns and natural scenes. One of my personal favorites is a mosaic that depicts an un-swept dining room floor, littered with pieces of uneaten food and refuse as though a dinner party had just ended.

In all probability, block-printed paper made its first appearance in China more than a thousand years ago. Printed wallpaper was first manufactured in America in the early 1700s. Later in that century, Louis XVI issued a decree in France that required a wallpaper roll to be about 34 feet long. Two Frenchmen responded in 1785 by inventing the first machine for printing continuous rolls of wallpaper.[45]

The most powerful indication in more recent times of the predisposition that people have for adorning their walls with graphics is evidenced in the famous 1930s Farm Security Administration photograph by Walker Evans of a cleanly swept sharecropper's shack, its walls covered with printed newspaper advertisements that had been pasted on them for decoration. Wallpaper enjoyed its greatest popularity during the 1920s, but fell out of fashion during the Modernist period following World War II. When I was a child in the 1960s, wallpapered rooms had the musty odor of a bygone era. Plain painted walls created the proper ambiance for the space-age family. With the thankful death of Modernism, wallpaper, now known by the more upscale term *wall coverings*, has made a dramatic comeback.

Commercial wall coverings must be produced in narrow rolls that have continuous repeating patterns that can be hung vertically in strips to form a continuous horizontal pattern. Three mechanical printing processes are used to print most modern wall coverings:

flexography, rotary screen, and gravure. Flexographic presses used to print wall coverings employ special laser-engraved rubber cylinders. The engraved cylinders can transfer a continuous graphic pattern to a roll of paper or plastic. One cylinder is needed for each color in the pattern. Gravure and rotary screen printing can also produce a continuous pattern on rolls of substrate. All three processes are capable of printing on paper and plastic substrates. Because the cylinders for all three processes are expensive to manufacture, similar economies of scale apply as with gravure-printed vinyl flooring. Digital alternatives to these mechanical processes have the same potential to fundamentally change the way manufacturers serve commercial and consumer markets.

Three digital printing processes are good candidates for replacing conventional analog processes in the manufacture of wall coverings: electrophotography, inkjet, and digital photographic printing. Color electrophotographic printing on continuous rolls is being used to produce niche wall covering products such as personalized border prints that can be installed along the top or bottom edges of walls to add a decorative touch to a room. HP and Xeikon manufacture electrophotographic printers that are suitable for printing photographic-quality color images in continuous patterns on rolls of paper or plastic. The printed surfaces need to be laminated for protection because the fused toner will not stand up to the abrasion associated with normal use. The cost of electrophotographic toners is also much higher than the printing ink used in the conventional processes. The current opportunity for electrophotography seems to be in customized or personalized applications, where the increased cost of materials is justified.

Wide-format inkjet printing on plastics using UV-curable inks is another viable candidate for production of custom wall coverings. The ability to print on wide rolls of material is a potential advantage in some applications. However, there is good reason why rolls of wallpaper have remained relatively narrow, even though the conventional printing processes used to produce them are capable of printing on much wider rolls. Hanging a 24-inch-wide strip of wallpaper is hard enough to do. If the rolls were much wider, they would be impossible to install.

A third digital printing process also has some potential for the manufacture of wall coverings for specialized applications. Wide-format, roll-fed digital photographic printers that employ lasers to image directly onto photographic paper can be used to produce continuous rolls of printed material. For applications requiring the highest photographic print quality, this offers the best solution. A resin-coated or plastic-based photographic print, coated or laminated for protection, provides a permanent and durable surface for wall coverings. Both inkjet and digital photographic printing are currently used primarily to produce high-quality pictorial wall coverings for business and commercial spaces. Consumer markets for digitally-produced wall coverings are not yet significant, but this will likely change in the next decade.

CHAPTER FIFTEEN

NON-GRAPHICAL APPLICATIONS OF PRINT

EVERY NEW PRINTING TECHNOLOGY THAT HAS BEEN DEVELOPED, from the first wooden blocks used by ancient Chinese and Korean printmakers to the most advanced digital inkjet and electrophotographic devices of today, was first intended to create graphics. Most of these processes work by precisely-controlled deposition of thin layers of material onto media that alter the way light is reflected from the printed surface. The finer the control over the placement of the material, the more graphic information can be encoded in each unit area of the printed surface. Printing technologies reach their maturity in the realm of image quality when they are capable of controlling the distribution of material with such precision that the amount of image information that can be reproduced exceeds the resolving power of the human eye operating at the expected viewing distance. For printed media such as magazines and books this distance is somewhere between twelve and eighteen inches. For billboards the expected viewing distance may be several hundred feet.

As it turns out, technologies that can control the deposition of thin layers of material with enough precision to satisfy the requirements of the human visual system at normal reading distances are the most sophisticated industrial coating processes in existence. Processes like lithography or flexography can deposit ultra-thin layers of material (on the order of one micron in thickness), controlling the exact placement of material across a large two-dimensional surface. This makes it possible to reproduce detail much finer than can be resolved by the eye. This capability can be expressed in terms of the number of discrete lines that can be printed in a given linear measure such as an inch or a centimeter. Lithography, for example, may approach 200 lines per centimeter on smooth non-porous substrates.

What applications might there be for printing processes beyond the reproduction of graphics? This is a question that has been getting a lot of attention lately. A good example of an existing non-graphic application is the use of screen printing to produce the etching stencils for printed circuit boards or to print circuit patterns directly onto boards and ribbons with conductive inks. The technology was originally developed for graphic applications, but later proved to be a perfect mechanism for laying down etching resists and circuit patterns.

One new potential application is the production of electronic components that will be incorporated into packaging materials in the next decade. The printing industry first encountered the need to add non-graphic functional features to printed products in past decades when *barcodes* were incorporated in packaging, labels, and publications, and when *Magnetic Ink Character Recognition* (MICR, pronounced "Miker") features were added to checks. Even though both barcodes and MICR printing were both graphic elements in the sense that they were intended to be seen and read by people, their performance as information-encoding features that could be machine-read was paramount. These features represented the first time the printing industry had to deal with standards of print quality that were not derived from visual requirements. A MICR code on a check can be beautiful to look at, yet fail miserably in its intended use. The same is true of a barcode.

The next generation of machine-readable coding to be incorporated into many printed products is known as *Radio Frequency Identification*, or RFID. The basic concept of RFID was developed during the Second World War, and exists today in many common applications. Unlike a barcode or the magnetic strip on a credit card, RFID technology does not require a direct line of sight or physical contact with the reader to work. An object or person carrying an RFID tag can be identified by a reader as it passes nearby. The technology is currently used to identify motor vehicles as they pass through toll booths, and to track rail cars and livestock as they move from place to place. Most current applications use active RFID tags, meaning they are powered by small batteries and transmit a signal continuously. In addition to active tags, there are also passive tags. Passive tags require no on-board power and last indefinitely. The newest RFID tags are hybrids called semi-active tags. These combine a battery and antenna that can be printed by screen or flexography onto a plastic substrate. A tiny semiconductor chip must then be attached to the printed components. This presents a fabrication challenge that requires great precision and cleanliness.

The move toward adoption of RFID technology accelerated in 2003 when Wal-Mart announced that it would require its largest suppliers to include RFID tags on all cases and pallets within two years. This unleashed a torrent of speculation about the possibility that, at some point in the near future, RFID tags will be as universal on packaging as barcodes now are. All it will take is for Wal-Mart to wave its powerful hand, and most product manufacturers will have no choice but to comply. At 2004 costs for chips that are fabricated entirely from electronic components, the burden of having to comply with a mandate like this would put many manufacturers out of business. Printing all or part of the tag using conventional printing equipment modified for the task is an attractive possibility. It has already been demonstrated that antennas for passive tags can be printed with conductive flexographic inks. Thin batteries can also be fabricated on film substrates using the screen printing process. It is not currently practical to print electronic components to replace silicon chips, but there is a considerable amount of research being conducted around the world in this area.

Beyond RFID, there are a number of potential opportunities for using printing technologies in the manufacture of electronic components. Epson, for example, has demonstrated the use of inkjet print heads to apply the dye masks on organic light emitting diode (OLED) color displays. Eastman Kodak has pioneered work in the use of flexible plastics for the fabrication of color displays. Scientists at Kodak are quick to point out that it was Kodak that transformed photographic media from glass plates to flexible plastics more than a century ago, and that the same evolution must happen in the fabrication of computer displays. Their vision is eventually to be able to "print" large flexible digital displays at far lower cost than current semiconductor fabrication methods allow.

CHAPTER SIXTEEN

A NEW INDUSTRY
EMERGES

AT THE BEGINNING OF THE NEW MILLENNIUM, there were a number of attempts to place the achievements of the previous thousand years into some kind of perspective. One such attempt came in the form of a book entitled *1,000 Years, 1,000 People: Ranking the Men and Women who Shaped the Millennium*, published in 1998.[46] This book was the culmination of a regrettable cultural trend toward ranking the relative importance of people that *Time* magazine started back in 1927 when it named Charles Lindbergh the first annual "Man of the Year." In the book, the authors presented a ranked list of the 1,000 most important people of the past millennium.

On this list, Wilbur Wright is ranked 23rd and his brother Orville is 24th. Hitler is number 20, slightly more important than George Washington at 22. Charles Dickens at 70 edges out Suleiman the Magnificent at 71, and Joseph Stalin at 82 just beats Joan of Arc at 83. The number one person on this list, the most important person in the world during the entire second millennium, was Johannes Gutenberg, the inventor of printing from movable type. Gutenberg also scored the top person of the millennium honor in a poll conducted in 1999 by National Public Radio. These polls were celebrated with great fanfare and pride by people in the printing industry, although not without a hint of defensiveness in some cases. "The new media may be getting all of the attention, but our guy, Johannes, won the grand prize of the millennium! I guess Bill Gates and the Google guys will have to wait another thousand years for their next chance to win!"

The idea that print is an old medium and the Internet is a new medium is an impediment to understanding what is actually happening to graphic communications in our time. There are plenty of examples of Internet-based communications that are strictly "old media" and a growing number of examples of print-based communications that are at the forefront of the new media. The most useful way to distinguish new from old is to focus on the nature of the connection between media producer and media consumer. If the connection is primarily a one-way connection, where content is designed and pushed from producer to consumer, the medium is old. New media are those that enable a dialog between producer and consumer, and where content is determined as a result.

Most of the websites currently in existence are electronic versions of traditional print media products that effect simple one-way communications between producer and consumer. The only information that comes back to the producer from the consumer is the occasional email and a click of the site visit counter. A website that is nothing more than an electronic brochure is an example of old media in new media clothing. For certain applications this simple old media website is exactly the right solution to the problem. Old media solutions are still sometimes the best solutions.

What about new media solutions that leverage the power of print? Two basic models have emerged. Print with customized content can be generated and mailed to an individual as a result of an interaction between the individual and a website. Many companies have established interactive websites tied to digital print production and mailing facilities that can be used to deliver personalized messaging and printed products to customers.

It is also increasingly common for print to point to the Internet to add an interactive component to advertising. Most print advertisements now include a web address that points the reader to a more extensive and possibly interactive body of information. Until recently this was entirely at the discretion of the individual advertiser and the phenomenon proliferated at the grass roots. This changed in 2004 when the publisher Condé Nast introduced a website to service all of the advertisers in the September issue of *Vogue* magazine and allow readers to use the magazine as an index to the website. When you went to the website, you could reference most of the products advertised in the magazine by brand name or product category. When you found the ad page image, you could click on the specific product of interest and obtain pricing information and the location of the nearest stores where you could buy the product. The website linked to the *Maps on Us* service to draw a map to the store.

The September 2004 issue of *Vogue* began a new chapter in the long history of magazine publishing. The seamless integration of printed magazine and website constitutes a powerful new medium that is a true hybrid. This new hybrid medium combines the strengths of the two component media to create something far more powerful than either one of them could be alone.

In retrospect it makes perfect sense that this new medium would have made its debut in the service of the fashion industry. There is no more elegant and impressive way of communicating the look of new fashion designs than with still photography. Fashion photography reproduced in a magazine ad is the quintessential example of the material medium of print directly referencing the material world. The production standards for *Vogue* are the absolute zenith of the printing craft and provide the ultimate platform for the display of photographic art. The publisher has harnessed the power of print to create desire and bound it to the interactive capabilities of the web to guide the customer to the front door of the retailer, informed and ready to spend money.

It makes no sense to try to deconstruct this new hybrid medium into its component parts and then to regard one part old media and another part new. It might be helpful to give each new hybrid medium a new name. However, this can lead to strange new words that sound ridiculous when uttered by serious people. My personal favorite is a term that was coined by Xerox Corporation to describe a seminar on the web where participants received bags of custom-ordered snack food as part of the experience. The name of this new hybrid medium? A *Snackinar*.

If we try to think of clever names for each new hybrid media product, we will soon grow weary of the task. We need to abandon the comfort and security of fixed generic terminology altogether, to freely describe emergent hybrid media. Any reluctance we may have to let go of old media language hampers our ability to clearly see the future unfolding before our eyes.

The generic terminology that served to describe old media

categories for hundreds of years must be replaced by a more intelligent way of naming and distinguishing media types. Fortunately, we can resort to the time-honored method of naming things that are unique and give each new media product a proper name of its own. The name that Conde Nast gave to its first hybrid magazine/website was *ShopSeptemberVogue.com*. *ShopSeptemberVogue* was made of components that can be described using old media terms. However the fact that *ShopSeptemberVogue* had a print component is as relevant to understanding its true nature as the fact that I have a set of vocal cords is to understanding mine. On the component level, I look about the same as every other person walking the earth and *Vogue* magazine (minus the perfume samples) looks like every other magazine. However, taken as a whole, *ShopSeptemberVogue* was as unique in the world of new media as I am unique in the population of authors of books about the new medium of print.

Once we make the leap from seeing the world of new media through old media eyes to seeing each new medium as a unique hybrid organism, we are better equipped to understand the technological requirements of print in its new role.

DIGITAL PRINT: THE GREAT ENABLER

I chose to use *Vogue* magazine to introduce the concept of hybrid new media precisely because it is produced by conventional means that have long been associated with the old medium of print. If a fixed-content print component of a hybrid new medium needs to be manufactured and distributed in large quantities at low cost, conventional printing processes are the appropriate solution. This will remain true for a long time to come.

For applications where the content of what is printed varies with each impression, or where quantities of unique printed units are very low, digital printing processes are required. The pace of digital print technology development has been blinding during the past two decades, but there are still powerful pressures on the manufacturers for improvement. Digital processes dominate some markets almost completely and hardly have a presence in others. A majority of outdoor advertising is now produced digitally because the higher technology and material costs of digital are more than offset by the lower labor costs and faster changeover of displays. On the other hand, nearly all packaging is produced by analog processes such as offset lithography, flexography, and gravure because no digital processes currently exist that can deliver the required graphic quality in large quantities at the low costs required.

If we look for a rule that will predict where conventional analog printing processes will continue to dominate and where digital processes will replace them, we need to look at the markets served by print. Let me propose a simple rule. Mass markets for standardized consumer products will continue to be served by conventional analog print, and mass markets served by customized consumer or professional products will be served by digital print. For as far as anyone can see into the future, these two different types of markets will co-exist, and thus both conventional and digital print will be with us for a long time to come.

The future of analog print serving mass markets is determined by the demand for standard products worldwide. The most promising opportunities for growth are in the developing world. The manufacturers of conventional print production technology and the suppliers of conventional print therefore focus most of their attention on places like China, Russia, Eastern Europe, and India. In the U.S., conventional print serves mature consumer markets full of overweight, overindulged people trying to cut back on their intake of everything. There is only so much capacity for future growth of mass markets in this part of the world. The same can be said of Western Europe and Japan.

Given current trends in mass manufacturing and distribution of consumer products, and projecting forward a few decades, the vision of the future that comes to mind is one of large automated factories, highly efficient distribution systems, fully optimized supply chains, and Wal-Mart. The challenges facing the printing industry that serves these markets will be to get good enough, fast enough to keep up with Wal-Mart. The implications are far reaching.

I'll give one example to illustrate the point. The industry that manufactures packaging materials and sells them to consumer product companies like Frito-Lay and Gillette is under constant pressure to reduce the amount of time required to get a new package design on the store shelves. Packaging is increasingly viewed by consumer product manufacturers and retailers as the final, and most critical, opportunity to sell the product. A printed food package, for example, enables the manufacturer to communicate with potential consumers walking down the supermarket aisle. The communication is effective if the consumer purchases the product. Now imagine how excited the food industry would be if it were suddenly possible to change the graphics on packages as they sat on store shelves by simply uploading the new graphics to a web server! This fantasy vision is already a reality in publishing. If the *New York Times* can change the content of the newspaper while people are reading it everywhere in the world instantaneously, why shouldn't Frito-Lay want to do the same with Doritos bags?

Packaging manufacturers know that the pressure to get to market faster will never let up until this vision is fully realized. They understand the true value of rapid service to their customers and they continuously strive to improve their capabilities in this regard. The printing industry that serves mass markets must fully embrace the principles of lean manufacturing that are the guiding forces throughout the mass market supply chain. The companies that do this most effectively will be able to stay in the game. A good predictor of success might be something simple like how closely the top management of a company follows every move and utterance of Wal-Mart. I offer this because it is relatively easy to determine in casual conversation.

LESS IS MORE

One of the primary goals of lean industrial practice is to reduce the amount of waste produced at every step of the process. Print is distinguished among all manufactured products in that most of it ends up in a landfill or in a recycling stream shortly after it is produced. This may occur after it has served a brief but useful mission as in the case of packaging, magazines, newspapers, and books. However, vast quantities of some categories of print end up in the waste stream without ever having been used in any way. These include unsolicited direct mail, catalogs, and newspaper inserts. In these markets, the goal is to reduce the volume of waste by increasingly intelligent targeting strategies.

Five targeting strategies have been identified by Vertis Corporation, a leading supplier of mass media advertising. Vertis arranges these five strategies in a pyramid. Each layer of the pyramid requires a more sophisticated approach to targeting.[47] From lowest to highest, the five targeting strategies are:

1. **Geographic targeting:** Targeting a specific zip code or newspaper distribution zone.
2. **Demographic targeting:** Targeting age, income, and gender groups.
3. **Lifestyle targeting:** Targeting communities characterized by common recreational characteristics, such as golf or boating communities.
4. **Psychographic targeting:** Targeting groups based on inferences made from analysis of purchasing patterns.
5. **One-to-one targeting:** Targeting the individual based on unique knowledge.

Vertis Corporation's targeting strategies.

As you work from the bottom of the pyramid to the top, the difficulty and cost increases, but the effectiveness also increases. In the words of Don Roland, chairman of Vertis Corporation, "By reducing the volume of print and increasing its effectiveness, you are actually increasing the value of print. Why does an advertiser advertise in any medium? Because it produces! If you make print more effectively targeted, while it sounds like you're reducing print, you're actually increasing print. The advertiser is more likely to use print, to increase page counts, increase frequency, go upscale, because of the effectiveness of what you've done."

Generally speaking, as the sophistication of targeting strategy increases, the printer must play a greater role in developing the overall business strategy of his customer. The printing industry historically provided goods and services to customers after the procurement decision had already been made—long after the business strategy was established. Today's most progressive companies offering targeted services close to the top of the pyramid are becoming strategic partners of their customers. The notion that high volumes are good, higher volumes are better, and who cares whether most of it ends up in the landfill, is a rapidly-disappearing remnant of old media thinking.

THE EMERGENCE OF A NEW INDUSTRY

While the existing industry tackles the challenges of squeezing cost out of existing supply chains and improving the efficiency of the print itself, the stage is being set for the creation of a new industry that will produce a range of products and services that have never existed before. The five fundamental technology enablers of this new industry are:

- Production digital color printing
- Computational power
- The Internet
- A broad-band connected customer base
- Intelligent software to flow work from the customer base to the business

A sixth enabler is not technological, but cultural. Some of the most powerful cultural inhibitors to the rapid expansion of this new industry are the entrenched attitudes and practices within large organizations that favor old media solutions to new economy problems.

The first technology enabler is production-capable digital color printing. When the first digital production color printers were introduced to the world in the early 1990s, they captured the imagination of the industry before proceeding to break a lot of hearts and empty a lot of wallets. The devices were ingenious, temperamental, unreliable, and slow. They were capable of producing high-quality printing when compared to earlier digital devices, but fell short of the benchmark "offset quality" to which they were inevitably compared. Worse still, the computer software and hardware systems that were used to prepare and feed data to the devices were incredibly sluggish and prone to crashing. Everyone who lived through that first few years of the technology can tell a horror story about waiting hours for a file to process only to have the computer lock up just as the little progress bar reached the end of its long, slow, transit across the bottom of the screen. I remember, on more than one occasion, yelling unprintable words at the top of my lungs as I sat alone, in a lab, in the middle of the night.

But as fraught with problems as these early devices were, they were capable of doing something that had never been possible before. It was possible to change the images that were printed instantaneously without stopping the press. There were no material setup costs to changeover from one job to the next. You could effectively produce a run of one!

This was going to launch a revolution. It was just a matter of time. For the next decade, the major developers worked feverishly to improve the printing devices, the software and hardware systems that drove the devices, and the technology for binding and finishing the printed product. Today three American companies, Xerox, Kodak, and HP, offer high-speed color digital printing devices that produce quality indistinguishable from offset for publication printing. I have to be careful here because there are always going to be experts who can tell the difference between the best digital print and offset. Fortunately, these people are mostly old media types whose power is rapidly fading into the sunset. Goodbye, and good luck, guys!

In addition to these publication printing devices, there are a number of other digital color printers available for applications ranging from large-scale outdoor advertising to high-speed color printing of billing statements and direct mail. A growing number of innovative companies are building specialized systems for applying offset-quality color graphics to a wide variety of products.

The second technology enabler is computational power. The most robust and reliable digital printing devices are of little use if you can't feed them data fast enough to maximize their productivity. The exponential improvements in computing power and storage capacity over the past decade have largely solved the problems that plagued the early systems. Current generation front-end systems are capable of feeding the machines with a continuous stream of variable image data at the speed required to keep the machines running constantly at full speed. In the mid-1990s the industry was obsessed with how to improve computational performance. Today, the question has largely gone away, thanks to all of the crazy people in Silicon Valley who consistently work twelve-hour days, seven days a week.

The third enabler is the Internet. All the computer and digital printing power in the world isn't going to do a company much good if it remains dependent on a stable of hard-partying salespeople to roam the world looking for customers to "bring work to the presses." This is also an old media construct that does not offer any value to an emerging industry that can only thrive if transaction costs are driven out of the process altogether. Business must be conducted over the Internet. A production color digital printing press without the Internet is about as useful a Lamborghini in a wilderness rainforest.

The fourth enabler is broadband Internet connectivity. To conduct graphic-intensive business effectively over the Internet requires a high percentage of the target customer base to have broadband connection. For business-to-business services, broadband is now assumed to be universal. For consumer-oriented businesses, the percentage of penetration of broadband may vary depending on the anticipated customer base. Broadband is a critical threshold for almost all digital publishing applications. Dial-up just doesn't cut it.

The fifth enabler is software that creates a functional user interface and an automated workflow that drives print production and distribution. This is where most of the creative energy of the industry will be expended during the coming years and where nearly all of the value is created. Anyone with a bank loan can buy a Xerox iGen3 or Kodak NexPress digital color press. However, success depends on a far larger investment in the design of software that will attract and retain customers. The imperative for ease-of-use presents a hard threshold that a user interface must cross before an Internet business will flourish. The most important employees in Internet-based print services companies are the software engineers. In one small Internet print services company I visited recently I counted five software engineers and one press operator.

With all five technology enablers in place, the Internet-based print services provider faces one final and formidable challenge: how to overcome the cultural resistance to new ways of doing business. This resistance varies with organizations and individuals, but appears to increase with the size of the organization. Old media procurement people tend to look with disfavor on new media solutions that promise to put old media procurement people out of work. Smaller organizations that devote less overhead to the procurement of media services have less inertia in this regard. Individuals and consumers who use print communication services for their own purposes are most enthusiastic about new services that will save them time and money.

Organizational resistance to changes in procurement practices can be a significant impediment to growth opportunities for Internet-based print services providers. To overcome this impediment, the people who are paying for print communication services and who are responsible for the return on the investment must be educated about the potential advantages of adopting new print communication strategies. If you are a digital print services provider looking for ways to educate your customers, I am prepared to offer one concrete suggestion. Buy this book in bulk quantities and mail it to the key people in every organization with which you hope to do business in the future. The publisher will give you a great price on large quantity orders.

THE EMERGING NEW MEDIUM OF PRINT

So what kinds of things might we do with these ingredients in the near future? Here are a few possibilities:

A musical instrument dealer records the contact information and initial transaction information of all new customers in a Microsoft Access database. Each subsequent transaction is recorded and stored as a new record in the database. His inventory of high-end electric guitars made by one of the leading manufacturers has grown too large, and he decides to run a fifteen percent off sale on the entire brand for 36 hours over a weekend to reduce the inventory. He sorts the transaction database by brand of product purchased and date of purchase to generate a mailing list of customers who have purchased something manufactured by that company within the past two years. He creates a new contact file of these customers and engages the services of a digital print services provider to produce and mail a postcard invitation to the exclusive sales event. The postcard serves as a personalized coupon for the discount. The print services provider's website allows the dealer to choose a postcard template from a rich selection of different designs and construct the personalized promotional message with a simple, menu-driven design application. The dealer chooses the template, keys in the promotional offer, and uploads the mailing list. He also indicates the date the postcard should appear in his customers' mailboxes. The print order enters a production queue at the print services provider's facility and is automatically printed, finished, and presorted for mailing just in time to meet the delivery requirements.

A wedding photographer offers a new service to her clients. After the wedding they can browse her entire collection of wedding photographs on the Internet and highlight the ones they want to include in a small, elegantly bound album that doubles as a thank-you note. Several designs are available. Each design is accompanied by a matching envelope for mailing. The client chooses a design from a selection and provides mailing addresses for the entire wedding guest list. The order is transmitted from the photographer's website to a digital print services provider where it is produced and shipped to the client within 48 hours. The proper postage and mailing addresses are included on the envelopes. The client writes a personalized note in the front of each album, seals it in the matching envelope, and drops it in the mail.

You are on vacation with your family. You are carrying a mobile phone that has a built-in three-megapixel digital camera, thumb keyboard, and wireless Internet connectivity. You take a funny picture of your kids posing next to a chrome-plated statue of Lawrence Welk, and decide to send it to some of your relatives and friends. You type a brief message describing where you are and that you are all having a great time. You scroll down through your contact list and highlight the names of the people you want to receive the photo. You press the "mail postcard" button and put the phone back into your pocket. Your order is transmitted over the Internet to a digital print services provider. The postcards are printed and mailed within 24 hours. You are billed for the service by your phone company.

Flipping through a home furnishings magazine looking for ideas about a new look for your kitchen floor, you find the perfect pattern in an advertisement for one of the major floor covering manufacturers. You go to the magazine website and find the ad, click on the pattern you like and input the dimensions of your floor. You are presented with a selection of different durability grades and the exact price of each grade for your kitchen. You choose the durability grade and submit your order directly to the manufacturer. The manufacturer mails a small sample of the pattern to you for approval. If you approve, you go back to the website to confirm your order and schedule an installation date. The manufacturer prints your order on-demand using special machinery that incorporates wide-format digital inkjet printing to produce the graphics inline with the manufacturing process. Your completed order is shipped to a local installer who shows up on the scheduled date to install your new floor.

A native of Syracuse, New York wins a gold medal in skateboarding at the 2008 summer Olympics in Beijing. A leading manufacturer of sportswear wants to capitalize on the local pride of Syracusans with a public message of congratulations. The company prepares a simple graphic saluting the Olympian's accomplishment with the intent to purchase a three-hour time block during rush hour the next day on four billboards along the major east/west arterial running through the center of Syracuse. The billboards are digitally-controlled, self-printing signs owned by one of the major outdoor advertising companies. The company auctions one-hour time slots on the billboards, closing each auction 12 hours before the time slot begins.

A product manager in a major food manufacturing company wishes to change the messaging on a popular brand of children's snack food to echo a new catch phrase that has swept the population of seventh and eighth graders. The product manager has an in-house designer add a burst to the front of the package containing the catch phrase spelled out in brilliant orange letters. These changes are transmitted automatically via the Internet to converting plants where new flexographic plates are imaged with the altered design. One week later the burst begins to appear on newly-stocked packages throughout the country.

Once you understand the true nature of the new medium of print, you begin to realize that the possibilities for future business opportunities are nearly boundless. The only necessary condition in each case is the need or desire for some kind of material communication product.

We are nearly at that point with this book. When I finish writing these last few paragraphs, the content of this book will be complete. If this were only a few years ago, we would be facing a long and difficult path to transform the content into a printed product and get it into your hands. Today we can take advantage of the power of the new medium of print to publish the book on the same day it is completed and make it available to anyone in the world who has access to the Internet.

In the interest of full disclosure, there are a few things that we still need to do before this content is ready for publishing. The text must be edited. The book must be designed. The text and graphics must be laid out in paginated form by a designer. Some of this work can be automated. Microsoft Word helps with some of the editing functions such as spell checking and grammar checking. However, these automated functions cannot substitute for a skilled editor. Layout and design of the pages can also be automated using templates and style sheets. For some kinds of publications, fully automated systems transform structured content into finished pages without any human intervention. For a book like this one, full of photographs and illustrations, some intervention is almost inevitable to ensure a graphically elegant presentation of the content. The generation of the table of contents and index can only be completed after the book is in its final paginated form.

So, even though I will finish writing this text before the cock crows, there remains a lot of hard work to be done before the content is in its final form, ready for production. Let's therefore jump ahead to the moment in the near future where the content and formatting of this book will be truly finished. Let's take up the story at the point where a perfect Adobe PDF version of this book exists on my hard drive and I am sitting with my feet up on the desk, cigar in hand.

It is now time to invoke the powers of the new medium of print to demonstrate, in one final dramatic flourish, all of the wonderful possibility that this book has promised. It is time the author puts his money where his mouth has been. So let us publish, and be done with it!

I will use an Internet service for publishers, called Lulu. The company was founded by Robert F. Young, a pioneer in the *open source* software movement and the founder of one of the leading software companies in the *Linux* world, *Red Hat*. Open source refers to the source code used to create the Linux operating system. The idea of open source is that by making the source code open to everyone who might want to develop software for the Linux system and allowing people to modify the source code itself, the system will grow and improve much faster than if the source code remains the proprietary secret of a single Microsoft-like company.

Lulu extends the open source idea into the world of publishing. Lulu allows content owners to freely access a suite of tools and services that enable them to make their content available for purchase in commercial-grade printed form to anyone in the world within a few hours. Lulu can work with files in dozens of formats. These include common word processing programs like MS Word and WordPerfect, as well as tagged formats like RTF and XML. You can upload the content of a book in one large file, or in pieces and let Lulu assemble them. You can design your own cover, or pick one from the Lulu gallery.

If you want to precisely control the appearance of the book, the only correct choice is Adobe PDF. I uploaded this book in the form of PDF files that were generated from Adobe InDesign. The text was uploaded first, and the cover measurements were generated based on the number of pages. The book was designed in the standard size of 6 by 9 inches. Lulu offers a choice of either black-and-white or color printing for the text. All covers are printed in color.

Once the files have been uploaded, Lulu converts them into a common PDF that is compatible with all subsequent interactive and production operations. To publish the book, you need to preview and approve the final appearance of the cover and establish your royalty. Here's where Lulu reveals its simple but revolutionary business model. As the publisher, you have complete freedom to determine your royalty. Lulu calculates the base price of the book based on page count, size, and whether the book will be printed in color or black and white. You add the profit to this number to determine the final price. Lulu takes 20 percent of this profit and pays you the remaining 80 percent as a royalty for each book sold. You receive a monthly royalty payment from Lulu through PayPal. It's that simple!

Here's an example of how the finances work. Assume that the base cost of your book is $10. You decide that you want to sell the book for $20. This yields a profit of $10. Lulu takes 20 percent ($2.00) commission, and pays you $8.00 royalty each time someone buys your book. If the book doesn't sell at $20, you can lower your royalty at any point. You can also raise your royalty at any time. Lulu doesn't care what you decide to do. If you think there is a market for your book priced at $200, go ahead and price it that way. Lulu will be happy to take its 20 percent of whatever you decide the profit should be. And the most surprising aspect of this business model is that it works the same no matter how many or how few books you sell. In fact, if someone buys your book in large quantities, they can even obtain discount pricing.

Once you have established your royalty amount, you simply press the *publish* button, and your book is instantaneously available for purchase by anyone in the world. One minute after pushing the publish button, if someone in Seattle finds your book on the Lulu website and orders it, the book will be produced and shipped in a matter of a few days' time. When an order for your book comes in, Lulu automatically transmits the file over the Internet to Color-Centric, a company located in Rochester, New York. ColorCentric prints and binds the book, and ships it directly to the purchaser. The system is so highly automated that nobody at Lulu or ColorCentric inspects the files or the printed books before they are shipped. Lulu and ColorCentric have created a tightly integrated system that is completely transparent to the publisher and to purchasers of books. If you want to buy this book from Lulu, go to Lulu.com and search for the title words "New Medium of Print."

AUTHORSHIP LOST AND AUTHORITY REGAINED

There remains one final sacrificial act to be performed before this book is complete. The book must transcend its old-media body completely and be born again as an exemplar of the new medium. This requires a more thorough conversion of the soul than merely transitioning from a traditional to a print-on-demand publishing model. The print-on-demand version of this book has the same DNA structure as the traditional version. (Both were generated from the same InDesign file.) Thus print-on-demand publishing does not change the essence of the book. Nor does it alter the relationship of author to reader. I am still the author and you are still the reader. It is now time to end this one-way relationship and replace it with something better.

Unfortunately I cannot simply sacrifice this book on the altar of the Internet and let it escape its earthly bounds completely. That would be the easy way out. I could create an interactive forum and post this content as a way of starting a number of simultaneous discussions on the various topics of the book. But if the contents of the entire book were available online for free, it would be more difficult to sell printed copies. At the moment our business plan cannot succeed without such sales. It might be possible to use this content as the starting point for a new website that would eventually attract enough visitors to become attractive to advertisers. But that's not what we had in mind when we started this project.

How can we preserve the value of the printed book, while allowing it to gain the benefit of interactivity made possible by the Internet? Here's how we propose to square the circle. The conversation starts with the printed book. The easiest and most enjoyable way to get into the conversation is to buy the book. The interactivity will occur online on the following message board: print.rit.edu/cost. Come and join us there now! The most insightful commentary that emerges from our conversations will become new content in subsequent print editions of the book. The book will gain authority as the author's initial contribution is joined by the accumulated insights and observations of its readers.

In this way I can take comfort in the fact that the end is really the beginning. As I prepare to stop writing and press the publish button, I feel like a happy parent sending a child off into the world without a clue or a desire to predict what it will become, but with the assurance that, as it succeeds, it will occasionally send some good things back home.

REFERENCES

The Association for Suppliers of Printing, Publishing and Converting Technologies (NPES). *www.npes.org.*

Beech, Rick. *The Origami Handbook.* London: Hermes House, an imprint of Annes Publishing Limited, 2002.

Boorstin, Daniel J. *The Americans: The Democratic Experience.* New York: Vintage Books, 1974.

Cappo, Joseph. *The Future of Advertising: New Media, New Clients, New Consumers in the Post-Television Age.* New York: McGraw-Hill, 2003.

Cost, Frank. *Pocket Guide to Digital Printing.* Albany, NY: Delmar Publishers Inc., 1997.

Cost, Frank, et al. *Book Printing Study.* RIT, 2002, unpublished.

Costello, Frank, president, Magazine Publishing Services, RR Donnelley. Interview with the author, September 2004.

Direct Marketing Association (DMA). *www.the-dma.org.*

Doyle, Nicholas. *PDF Capability Study,* MS Thesis. Rochester, NY: Rochester Institute of Technology, 2004.

Eldred, Nelson R. *Package Printing.* Plainview, NY: Jelmar Publishing Co., Inc., 1993.

Elyjiw, Zenon. *Sixty Score of Easter Eggs: A Comprehensible Album of Ukrainian Easter Eggs.* Rochester, NY: privately printed, 1994.

Elyjiw, Zenon. "Ukrainian Pysanky: Easter Eggs as Talismans," *The Ukrainian Weekly*, April 16, 1995.

Flexible Packaging Association (FPA). *www.flexpack.org*.

Flexographic Technical Association (FTA). *www.flexography.org*.

Flexography: Principles & Practices, 5th Edition (6 volume set). Ronkonkoma, NY: Flexographic Technical Association, 2000.

Floss, Dennis, assistant managing editor/presentation, *Democrat and Chronicle*, Rochester, New York. Interview with the author, Spring 2004.

Gerling, Curt. *Smugtown, U.S.A.* Webster, NY: Plaza Publishers, 1957.

Glover, John D. Prepared Witness Testimony, House Committee on Energy and Commerce, Subcommittee on Oversight and Investigations. June 7, 2001. *energycommerce.house.gov/107/ hearings/06072001Hearing267/Glover403.htm*.

Gottlieb, Agnes Hooper et al. *1,000 Years, 1,000 People: Ranking the Men and Women Who Shaped the Millennium.* New York: Kodansha America, 1998.

Graphic Arts Technical Foundation (GATF). *www.gatf.org*.

Gravure Association of America (GAA). *www.gaa.org*.

Hayssen Packaging Technologies. *www.hayssen.com*.

Holweg, Matthias and Frits K. Pil. *The Second Century: Reconnecting Customer and Value Chain Through Build-to-Order.* Boston: MIT Press, 2004.

Infotrend/CAP Ventures. *www.capv.com*.

International Cooperation for the Integration of Processes in Pre-press, Press and Postpress (CIP4). *www.cip4.org.*

I.T. Strategies, Inc. "U.S. vs. Worldwide Value of Printed Product." U.S. Census of Manufactures: Commercial Printing. "U.S. Industry Outlook: 1999." Additional Sources.

Jacobson, Gary and John Hillkirk. *Xerox: America Samurai.* New York: Collier Books, MacMillan Publishing Company, 1986. ISBN 0-02-033830-9.

Kapr, Albert and Douglas Martin. *Johann Gutenberg: The Man and His Invention.* Aldershot, Hampshire, UK: Ashgate Publishing, 1996.

Kipphan, Helmut et al. *Handbook of Print Media.* Berlin: Springer-Verlag, 2001.

Kleper, Michael L. *The Handbook of Digital Publishing, Volumes 1 and 2.* Upper Sadler River, NJ: Prentice Hall Professional Technical Reference, 2001.

Koren, Leonard. *13 Books (notes on the design, construction & marketing of my last . . .).* Berkeley: Stone Bridge Press, 2001.

Lemay, J. A. Leo and P. M. Zall, editors. *Benjamin Franklin's Autobiography: An Authoritative Text, Backgrounds, Criticism.* New York: W.W. Norton & Company, 1986.

Leonard, Devin. "Nightmare on Madison Avenue." *Fortune* 149 (June 28, 2004): 93.

Lileks, James. *The Bleat. www.lileks.com.*

Magazine Publishers of America (MPA). *www.magazine.org.*

National Association of Printing Leadership (NAPL). *www.napl.org.*

National Endowment for the Arts. "Reading at Risk: A Survey of Literary Reading in America," *Research Division Report #46*, June 2004.

New York Insideout Guide. Winford, England: Mapgroup International, 2003.

Nord, David Paul. *Communities of Journalism: A History of American Newspapers and Their Readers.* Champaign: University of Illinois Press, 2001.

North American Industry Classification System (NAICS). *www.naics.com.*

Outdoor Advertising Association of America, Inc. *www.oaaa.org.*

Owen, David. *Copies in Seconds: How a Lone Inventor and an Unknown Company Created the Biggest Communication Breakthrough Since Gutenberg—Chester Carlson and the Birth of the Xerox Machine.* New York: Simon & Schuster, Inc., 2004.

Paxton, Bradley, CEO of ADI (Advanced Digital Imaging), LLC. Interview with the author, July 2004.

Perception Research Services, Inc. "The PRS Eye Tracking Studies: Validating Outdoor's Impact in the Marketplace 1999-2000." Outdoor Advertising Association of America, Inc. *www.oaaa.org.*

Printing Industry Association/Graphic Arts Technical Foundation (PIA/GATF)'s Graphic Arts Information Network. *www.Gain.org.*

Pollard, Michael. *Johann Gutenberg.* Watford, UK: Exley Publications Ltd., 1992.

Quaknin, Marc-Alain and Josephine Bacon. *Mysteries of the Alphabet: The Origins of Writing.* New York: Abbeville Press, 1999.

Rebecca Schunck Wallpaper Installation and Removal. *www.wallpaperinstaller.com.*

Roland, Donald E., chairman and CEO of Vertis. Interview with the author, February 2004.

RR Donnelley Logistics. *www.rrd.com/rrdl.*

Senefelder, Alois. *The Invention of Lithography.* Translated by J. W. Muller (1911). Pittsburgh: GATF Press, 1998.

Sharma, Abhay. *Understanding Color Management.* Clifton Park, NY: Thomson Delmar Learning, 2004.

Steinberg, S.H. *Five Hundred Years of Printing, 4th revised edition.* New Castle, DE: Oak Knoll Press, 1996.

Sullivan, Louis H. "The Tall Office Building Artistically Considered." *Lippincott's Magazine*, March 1896.

Technical Association of the Graphic Arts (TAGA). *www.taga.org.*

Thompson, Bob. *Printing Materials: Science and Technology.* London: Pira International, 1998.

United States Army Field Manual. "Psychological Operations, Tactics, Techniques, and Procedures," FM 3-05.301. December 2003. Restricted access.

United States Postal Service. *www.usps.com.*

United States Postal Service. *Household Diary Study: Mail Use and Attitudes in PFY 2003.* Austin, TX: NuStats, April 2004. Contract #102590-99-B-1720. *www.usps.com.*

Warde, Beatrice. *The Crystal Goblet: Sixteen Essays on Typography.* London: Sylvan Press, 1955.

What They Think. *www.whattheythink.com.*

Wines-Reed, Jeanne, and Joan Wines. *Scrapbooking For Dummies.* Hoboken, NJ: John Wiley & Sons, 2004.

Witkowski, Trish. *Fold: The Professional's Guide to Folding,* Volumes 1 and 2. Reisterstown, MD: Finishing Experts Group, 2002.

ENDNOTES

1. Costello, in conversation with the author, September 2004.

2. Holweg and Pil, *The Second Century.*

3. Paxton, in conversation with the author, July 2004.

4. Quaknin and Bacon, *Mysteries of the Alphabet.*

5. Doyle, *PDF Capability Study.*

6. Senefelder, *The Invention of Lithography.*

7. Beech, *The Origami Handbook.*

8. *New York Insideout Guide.*

9. Witkowski, *Fold: The Professional's Guide to Folding.*

10. LeMay and Zall, *Benjamin Franklin's Autobiography*, p. 85.

11. USPS, *www.usps.com/communications/organization/ postalfacts.htm.*

12. USPS, *www.usps.com/businessmail101/classes/periodicals.htm.*

13. USPS, "The Household Diary Study: Mail Use & Attitudes in PFY 2003," *www.usps.com/householddiary/_pdf/ HDS2003ES.pdf.*

14. Ibid.

15. RR Donnelley Logistics, *www.rrd.com/rrdl.*

16. RR Donnelley Logistics, *www.donnelleylogistics.com/ Default.asp?URL=http://www.donnelleylogistics.com/NewsDet ail.asp?NewsID=3286&AltParentID=135.*

17. Costello, in conversation with the author, September 2004.

18. Cappo, *The Future of Advertising.*

19. NAICS, *www.naics.com.*

20. Pollard, *Johann Gutenberg.*

21. Doyle, *PDF Capability Study.*

22. Cost, *Book Printing Study.*

23. Warde, *The Crystal Goblet: Sixteen Essays on Typography.*

24. Sullivan, "The Tall Office Building Artistically Considered."

25. Nord, *Communities of Journalism: A History of American News-papers and Their Readers.*

26. Cappo, p. 68.

27. Wines-Reed and Wines, *Scrapbooking For Dummies.*

28. Boorstin, *The Americans: The Democratic Experience.*

29. National Endowment for the Arts, "Reading at Risk."

30. Gerling, *Smugtown, U.S.A.*

31. Lileks, *The Bleat,* April 28, 2004, at *www.lileks.com/bleats/ archive/04/0404/042904.html*

32. Floss, in conversation with the author, Spring 2004.

33. Roland, in conversation with the author, February 2004.

34. U.S. Army Field Manual, FM 3-05.301, restricted access.

35. Gerling, *Smugtown, U.S.A.*

36. Outdoor Advertising Association of America, Inc., "Facts and Figures," *www.oaaa.org/outdoor/facts.*

37. ———. "Outdoor Advertising Expenditures, 1970-2003," *www.oaaa.org/outdoor/facts/Historical_Expenditures.pdf.*

38. ———. "The PRS Eye Tracking Studies: Validating Outdoor's Impact in the Marketplace, 1999–2000," *www.oaaa.org,* through an advanced search using PRS Eye Tracking Studies as keywords.

39. ———. "Code of Principles," *www.oaaa.org/government/ codes.asp.*

40. Hayssen Packaging Technologies, *www.hayssen.com/ content/menus/hpt/hay_ultimast.aspx.*

41. Jacobson and Hillkirk, p. 65.

42. Ibid, p. 67.

43. Glover, Prepared Witness Testimony.

44. I.T. Strategies, *U.S. vs. Worldwide Value of Printed Product.*

45. "Wallpaper History," *www.wallpaperinstaller.com/wallpaper_ history.html.*

46. Gottleib, et al., *1,000 Years, 1,000 People.*

47. Roland, in conversation with the author, February 2004.

ABOUT THE PRINTING INDUSTRY CENTER AT RIT

The Printing Industry Center at RIT is dedicated to the study of major business environment influences on the printing industry, precipitated by new technologies and societal changes. The Center addresses the concerns of the printing industry through educational outreach, research initiatives, and print evaluation services. The Center serves as a neutral platform for the dissemination of knowledge that can be trusted by the industry, as a place for printing companies and associations to share ideas, and as a meeting ground for building the partnerships needed to sustain growth and profitability in a rapidly changing market.

With the support of RIT, the Alfred P. Sloan Foundation, and our Industry Partners, it is our mission to continue to develop and articulate the knowledge necessary for the long-term economic health of the printing industry.

Printing Industry Center
Rochester Institute of Technology
55 Lomb Memorial Drive
Rochester, NY 14623
http://print.rit.edu

The research agenda of the Printing Industry Center at RIT and the publication of research findings are supported by the following organizations:

Adobe

creo

RR DONNELLEY

+HEIDELBERG-

Kodak

MeadWestvaco

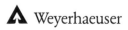

INDEX